CRIES
FROM THE
JUNGLE

Bastiaan Opdenkelder

CRIES FROM THE JUNGLE

Experiences from
Dutch Indonesian Families
in Manokwari

The first settlers in New Guinea (Manokwari)
Their life in captivity by Japanese soldiers
Liberation by the U.S. Alamo Scouts
Heroic actions by Dutch Indonesian military

Produced by
LYO PRODUCTIONS
Grimsby, Ontario
Canada

Bastiaan Opdenkelder is a Dutch-born writer
Married to Louise (Beynon) born in Manokwari
Two daughters: Claudia and Griselda
Immigrated to Canada in 1980
Two grandchildren: Mya and Francesco
Frequent traveller to South East Asia

ISBN 978-1-7777668-0-1

Canada 2021

TABLE OF CONTENTS

Foreword 9

Acknowledgements 11

Indo or Indo Dutch or Dutch Indonesian or Eurasian.................13

Netherlands New Guinea or Dutch New Guinea.........................19

Papuans the Indigenous Peoples of New Guinea......................23

CHAPTER 1 Beynon Family to New Guinea in 1933 25
Reasons for Transmigration. The SIKNG and KNG

CHAPTER 2 Manokwari 1930....................................29
Where Is Manokwari? Letters From Early Settlers

CHAPTER 3 Mauretz Christiaan Kokkelink............................41
Mauretz Travels to Manokwari. The First Days in the Jungle

CHAPTER 4 Paula Mellenbergh 53
With My Father to Manokwari in 1937
Japanese Warships Are Nearing the City

CHAPTER 5 Jean Victor de Bruyn (Jungle Pimpernel)..............59
Working and Living With the Papuans. White Piglets

CHAPTER 6 Manokwari 1936....................................69
Life of the Settlers. The War Is Near

CHAPTER 7 Japan Attacks the United States............................77
The History and Possible Reasons Why?

CHAPTER 8 The Netherlands Declare War On Japan...............81
Queen Wilhelmina Speech
Karel Doorman Attacks Japanese Fleet

CHAPTER 9 Japan Invades New Guinea.................87

CHAPTER 10 Manokwari 1942.................93
Hans Fuhri Captured and Beheaded

CHAPTER 11 Japan Trained Papuans to Become Spies.............99

CHAPTER 12 Evacuation to Camp Oransbari.........105
Captain Geeroms Takes Troops Into the Jungle

CHAPTER 13 Pieter Petrus de Kock 113
Pieter de Kock Guides His Team Into the Jungle

CHAPTER 14 Coosje Ayal.......117
Vivid Memories of Her Time With the Guerrilla Fighters

CHAPTER 15 Pieter Petrus de Kock.......123
Shots Fired. Sergeant Kokkelink Takes Command

CHAPTER 16 Paula Mellenbergh.......131
Leaving Manokwari to an Internment Camp

CHAPTER 17 Meity Kneefel.......133
My Parents' Memories in a Japanese Internment Camp

CHAPTER 18 Sergeant Zeelt Report of Internment Camp.......145
Women and Children of Guerrilla Fighters Were Imprisoned Here

CHAPTER 19 History of the Alamo Scouts of the U.S. Army 163

CHAPTER 20 Operation Oaktree 1942-1944 167
Jean Victor de Bruijn Fought With Papuans Against the Japanese

CHAPTER 21 Louis Rapmond 173
His Heroic Actions Saved Many Lives in New Guinea
Working with the Alamo Scouts

6

CHAPTER 22 Liberation of Camp Oransbari 1944 193
Oral History of the Alamo Scouts Liberating Camp Oransbari

CHAPTER 23 NEFIS and NICA Explained 213
Netherlands East Indies Forces Intelligence Service
Netherlands Indies Civil Administration
In Memory of Johannes Bernardus Herman Willemsz.-Geeroms

CHAPTER 24 Maurits Chistian Kokkelink 223
Lieutenant Razak Picks Up Sergeant Kokkelink
and His Guerilla Fighters

CHAPTER 25 Coosje Ayal - Liberated 227
Arrival in Hollandia. Move to the Netherlands

CHAPTER 26 Pieter Petrus de Kock 231
Hero's Welcome in Australia
Back to New Guinea

CHAPTER 27 Maurits Chistian Kokkelink 233
Back to the Jungle of New Guinea

CHAPTER 28 Meity Kneefel 249
Liberation of My Parents' Internment Camp

CHAPTER 29 Pieter Petrus de Kock 257
A letter from Queen Wilhelmina. Receiving the Bronze Lion

CHAPTER 30 Stichting Imigratie Kolonisatie NNG 1947 267
Original Settlers Want to Return to Manokwari

CHAPTER 31 Repatriation of Indos to the Netherlands 269

CHAPTER 32 Hans Fuhri – Reburial 1949 275

CHAPTER 33 The West New Guinea Dispute..........277

CHAPTER 34 Beynon Family 1948 - 1962 289
Beynon Family Back in Manokwari

CHAPTER 35 Papua Volunteer Korps 283

CHAPTER 36 The Morning Star..........................299
History of the Liberation Flag of the Papuan
Independent Movement in West Papua

CHAPTER 37 The Birds of Paradise 301

CHAPTER 38 Indos in the United States.............307
Many Dutch Indonesian Families Moved to the United States
Several Written Letters of Their Experiences of the Move Out
(Reasons Why) of the Netherlands

CHAPTER 39 War Stress Affects Future Generations.............315
Many Indo Families Have Experienced the Negative Emotions
After the Pacific War

CHAPTER 40 Pasir Putih (Beautiful Beach in Manokwari).319
Alex Bal Poem

Honouring Pieter Petrus de Kock - 103 years old! 323

Beynon Family 325
The Family Tree of Theodoor and Marie Beynon

Family Pictures..327

Vaarwel mijn Dromenland 334

8

FOREWORD

Writing a book on the Pacific War and especially on the history of my wife's family (Beynon) has always been on my to-do list and finally after many years of research, I am proud to present this manuscript.

Being born in the Netherlands automatically created an interest in Dutch history and especially the East Indies. I remember my grandfather Bastiaan talking about Java and the tea plantation that his brother had that he visited in the early 1930s.

My grandfather often took my brother and I to the *'Museum voor Land- en Volkenkunde'* now called *'Wereldmuseum'* in Rotterdam, close to the harbour. My first introduction to Indonesian artifacts and culture.

In my teenage years, I became very interested in girls who were not typical Dutch (white, blond hair, blue eyes) but rather in girls with a golden brown skin color (Indos) and brown eyes.

My grandfather was quite pleased when I introduced my future wife to the family in Rotterdam. Louise who was born in Dutch New Guinea lived that time in Breda.

It was during the Independence of Indonesia, August 1945, and closely thereafter that thousands of Indo families were forced to move to the Netherlands. Followed in the early 60s by many more from Dutch New Guinea.

In my school we welcomed several Indo boys and girls, and I was interested in their history as well as their musical talents *'Indo Rock.'*

I loved being invited to their homes which included an

invitation to try food that was different from Dutch meat, potatoes, and vegetables. I loved the taste.

Meeting Louise for the first time, my wife of over fifty-five years now, I was introduced into her extended family. After several years of dating and doing my military duties with the Marechaussee (MP), we became serious and decided to get married in Breda (1970).

Louise, the youngest sibling of the Beynon family, supported me through this project, and pushed hard to make sure I completed this book. The family did not really talk much about the Pacific War. As years passed, bits and pieces of information of their internment by the Japanese in Oransbari - south of Manokwari - became of more interest to me.

Several years ago, I received an email from a friend in the Netherlands requesting information about the Beynon family who were liberated from an internment camp!

That's when I met Lance Zedric in Chicago who belonged to a group called the Alamo Scouts Historical Foundation. I went to visit him during a gathering and was introduced to some members who were part of the liberation of numerous camps along the Pacific Coast Line. With that additional information, I was able to gather more details on the tragic events happening inside the Japanese internment camps. He also gave me a big historical view of the Alamo Scouts and their reconnaissance work during the Pacific War.

The schedule of events before, during, and after the internment of the Beynon family in Oransbari is the main theme of this book, but I have added additional stories from others, some of who were the first settlers to New Guinea and/or have been in the same or other internment camps during the Japanese occupation.

ACKNOWLEDGEMENTS

I would like to thank all the people who have contributed to my research and have previously written books or articles about the period prior, during, and after to the Pacific War in New Guinea (Manokwari), the daring liberation of the internment camp in Oransbari by the Alamo Scouts, and the guerrilla group who fought in the jungle and was aided by Papuans and also liberated camps at the Prafi River just to the north of Manokwari.

Lance Zedric and Michael F. Dilley: *Raid on Oransbari*
Lance Zedric: *Silent No More*
Tom Womack: *The Manokwari Garrison*
P. P. de Kock: *De ongelijke strijd in de Vogelkop*
M. Ch. Kokkelink: *Wij Vochten in het Bos*
English translation: We Fought in the Jungle
C. Giebel: *Morotai*
Tjaal Aeckerlin: *Paradijsvogels en Kroonduiven*
Jan Derix: *Bapa Papoea*
Bas Kreuger: *Kais*
Dennis Kloeth: *Terug naar Manok*
Frans Peereland: *Opgegroeid in Nederlands Nieuw-Guinea*
Lloyd Rhys: *Jungle Pimpernel*
Alex Ball: *De Laatste Indo*
Manokwari Geheugen, Manokwari Tempo Dulu,
Komunitas Manokwari Tempo Dulu
Wikipedia: the Free Encyclopedia
Doni Weidema, Roy Kneefel, Han Dehne, Bert Beijnon, Beangy Jaspers, and Marcel Ravenhorst
Tyler Bennett - T Dot Creative
Agus Gunawan - Cover Picture
Special thanks to Mary Nardi and Jean Ryan for editing

• *September 1933. The Beynon family leaves for their new adventure*
Boarding at Tandjong-Priok (Batavia) to Manokwari (New Guinea)
Top left to right: Emmi (11), Mama, Suze (1) in her arms, and Papa
Bottom left to right: Eddy (3), Margaretha (6), Hendrika (5) and Johan (8)

• *Picture of the Beynon family taken right after the liberation: Left to right:*
Eddy, Margaretha, Jeanne, Olga, Papa, Guus, Carla, Mama, Nancy,
Hendrika, Suze. The oldest brother Johan (Nono) is not in this picture

12

INDO or INDO DUTCH
DUTCH INDONESIAN
or EURASIAN

*In this book, I will use some of these names to refer to
Dutch mixed with Asian ancestors.*

Dutch-Indonesians are ethnic Dutch with a family history
in the former Dutch East Indies, present-day Indonesia.
Dutch-Indonesian people can be roughly divided into two
groups: *Indo-Europeans* and *totoks*. 'Indo' is derived from
the Greek *Indoi* which refers to India and, in turn, is derived
from *Indus* (the River). Indo-Europeans, or abbreviated
Indos, are descendants of Europeans who lived in the Indonesian region.

The name *Indo* is not derived from or an abbreviation for
Indonesia and/or its inhabitants.

For three centuries, there was intensive migration between the Netherlands and the Dutch East Indies. Partly due
to mixed marriages, a new population group emerged. A demographic reconstruction of the number of Indos shows that
at the time of the Japanese occupation (1941) there were
about 300,000 Indos living in the Dutch East Indies, out of a
total population of more than sixty million.

After the war and the independence of Indonesia, the
lion's share of the survivors migrated to the Netherlands. In
1984, the highest number of Indos (living anywhere in the
world) was reached (616,000 of which 309,000 were the first
generation). Around the year 2000, 582,000 Indos were still
alive. Of these, an estimated 458,000 live in the Netherlands.

The second generation is considerably larger.

During the Second World War, the Dutch East Indies were occupied by the Japanese. After the Japanese surrender, the Dutch authorities had little time to think about the establishment of a post-war Dutch East Indies; two days after the surrender, the Indonesian nationalists proclaimed the *Independent Republic of Indonesia.* New Guinea remained under Dutch control until 1963.

During the construction of the Dutch colonial empire in the Indies, the Ambonese played a special role. This population group, from the archipelago around Ambon in the South Moluccas, had always strongly identified with the colonial administration, and a large part of this group adhered to the Christian faith.

After the independence of Indonesia in 1949, a rebel movement emerged on Ambon, which in April 1950 proclaimed the *Republic of the South Moluccas Republic Maluku Selatan, RMS.* The uprising failed, and in the aftermath of the conflict, several thousand Moluccan former soldiers of the Royal Dutch Indonesian Army were told by the Dutch government to come to the Netherlands with their family members.

First-generation Indos are people who themselves have been exposed to the colonial culture of the former Dutch East Indies for part of their lives, and who have brought this culture elsewhere through migration.

Second-generation Indos are people born to one or two first-generation Indo parents, i.e. persons who have not themselves experienced the colonial culture, but who, as children, have heard many stories about it.

Those who settled in the Netherlands from the Indonesian archipelago before 1967 did so from an emotional connection with the Netherlands. The border of 1967 coincides with the date until when the *spijtoptanten* (regret optants) could still choose Dutch nationality and arrival to the Netherlands.

14

This group of people surrendered their Dutch citizenship at or after independence in 1949, but later returned to it.

Within the first generation of the total group of Indo people, different groups can be distinguished. The most important of these are the following:

a) persons who stayed in the Dutch East Indies during or after the Second World War and had the status of Dutchman;

b) persons who stayed in the Dutch East Indies before the Second World War, had the status of Dutchman there, but had left the Indies before the war. In almost all cases, this was to the Netherlands;

c) persons who stayed in the Dutch East Indies during or after the Second World War did not have the status of Dutchman, but still obtained that status by permanently settling in the Netherlands afterwards;

d) persons from the Moluccas (the Moluccans) who were forced by the Indonesian government to choose between Indonesia and the Netherlands, and came across to the Netherlands. They were in a closed Dutch-Indonesian/Moluccan culture in the Netherlands for a long time, because they lived under the assumption that their stay in the Netherlands would only be temporary. They are a unique and separate group compared to the previous three categories.

The largest group of Indos comes from those who stayed in the Dutch East Indies during the Japanese occupation and had the status of *belanda* (Dutchmen), that is, persons with a Dutch passport and the persons were treated as such.

At the 1930 Census in the Dutch East Indies, four population groups were distinguished: Born Dutch, Europeans, Chinese, and Other Foreign Easterners. Europeans included all Westerners, including non-Europeans such as Americans and Australians. In order to obtain the same legal status as Europeans, for example, with a view to the permissiveness of trading or access to certain European schools, natives, Chinese, and Other Foreign Easterners had the option of requesting equalization from the Governor-General.

The transition to the European group could also take place through adoption, a concept that was replaced by recognition in 1867. If a man recognized the child of a woman from another population group as his own, this child was included in the father's group. In this way, children of non-European mothers became European every year. Descendants of these children in the male line were also considered Europeans.

Therefore, the legal position of the man was decisive for that of the woman and the children. A non-European woman was automatically granted European status by marrying a European man. The legitimate children of a European father were also automatically part of the European population. The marriage surplus is the difference between the number of women who joined the European population as a result of marriage to a European man and the number of European women who left the European population through marriage to a non-European.

1942–1945: Everywhere in the archipelago, except on the island of Java, all Europeans (including the Indo-Europeans, with the exception of Japanese allies and citizens of neutral countries) were interned almost immediately, or assigned a different place of residence.

All Allied soldiers present were taken prisoner of war and employed. The citizens of Allied or other Western countries were also interned. Among the prisoners of war and internees was a group of passers-by who happened to be present in the archipelago in March 1942.

In internment, the men were almost always separated from the women and children. Young, healthy men were put to work. Older and sick men and boys aged eleven to sixteen stayed in men's camps. The largest group, especially the Indo-Europeans, stayed outside the camps during the occupation. This mainly concerned persons who, on the basis of a pedigree certificate, could prove that they had mostly Asian blood and therefore could be considered as *brothers of the Japanese*. In addition, there were Europeans who kept the railways and postal services running for the Japanese. In general, most of the Europeans spent at least part of the war years, and a significant number even the entire war period until August 1945, in Japanese camps.

A second group of Indos was made up of persons who lived in the Dutch East Indies in the years leading up to the Second World War, but left Indonesia before the outbreak of the war. In contrast to the population described in the previous paragraph, this group did not spend the war in the Dutch East Indies, but elsewhere (usually in the Netherlands).

The population of Indos in the pre-war Netherlands consisted mainly of pensioners and students who had been sent to the Netherlands for their education. The group of Indos who spent the war in the Netherlands as a student was large. The members of this group are referred to as *Katjangs*. On 1 January 1946, the number of *Katjangs*, or Indos, in the Netherlands, can be roughly estimated at approximately 34,000 people, concentrated in the age group fifteen to thirty years.

1946–2001: There are other population groups who fall under the broad concept of Indonesian Dutch. These persons who were not yet Dutch citizens during the Second World War, still obtained that status after the war by permanently settling in the Netherlands. With the exception of the *Katjangs*, all Indos were in the Dutch East Indies at the end of 1945. Over the years, most have left Indonesia, mainly to the Netherlands, and some to countries such as Australia, New Zealand, Canada, and the United States.

Finally, there are the Moluccans, who form a special category in the demographic history of the Indonesian-Dutch. The majority of Moluccans did not meet the naturalization requirement in 1967 because, even after 1968, children were stillborn in designated residential housing, and therefore within the first generation continued to grow.

The total number of Indos reached its peak in 1984, with 616,000 people. The first generation has been declining in size since 1968. The second generation had reached its high point in 2001, with 336,000 people. The fact that there are still first-generation Indo people is due to the fact that the children born between 1965 and 1980 in Moluccan housing are counted as the first generation.

The large second generation is related to the number of births in the period 1960–1980. The second generation of Indos is also ultimately doomed to extinction. However, this will not be the case until the end of the 21st century.

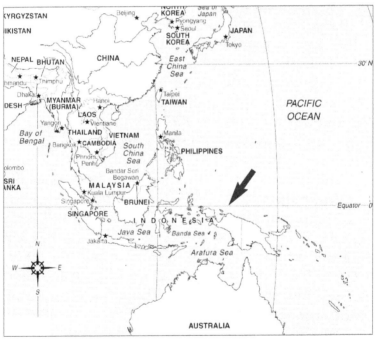

• *Map of South East Asia. The arrow indicates New Guinea (Indonesian: Papua (Irian). It is the world's second-largest island and with an area of 785,753 km2 (303,381 sq mi), the largest island in the Southern Hemisphere.*
The west side of the island (West Papua) was called Netherlands New Guinea until May 1 1963.
The history in this book is about that part of the island.

NETHERLANDS NEW GUINEA
or DUTCH NEW GUINEA

Netherlands New Guinea refers to the West Papua region of Indonesia which was part of the Dutch East Indies until 1949.

From 1949 to 1962, it became an overseas territory of the Kingdom of the Netherlands. It was commonly known as Dutch New Guinea. It contained what are now Indonesia's two easternmost provinces, Papua and West Papua, which were administered as a single province prior to 2003 under the name Irian Jaya.

Until after World War Two, the western part of the island of New Guinea was part of the Dutch colony of the Netherlands Indies. The Netherlands claimed sovereignty over New Guinea within the Netherlands Indies through its protection over the Sultanate of Tidore, a sultanate on an island west of Halmahera in the Maluku Islands.

In a 1660 treaty, the Dutch East India Company (VOC) recognized the Sultanate of Tidore's supremacy over the Papuan people, the inhabitants of New Guinea.

This may have referred to some Papuan islands (Raja Ampat) near the Maluku Islands as well as coastal areas like Fakfak, through familial relations with local rulers, however, Tidore never exercised actual control over the interior and highlands of New Guinea.

In 1828, the Netherlands established a settlement in Western New Guinea and proclaimed sovereignty over the part of the island lying west of 141 degrees longitude.

In 1872, Tidore recognized Dutch sovereignty and

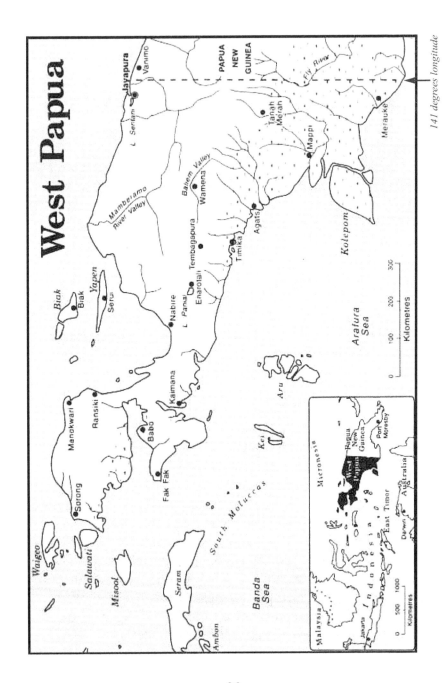

West Papua

141 degrees longitude

granted permission to the Kingdom of the Netherlands to establish administration in its territories, legitimizing a claim to the New Guinea area. The Dutch established the 141st meridian as the eastern frontier of the territory *(see map)*.

In 1898, the Netherlands Indies government set up administrative posts in Fakfak and Manokwari, followed by Merauke in 1902.

The main reason for this was the extending of British and German control in the east. The Dutch wanted to make sure England and Germany would not move the border to the west. This resulted in the partition of the island of New Guinea.

In reality, most of New Guinea remained outside colonial influence. Little was known about the interior; large areas on the map were blank and the number of inhabitants was unknown, and numerous explorations were made into the interior from the turn of the 20th century on. The indigenous inhabitants of New Guinea were Papuans who lived in tribes and were hunter-gatherers.

Pre-World War Two economic activity was limited. Coastal and island dwellers traded to some extent, mainly with the Maluku Islands. A development company founded in 1938 by the Dutch government tried to change this situation but was not successful.

Until World War Two, New Guinea was considered unimportant territory within the Netherlands Indies.

During World War Two, Western New Guinea was occupied by the Japanese and later recaptured by the Allies, who restored Dutch rule.

During the Indonesian Revolution, the Dutch launched police actions to reclaim territory from the Indonesian Republic. However, the harsh methods of the Dutch drew international disapproval.

With international opinion shifting to support the Indonesian Republic in 1949, the Dutch managed to negotiate for the separation of Netherlands New Guinea from the broader

Indonesian settlement, with the fate of the disputed territory to be decided by the close of 1950.

In the following years, the Dutch were able to argue successfully at the UN that the indigenous population of Netherlands New Guinea represented a separate ethnic group from the people of Indonesia and thus should not be absorbed into the Indonesian state.

In contrast, the Indonesian Republic, as successor state to the Netherlands East Indies, claimed Netherlands New Guinea as part of its natural territorial bounds.

The dispute over New Guinea was an important factor in the quick decline in bilateral relations between the Netherlands and the Indonesian Republic.

The dispute escalated in 1962, following Dutch moves in 1961 to establish a New Guinea Council. Following the *Vlakke Hoek incident**, Indonesia launched a campaign of infiltrations designed to place pressure on the Dutch.

Facing diplomatic pressure from the United States, fading domestic support and continual Indonesian threats to invade the territory, the Netherlands decided to relinquish control of the disputed territory in August 1962, agreeing to the *Bunker Proposal* on condition that a plebiscite to determine the final fate of the territory be conducted at a later date.

The territory was administered by the UN temporarily before being transferred to Indonesia on 1 May 1963. A plebiscite, *the Act of Free Choice,* was eventually held in 1969, but the fairness of that election is disputed.

* *The Battle of Arafura Sea (Indonesian: Pertempuran Laut Aru), also known as the Battle of Vlakke Hoek (Dutch: Slag bij Vlakke Hoek), was a naval battle in the Vlakke Hoek Bay (Etna Bay) of the Arafura Sea in Western New Guinea on January 15, 1962 between Indonesia and the Netherlands.*

PAPUANS: THE INDIGENOUS PEOPLES OF NEW GUINEA

• *Arfakkers - one of the many tribes in New Guinea*

The indigenous peoples of New Guinea, commonly called Papuans, are Melanesians. There is genetic evidence for two major historical lineages in New Guinea and neighboring islands: the first wave from the Malay archipelago perhaps 50,000 years ago when New Guinea and Australia were a single landmass called Sahul; the second wave of Austronesian people from the north who introduced Austronesian languages and pigs about 3,500 years ago, and who left a small but significant genetic trace in many coastal Papuan peoples (only a minority of Austronesian-speaking Papuans have detectable Austronesian ancestry).

Linguistically, Papuans speak languages from the many families of non-Austronesian languages that are found only on New Guinea and neighboring islands, as well as Austronesian languages along parts of the coast, and recently developed creoles such as Tok Pisin, Unserdeutsch, and Papuan Malay. The term *Papuan* is used in a wider sense in linguistics and anthropology. In linguistics, *Papuan languages* refer to the diverse, mutually unrelated, non-Austronesian language families spoken in Melanesia, the Torres Strait Islands, and parts of Wallacea.

In anthropology, *Papuan* is often used to denote the highly diverse aboriginal populations of Melanesia and Wallacea prior to the arrival of Austronesian-speakers, and the dominant genetic traces of these populations in the current ethnic groups of these areas.

Research has shown 826 languages of Papua New Guinea and 257 languages of Western New Guinea, a total of 1,073 languages, with twelve languages overlapping.

CRIES FROM THE JUNGLE

Beynon Family to New Guinea in 1933

1

In September 1933, Theodoor Beynon (1902-1984) and his wife Marie (Retelaer) (1905-1976), who both were born and raised in Batavia (Java), transmigrated due to an initiative of the Dutch colonial government. They had six children: Emmi 1922, Johan (Nono) 1925, Margaretha (Nini) 1927, Hendrika (Ika) 1928, Eddy 1930, and Suzanne (Suze) 1932, who were all born in Batavia.

In the early nineteenth century, the government wanted to reduce poverty and overpopulation on Java, to provide opportunities for hard-working people, and to provide a workforce to better utilise the natural resources of the outer islands.

The ethnic group that was most interested in New Guinea before the war were the Eurasians and/or Indo people. Before the war, 150,000 to 200,000 Eurasians were living in the Netherlands Indies. They were of mixed European and Indonesian descent and identified with the Netherlands and the Dutch way of life.

In the colonial society of the Netherlands Indies, they held a higher social status than indigenous Indonesians *(inlanders)*. They were mainly employed as office workers.

When the educational level of indigenous Indonesians rose, more and more Indonesians got jobs previously held by Eurasians.

The Eurasians were forbidden to own land on Java. This resulted in mental and economic problems for the Eurasians.

Some of the character traits required for a choice to migrate to New Guinea included a perfect health and a high level of energy and, of course, durability to sustain very dif-

25

ficult times in the beginning years. I believe both Theodoor (later in the book we change his name to Paatje Beynon), and his wife Marie (Marietje), must have had a great deal of energy to take six young children to a land that only a few colonists before them had entered. They hoped to build a better future for themselves and the children.

In 1923, the first plan to designate New Guinea as a settlement territory for Eurasians was devised. In 1926, a separate *Vereniging tot Kolonisatie van Nieuw-Guinea* (Association for the Settlement of New Guinea) was founded. In 1930, it was followed by the *Stichting Immigratie Kolonisatie Nieuw-Guinea* (Foundation for Immigration and Settlement in New Guinea).

These organizations regarded New Guinea as an untouched, underdeveloped island that could serve as a homeland to the sidelined Eurasians, a kind of tropical Holland where they could create an existence.

The first KNG and SIKNG settlers went in 1930 to Hollandia and Manokwari. Other settlers followed but were not necessarily part of the organized groups.

In the early 1930s, through negotiations with the Sultan of Tidore, the SIKNG was given a contract for settlements (60 parcels of 10,000 kilometers) in the northern area of New Guinea (Manokwari and surrounding area).

The associations succeeded in sending settlers to New Guinea and in 1938 successfully lobbied for the establishment of a government agency to subsidize the initiatives. However, most settlements failed because of the harsh climate and living conditions, and because the settlers were not always skilled in agriculture. In the Netherlands, some organizations promoted a kind of tropical Holland in New Guinea, but they were not very successful. The Beynon family signed up with the SIKNG and was given a large piece of land in the area to the north of Manokwari (Fanindiweg).

The KNG chose Hollandia as their main target of operation. Manokwari and Hollandia on the north coast were the original centers for the Eurasian colonization on New Guinea. Both areas were situated in the lowlands with a tropical rain climate, best suited for farming and a moist, hot, and a jungle-like climate. Manokwari received more rain than in Batavia and was perfect for farming. Unfortunately many settlers did not have enough initiative and/or energy to work hard. They liked to play soccer with the Papuans. This "promised land" did not match their expectations. In addition, many areas were dealing with malaria.

• ENGEO (First Electrical Company in Manokwari)
owned and operated by Mr. Hessing (picture inserted)

Dorey Bay of Manokwari

Dorey Bay is the name which Alfred Russel Wallace, a British naturalist, mentioned in his book *The Malay Archipelago.* He came to the Bay in 1858 to conduct research on birds of paradise and anything that was related to the natural history of New Guinea island. Since then, people who read his book have come from all over the world to Manokwari to see with their own eyes this beautiful Dorey Bay.

Here in Dorey Bay, tourists can travel around some small islands. The most famous is Mansinam. It is a small island that is located at the outermost part of the bay. Mansinam became the first to receive German missionaries who went to this Netherlands New Guinea to preach Christianity. Mansinam is considered by the indigenous Papuan people as "the island of civilization."

During World War Two, Japanese forces constructed many bomb shelters to defend Manokwari against their enemies, the Allied forces. The Imperial Japanese Army deployed 50,000 soldiers to Western New Guinea to reinforce their defense line in the Pacific. Lieutenant General Fusataro Teshima from the 2nd Army led the troops and chose Manokwari as his headquarters.

If you visit as a tourist, you can meet the villagers who live in Mansinam and Lemon islands. Dorey Bay is the best site for shipwrecks and deep sea diving.

Where Is Manokwari?
Letters from the Early Settlers

2

The city of Manokwari is situated on the northeast side of the Vogelkop (Bird's Head) and is protected by the Dorey Bay. The highest peaks around Manokwari are about 250 meters above sea level. The climate is warm, and the average temperature is twenty-six degrees Celsius. There is a significant rainy season and a shorter dry season.

In the beginning of the 1930s, the settlers spread along the coastline, south and northwest but always staying close to Manokwari. The areas of Ransiki and the Geelvink Bay and the Amberbaken to the north had the best soil in the area for farming. There were flat pieces of land in the hills that was good for deep *(intensive crop)* farming. One of these areas was called Warmangoapi. Most settlers stayed in the lower areas where the Papuan people worked on their small parcels of land. There is one large area behind Manokwari called Prafi which was situated towards the north coast. To the west there were the Amberbaken and the Kebarvalleys. And the very fertile area of Ransiki River to the south of Manokwari.

During the time the Beynon family arrived, about two hundred settlers were registered in Manokwari. The labor situation in Java meant more settlers transmigrated, and they chose to stay first in the many small *pasanggrahans* (government guesthouses, like a bed and breakfast) supplied by the SIKNG. They stayed together with other settlers without really doing any work. No-one in Java was informed of the hardships and all information published had only beautiful news from New Guinea. "Wild pigs are just walking around and ready to be shot."

• De Nieuw-Guineaer was in the beginning years the lifeline for colonists where information was gathered for the benefit of the SIKNG settlers.

One of the government appointed doctors one time said that never in the area of Manokwari did he see a wild pig. Another false statement was that "Food starts to grow by itself." In short, it was fantastic to be here! Something else that was interesting to mention is that there was no mention of alcohol abuse.

In *"De Nieuw Guineaer,"* a magazine of the time, an article stated the following message: "There was a malaria outbreak, and all people were taken into the hospital. Mr. G. died of Black Water Fever. No additional people were able to get into the hospital. The grandchild of Mrs. F. was born dead. Mrs. L. is already a week in coma. All settlements have many people who are sick. My wife and my youngest child are in bed with 40 degrees Celsius fever." But the article ended on an optimistic note: "The mental state of all settlers is with the exemption of a few, very positive."

Never a negative report back to Java! It was always the way of the SIKNG to report positive news from the settlers. It would attract more people to New Guinea!

The railways donated an iron storage facility in December 1933 in Manokwari. But in June 1934, there were only a few iron posts left. The iron was rusted and fell apart because of the weather. It showed the lack of maintenance initiative of these new settlers.

In March 1934, the government decided to stop sending new settlers to New Guinea, and many people who had failed in their efforts were transported back to Java.

In those years, in the total area around Manokwari, about 250 Eurasians were living with the 10,000 Papuans. The intent of the settlers was to have the Papuans work for them.

Outside of Manokwari, there were settlements in Pasar Poetih, Pami, Warbamboe, Mangoapi, and other places such as Wosi, Sowi, Sandani, Andai, Maroeni, and Oransbari.

31

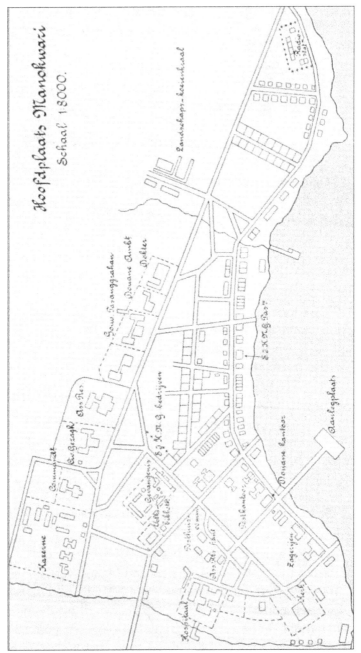

• *Map of Manokwari, approx 1933, published in De Nieuw Guineaer*

32

VIᵉ JAARGANG AFL. No 5 — 26 JUNI 1933.

TROPISCH NEDERLAND

VEERTIENDAAGSCH TIJDSCHRIFT
TER VERBREIDING VAN KENNIS OMTRENT
NEDERLANDSCH OOST- EN WEST-INDIË

ONDER REDACTIE VAN PROF. DR. A. W. NIEUWENHUIS, DR. Z. KAMERLING,
S. A. REITSMA, PROF. DR. B. G. ESCHER, C. K. KESLER EN H. F. TILLEMA.
Vaste medewerkers: G. J. STAAL, Oud-Gouverneur van Suriname, Prof. Dr. L. P. LE COSQUINO DE BUSSY,
H. CH. G. J. VAN DER MANDERE, M. C. VAN ROUVEROY VAN NIEUWAAL en vele anderen.
UITGAVE: N. V. DRUKKERIJ EN UITGEVERIJ J. H. DE BUSSY, ROKIN 60-62, AMSTERDAM

ABONNEMENTSPRIJS PER JAAR: FRANCO PER POST ƒ 12.—, VOOR HET BUITENLAND ƒ 15.—
LOSSE NUMMERS VOOR ZOOVER BESCHIKBAAR ƒ 0.50.

Stukken voor de redactie in te zenden: Jan van Goyenkade 44, Leiden.

In the above issue of the *Tropisch Nederland*, an article was written by Dr. Z. Kamerling about the *Colonization of New Guinea?* The following are some of his opinions:

""*Alle Begin is Moeilijk*' (All beginnings are difficult) and '*Aldoende Leert Men*' (With working you learn) are old Dutch proverbs, which became fully realized during the colonization of New Guinea. The beginning has proven to be very difficult, more difficult perhaps than the promoters had initially imagined. For a long time, it gave the appearance that it would be a hopeless, only failure-doomed endeavour. However, with great perseverance and unshakeable confidence, we have persevered and it is unmistakably, going into the right direction."

In December 1931, the Government decided to take measures to improve the quality of the settlers who signed up for the colonization of New Guinea.

About the current state of affairs in the *Vogelkop* colonization area of the Foundation for Immigration & Colonization New Guinea, we find in the *De Nieuw-Guineaer* publication of February 1933 a good overview:

"The average income of the SIKNG is 800 guilders per month. The settlers were not experienced farmers, but came from an office environment to agriculture out of necessity.

33

Among them are former government workers, policemen, su-
pervisors, sales people, soldiers, etc. In May 1930, the first
fourteen settlers left for Manokwari. After a short stop of settlers in mid-1931, there was another small upturn. Five more
families, consisting of nine adults and seventeen children,
have been sent to Manokwari. The colony is home to thirty-
six families, consisting of one hundred and fifty-six Europeans. Almost all families are, depending on their income, in
the possession of permanent or semi-permanent dwellings,
where they also have their planting of vegetables and other
edible crops, while livestock farming is also carried out. Almost all settlers own chickens, geese, pigs and goats; some
have even received cows from the landscape in sub-cultiva-
tion.

In March 1932, a *pasanggrahan* (guesthouse) was established in Manokwari to supply temporary accommodation to
settlers upon arrival. A cooperative *toko* (grocery store) was
attached to this *pasanggrahan*, from which the settlers can
meet their daily needs very cheaply. Replenishment of the
stock is coordination out of Makassar. This cooperative *toko*
was contractually managed by the settlers on October 1932,
considering the cooperative sale of the surplus product.

We must doubt whether, in the given time conditions, the
creation of a cooperative sales organization will produce favorable results. As long as there is no rebound in trade, the
excess product will find it difficult to sell. Its creation, on the
other hand, points to the favorable result that most settlers,
in terms of nutrition, can already self-suffice. However, for
the renewal of clothing, tools, etc., they must be able to count
on income from the sale of the surplus products.

They now have this income, but they are still too small
to be used to purchase the above articles. In our publications
we already mentioned the request to establish a European Primary School in Manokwari. In the meantime, the number of
children in need of primary education has now grown to fifty-
three. They are in the age from six to fifteen years.

A Delegate of the SIKNG, Mr. A. A. J. Hessing, after a personal research into the conditions and opportunities at Manokwari, decided to establish a Foundation with a rice peel and other small businesses for which it provides a proposal for the construction of a power plant. In a Government's decision, that concession was granted to him, so that in due course the inhabitants of Manokwari can also look forward to the use of electric light.

As soon as Mr Hessing comes here with the paperwork that he is ready to proceed, he leaves with his family for Manokwari and brings with him the first automobile, a unique one, for that place (apparently a Model T Ford).

It can be added immediately that, according to an Aneta telegram dated May 9, the Government is requesting the establishment of a European primary school at Manokwari and that already on May 11, from Surabaya, the head of the school, Mr. Bekker, and teacher, Mrs. Bekker, would leave. The school will start in July."

In addition to these messages, I have a few more. In the same February-number published settler letter, dated 22 October 1932: "When one is convinced of why one is going here - that is, one has to figure out his own self and that one comes here to help try to create for all Indo's each a homeland according to one's own strength. It is better to write all this in advance, because, as a rule, for a new settler, New Guinea is going to be a disappointment."

Apart from the coastal town of Manokwari, everything is jungle and jungle, which one sees on hilly land. The beautiful and suitable places for a settlement, either at a river, beach, or forest, on an altitude plateau, or in the valley near a spring or stream, one has to choose for yourself, these places are enough. Excellent building land to be found everywhere.

The settlers of the SIKNG here still live scattered in the city environment of Manokwari, further Fanindi, on the Manggoapi plateau, in the river valley Pami Manggoapi - where I myself have my place of pleasure - the Pami River near the beach, the Foundation Campong Warbamboe. Then there's Andai, a coastal town, which can be reached with a *prauw* (canoe) in about two hours from Manokwari.

It is not my job to list the pros and cons of each of these places. Self-assessment and research is, in my opinion, the safest. Any newcomer can do that once he is in Manokwari and has explored the region. Every settler here will then try to convince you why his surroundings are better and persuade you to become their neighbor, which is forgivable and understandable, but.... yet only indicates: it is equally beautiful here everywhere, just as good.

Upon arrival, you can go directly to our own *pasanggrahan*, also cooperative shop, or to the Government *pasanggrahan*, both in Manokwari. In the first one, the stay is free; in the other, the rate per person per day is one to two guilders. In both cases, the costs must be taken care of themselves, for this purpose, one can understand with the administrator.

What has already been achieved here is also disappointing. The houses are made of wild wood with *atap* (roofing made of straw) and decked walling. Who can afford it would have a house made with a zinc roof and constructed of iron wood, which can be obtained from the sawmill in Manokwari at a fair price — compared to Java (sixty guilders for first class and twenty guilders for second-class processed wood per kub. meter).

We mainly grow crops such as *djagoeng* (corn), *katjang tanah* (peanuts), *kedelee* (soy beans), *katjang idjoe* (mung beens), *native millet* (small seeds of a plant), *ketella pohong* (cassava), also vegetables for own use. Now we are so advanced, that the possible sale has been started through the intervention of our cooperative shop.

I hope that we have now entered a stage of systematic work, following an unpleasant and uncertain period of system lessness among the settlers. That the togetherness and cooperation is now being managed by the fact that, in particular, the support on a healthier basis, in relation to family size and work performance the settlers is, I believe, a logical consequence of the unrest periods of dissatisfaction and noise under the previous system. Are the people there *senang* (happy)? Generally I did, at least for many of us, I got on a question in question always the answer, which they do not want to go back under any circumstances.

Our impression is that we can make ends meet with a monthly income of at least twenty-five guilders for a family of three adults and two children. Of course, saving cannot be considered. Papuan workers' wages are different. On average, this is now twenty-five cents per day.

At Manokwari, there is a KPM-agent, customs, sawmill, coal shed, post office, Governor's Office (Assistant Resident, Commander), armed police with barracks, day care or canteen, hospital with Indonesian doctor, missionary churches, Government *pasanggrahan*, radio station, *passer* (market), ice factory, various Chinese *tokos*, Native *warongs* (stores), a Government indigenous school, and the prison. Every four weeks, it's only once on a Sunday, the KPM ship arrives.

The houses in Manokwari are connected to a water system. The cost of renting a house is from five guilders per month with guaranteed good housing. Subscription to water mains, if I'm not mistaken, something like two Dutch guilders and eighty cent per month. Wells are also there, but the water is less good on the coast. On my old plot at the Pami estate, I got from the well dug out by us at a depth of six meters, good drinking water.

Little can be said of the state of health, but my own opinion is not better or worse than anywhere else. Just one question: how many traffic accidents occur on Java from buses, taxis, trams, which are not happening here. Think of school-age children, cycling schoolchildren, etc. I've had it many times in Java before I went here, that I am taking a risk to settle here. 'Under the Papoeans? Headhunters? Man, you're out of your mind'." (end of his article)

The houses of the Eurasians in the city were mostly rented

out and owned by the Chinese. With smart investments the Chinese population were gradually increasing their wealth: First to rent the homes, and secondly by increasing sales in their grocery stores.

It was the intent of the SIKNG to make Manokwari a comfortable retirement area, a place where pensioners could stay just like Bandoeng and Malang. The expected advantage was that these people brought money so they would help the settlers by buying their products. Progress was going to take a lot longer as Manokwari had to deal with malaria, and the settlers did not have enough produce available for selling in the *pasar* (market) and stores.

Fanindi (the area were the Beynon family was settled) was an area to the north of Manokwari city. In 1935, fifty-one Indo-Eurasians and twenty-two children lived there. They lived a far distance from each other. Some of the younger generations worked in the city; others tried to make a living hunting or with the farming of chickens. But, there were also a few retired people.

We also need to mention the *Amberies* which is a name for all local people from different areas, such as Ternatanese, Ambonese, and Menadonese.

Playing soccer was a way of dealing with stress, and sometimes fishing or hunting, but there was not much else to do in Manokwari.

In the letters written by the settlers to the SIKNG, they posted a wishlist, "Please add: a telephone system, cinema, forms of transportation, such as horses and buggies, dog-pulled cars, cars, taxi's, busses, trains, light rail, *grobaks* (small food carts), electric light. We hope it will get better soon." But this longing for luxury could not be established in this area yet. It would take many years.

Randani was a new settlement and was about forty-five minutes from Manokwari close to the Dorey Bay. There were also small settlements in Wosi and Sowi. The biggest problem was still the malaria mosquito.

Andai was one of the oldest and largest areas outside of Manokwari. The nicest gardens were there as the settlers had more money to spend and had a better choice of the aboriginal labor force.

There was an old settlement right at the river in Pami where three energetic German brothers, Denningers, had six hundred acres in their possession. But eventually they lost their investment as well. The Javanese *koelies* (laborers) deserted and started to settle in another area of the land that was free for the taking. In 1933, the Denninger family moved away and the leftover Javanese workers took over.

Further to the south in Maroeni and Oransbari and as far as Momi, there were a few settlers. There was a constant change of people coming and going and/or trying their luck somewhere else again.

In 1934, the SIKNG received additional support from the government to help the settlers hire Papuan workers. The following crops were popular for farming in the beginning years: cassava, peanuts, and several kinds of legumes. With the rain, these crops did very well. The average wage for a Papuan worker in these years was twenty-five cents per day.

Theodoor Beynon was hired as a maintenance worker for the electricity department in Manokwari, after settling and building a home with a large farm for his family and creating a working opportunity for the Papuan people. His wife, Marie, loved farming but above all, her flower beds were admired by many. A healthy life-style and being responsible for your own rich agricultural land showed itself in the steady growth of the family union; Jeanne (1935), Nancy (1936), Olga (1938), and Gustaaf also known as Ventje (1940) were born.

Most settlers who took the opportunity to move to New Guinea were not successful, and therefore it is with a lot of respect to the Beynon family and others that they were successful and kept working towards a better future for their children.

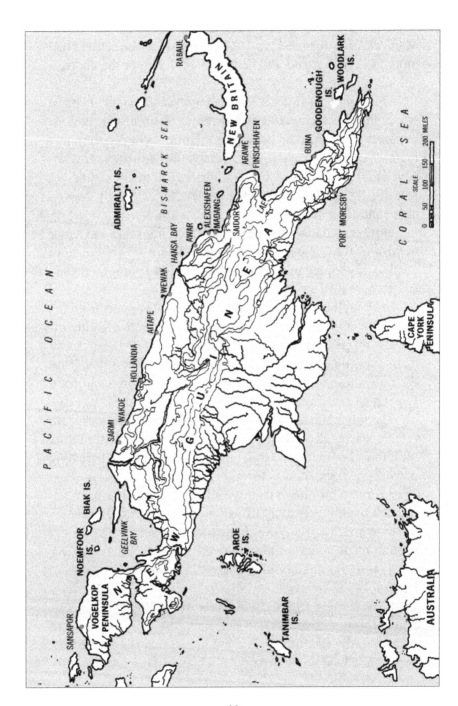

40

Mauretz Christiaan Kokkelink:
Travel to Manokwari and First Days in the Jungle

3

Many other famous Indos came to Western New Guinea in the early part of the 20th century to seek a better life. Mauretz Christiaan Kokkelink, an important part of the guerrilla fighters in New Guinea under the command of Captain Willemsz.-Geeroms when the Pacific War was fought against the Japanese invaders, travelled in October 1933 from Bandoeng to Manokwari.

Mauretz Kokkelink was an Indo, born and raised in Java. As a young man, he served for three years in the KNIL (Royal Dutch Indonesian Army). His army service was not a success, at least not for the KNIL. He had enough goodwill, self-confidence, and even recklessness, but blind obedience to commands, which at times made no sense, was against his feeling of being comfortable. He was not what the military would call a "good soldier." He was glad to hang up his uniform and put on civilian clothes. He did learn a few things as a soldier, including how to deliver an enemy neatly and efficiently to the other world!

Mauretz was also not successful in civil society. He did not learn a specific trade, and was restless and impetuous. He was a jack-of-all-trades.

The following is a vivid firsthand account of Kokkelink's arrival in New Guinea:

"When I decided to transmigrate to New Guinea, I did sell off all my possessions to pay for the fare on the boat to

41

Manokwari. It would leave me with five guilders to buy cigarettes.

There was no emotional attachment to Batavia. I was not married, and I did not have a girlfriend, well let us say not somebody serious, that I would be sad to leave behind.

With that, it was not a difficult move for me to change to a different part of Netherlands Indie, and I believed that with the five guilders, it would be easy to find myself a place to stay in that far away land. Ready to start my life as a colonist, I believed it would be a great opportunity to become very rich! I purchased a ticket as a deck passenger onboard a small KPM *(Koninklijke Pakketvaart Maatschappij)* boat and was anxious to start this journey at sea.

But the travel on a boat was not very exciting to me, and the calm ocean became my friend. Because of that, I was fortunate not to be struck by sea sickness.

Arriving at the shore of Makassar (the capital city of South Sulawesi, formerly known as Celebes), it was very hot. There was no wind, and the ocean was flat like a mirror.

I felt I needed to take that chance. I took off most of my clothes and jumped overboard to enjoy the cool ocean water. I was playing around for a while, and when I looked up at the railing of the boat, there were many spectators, but they were waving and shouting at me wildly.

I waved back as I did not understand a word they were saying. The boat was noisy with moving freight, and I ignored their waving and kept swimming around.

Suddenly, I did see close to me, that the water was full of action. It looked like a small submarine coming to the top. But hold on, it was not a submarine I saw, but a very large fish.

Sometimes it came to the top with his head and then again with his tail. Just like a shark, I thought. I was right. Of course, it was a shark!

Being about forty feet from the ship, I must have swum a new world record, and at the same time the people on board where throwing anything they could find on the ship at the shark to keep it away. They hastely threw down a rope ladder, and I climbed up very quickly, just in time.

Back on board, everyone came to me. Also, the captain of the ship. First, he gave me a tongue lashing, but right after he gave me a couple of shots of Dutch gin.

He took a couple himself.

'To recover from the shock,' he said.

After a trip of fourteen days, we came through Dorey Bay and approached Manokwari. We threw out the anchor about two hundred meters from the shore.

At first sight, New Guinea did not impress me. I did not see a clear difference with the coast of Java. There was a large shoreline with a thick bushy jungle and mountains behind it. Scattered around the landscape were very tall trees that were at least fifty meters high and stood very straight up in between the smaller trees. They created an overall majestic scene.

The ship was quickly surrounded by a large fleet of tree trunk-size *prauws* (canoes) and on it a bunch of wild-looking people. Some of them were totally naked.

I looked at them with great interest. So, these are the Papuans of which I heard of so much before. I was told that they loved to eat human flesh: raw, cooked, baked, or fried. Just take your pick.

I soon found out that this was their day of not eating humans. They screamed at us: 'Tobacco! Tobacco!'

From the limited batch of tobacco that I had with me, I threw a couple of packs of *van de weduwe* (strong Van Nelle Dutch tobacco). They caught them with a big smile and shared the packs between them.

The few passengers, who just like me, came to New Guinea as new settlers, were carried on land without hassle from customs, police, or other government officials.

This monthly visit from the KPM boat was a day of pleasant distraction for everybody. It meant two things for sure: fresh provisions and mail.

• *Asmat warriors in a 'battle prauw' (canoe)*

• *Arfakkers in Manokwari*

44

Yes, there was a radio station in Manokwari, but that was only used for official business. The KPM boat was still the only link with the rest of the world.

There was not much excitement for a young man like me in Manokwari during that time. But it was the largest settlement for new colonists in New Guinea.

Spread along the shore were about one hundred very primitive-looking houses with walls made of bamboo twine and palm roofs. Around each home, you did see empty oil drums that were used to catch rainwater for bathing and consumption.

I did not have much time to really look in more detail as the whole settlement of colonists came out to welcome us. Everyone talked to us like we had known each other for many years, and I was invited by most of them to come over and stay with them. And surely these were not rich settlers among them!

Because the *pasanggrahan* (guesthouse) of the government building was full, I accepted one of the friendly invitations and started as a guest in a settlers home for my first days in New Guinea.

As I mentioned before, the homes were not luxurious. Everything was home-made from old planks and caskets of which the names of the different companies were still legible. Closets and tables with engraved names like *Amstel Bier, Blue Band* Margarine, *Eysen Kaas* Cheese, and so on.

On the side of a children's crib, I read the warning: 'Keep away from boilers.' Very sensible.

The settlers did not look very healthy to me. Malaria was a frightening threat for everyone in this area, but the people were cheerful and content. That was a characteristic of a true pioneer.

The hostess prepared a small *rice table* (white rice, vegetables, a meat dish, and *sambal* (hot sauce). Not much different than what I was used to in Java. The biggest difference was that the meat was not fresh but came out of tins.

45

After dinner, I had a long conversation with the man of the house. He was a governor who lived in New Guinea for several years and therefore well-informed about all the important events happening in the surrounding area.

His stories were not very promising for success, but for someone like him with a small pension, it was a way of living that he chose and that was comfortable for him, he said. For a young man like me, he did not see an immediate rosy future.

The settlement of colonists numbered about 350 souls. A large portion of them were farmers: agriculture, horticulture, and breeding chickens. Not a business to get rich quick.

With the lack of machines, everything had to be done by hand: reclamation, irrigation, ploughing, sowing, all under the watchful eye of the warm sun.

In these years, the indigenous Papuan population were not very eager to work. The reason was that some tribes did not fully trust white people.

They were hesitant to connect with the Eurasian or *totoks* (white colonists). There was no need, and they were used to making a living out of hunting, fishing, and what nature provided for them to survive.

That meant that the colonists, in the beginning, did not have any help at all. Nobody to help on the land and no servants in the homes.

Everything had to be done by the settlers themselves, and women had to work as hard as men.

I did sleep well the first night in New Guinea, and it was smart of me to bring my own camp bed.

The next morning, I went for a walk in the area. There was not much to see. The government, according to the settlers, did not care much about Manokwari, and the rest of New Guinea was represented by an Assistant Resident who was in charge of a detachment of field police of about sixty men, mostly Indonesians although their commanding officer was European.

Beside the house of the Resident there was a small field hospital under the leadership of an Indonesian doctor. There was also a protestant church and an elementary school with two teachers.

The kids who finished elementary school were either ready to go to work or had to leave for Java to register for high school and university. But that was too expensive for most of the kids of the colonists.

While exploring the area, I talked to the people and got offered countless cups of coffee or a glass of *ajer djeroek* (water with fresh lemon). I did find out through these conversations that about forty German settlers were in Manokwari who had fled their country during the First World War and started plantations. One of the German settlers had started a small woodcutting business.

The most significant information was about the Japanese population that lived in Moni, about one hundred kilometers to the south of Manokwari, close to Geelvink Bay. It was a Japanese cotton factory which was equipped with the most modern equipment, and they even had their own telephone network and an electric power plant.

With a Japanese fleet of ships, the cotton was transported to other islands in the area. The representative in Manokwari, where we did not have this modern equipment, was a retired Japanese colonel by the name of Saito. His son finished school in Makassar and spoke fluent Dutch.

Our local government did not believe there was anything to worry about that Japanese factory; although, it was evident that they preferred to be in charge of their own settlement.

The colonists were not alarmed about it either.

We had no time to think about politics. We had to take care of our own livelihood first. Almost everything was in short supply which also included *patjols* (pickaxes) to work in the fields.

The fastest way to move around was on a bike. There were six bikes for a total of three hundred people to share.

Horses or mules were not known here. There were a few dogs, but a lot of cats. That was good because they were natural exterminators of the rats and snakes.

How primitive the colonist lived was evident in the wearing of their shoes. I brought American-made new shoes, and I did take them off to be part of the rest of the people, who were mostly barefooted. Most woman did not wear any shoes.

I understood very quickly, after just one day, that this was a place that required hard work. I did not have much money but also did not want to take advantage of other people.

My host knew of a possible solution. A friend of his did have a fairly large plantation. He was not a young man but, above all, not healthy so he surely could need a helping hand.

I finally realized that my dream of digging for gold and catching Birds of Paradise was going to happen soon. But I had to ask him: 'Is there any gold found here?'

He started to laugh and said: 'Of course but you have to go out and get it in the jungle, and if you do not mind taking a chance to end up on a tribal Papuan menu.'

That was not something I was looking for, so I decided to visit the plantation of the old man which was about six kilometers from Manokwari. I figured I could arrive there in about an hour. But I did not know this part of the world.

My friend told me to be careful for snakes and that was one of the reasons I put on my shiny shoes. That was a smart move as the road was full of sharp stones. I could have easily cut my feet.

The winding road took me through heavy mountainous terrain. Several times I encountered a group of Papuans who were armed with bows and arrows and many were carrying a spear. Mostly seeing them for a quick moment as they swiftly moved back into the jungle, like ghosts.

I got lost in the jungle, but luckily and after several hours, I finally did see a column of smoke in the distance.

I reached an area of several homes with Eurasian settlers who were all working the field.

I asked for the man I was looking for by name, and they told me he lived another fifteen minutes further through the jungle, but that I would not be able to find him by myself.

First I was offered a couple of cups of coffee and had to tell them the latest news from Java. After that they promised they would escort me to meet my destination.

In the twilight of the day, we sat in a circle in front of the homes, and once again it shows how small the planet really is. One of the colonists had served in the same military battalion and was listed before me. With some of the others settlers, I had common friends in Java.

One of the ladies said: 'You can stay and eat with us, but I am sure that when you get to your destination, the food that will be offered to you, will be much better.'

Liking that statement and while it was now really dark, I walked with one of the settlers into the dark. A wooden torch was used, as in these days we did not have a flashlight or lantern.

Finally, I found the family I was looking for. They were sitting at the dinner table: father, mother, two mature daughters, and a son of sixteen. We were invited to join them.

The home looked a lot better than the other homes I did see before. Bed frames made of iron, rattan chairs and even a couple of paintings on the wall!

The walls of the home were painted white and reflected-back the light of petrol lamps.

The house immediately felt like home.

After the meal, Mr. J. gave me his opinion on the reality of living in the jungle and again there was no mention of digging for gold or catching any Birds of Paradise.

He had twenty hectares of land but could only cultivate a small section of it as there were no helpers.

Working on a larger farm would not make sense as there was no means of transportation to bring his fruit and vegetables to market, and on top of that, there just were not enough customers to buy the products.

Another reason was that if there was a big rainfall, the roads would be impossible for wagons to pass.

In the area of Manokwari, there was no dry and wet season like on Java. Throughout the year, you could expect a long drought or weeks of rainfall.

Mr J. was better off than most settlers. He had an ox for ploughing and a couple of pigs and chickens, but again, he was not able to produce more than what he consumed for himself and the family.

Mr. J. said: 'Sometimes I am able to get some local Papuans to come and help with the removal of tree stumps. They are very good at that kind of work, but for agriculture, they have no idea what to do. We do that work ourselves, but don't forget we are dealing with malaria, and when that happens, we are out of commission for weeks, and the work is not being done.'

Most settlers were taking quinine, and they learned quickly never to sleep without a mosquito net. Mr. J.: 'If you are still interested to join us, you are most welcome!' I did think about it for a short time and told him I would accept the offer. There were just no other options available for me.

He laughed and said earnestly: 'You will have to live in our home and eat with us and eventually we will build you a little home. I can't pay you at the moment, but I promise you that you will be paid in different ways.'

In 1933, my journey as an agricultural farmer started. I have never had a feeling of disappointment that I decided to come to New Guinea. I learned to accept my faith and to be satisfied with what my decision has given me.

The area where I settled was called Mangoapi. It was on a plateau a couple of hundred feet above see level. Being there, the nights were cooler than in Manokwari, and the overall climate, I believed, was healthier.

The relationship with the other settlers in the area was excellent. 'Help yourself, but also help your neighbor,'was their motto.

After working with Mr. J. for several years, he gave me six hectares of his land as a payment. He said: 'I know what it means to have your own house and property, how small it may be. On top of that, I believe you eventually want to get married, and you have to show your wife what you have to offer.'

And he was right; the woman who I was hoping to share my land and home with was one of his closest family members. One of the plans swept away by the war.

In the following years, things did of course change as more colonist came to Manokwari. But not much changed in the living conditions."

• *Mama Beynon with some of her children: Second in the front her oldest daughter, Margaretha (Nini), and local children. One of the kids is hiding (left) in the bushes.*

• *Home of Arfakkers (Papuans) around 1920*

• *Papuans close to Mansinam Island*

Paula Mellenbergh:
With My Father to New Guinea in 1937

4

Paula Mellenbergh (born in 1931) whose father and uncle fought together with Captain Geeroms, remembers the decision of her father to transmigrate to Manokwari.

The world economic crisis which presented itself in the end of the 1920s was also influencing the economy in Java.

Many people who worked for the government and local businesses lost their jobs. It went from one day having a desk job to the next day trying to make money selling goods door to door.

Others had to deal with a sharp decline in their wages, and they had to sell their furniture to get extra income for the family.

The secondhand stores were overloaded with *Fongers** bikes and djati wooden dressers. In Indonesia, there was no social security or help for people losing their jobs.

My father had to deal with that as well. He was a chemical engineer and could have made a great career in either the sugar and/or rubber plantations, but there were no job opportunities available for him.

The people also had to deal with the discrimination of helping local people from non-Indo or Eurasian descent first to give them a job as they were much cheaper to hire.

---

* Fongers is an old Dutch brand of bicycles, mopeds and motorcycles. Fongers was based in Groningen from 1897. The company was a pioneer in the development of the classic Dutch touring bike. From 1884 -1910, Fongers manufactured high-quality bicycles reserved for the most powerful upper tier of the population.

It was during these years that the societies of colonists started to appear in the news. New Guinea, a mostly uninhabited island with a lot of opportunity for new settlers, was heavily promoted now.

The government wanted to create a new homeland for the Eurasians. My father believed that as well and wanted to be one of the first colonists there.

Our family moved to Kesilir, on the north-east side of Java, where we were prepared for the trip to New Guinea.

My father received a special training for settlers on how to set up a farming colony. He received a crash course in chopping, plowing, seeding, and feeding of livestock. His nephew, Richard, also joined with his wife and five children.

Some of the family members (mostly the women) tried to convince the men not to take that big step. But my father made up his mind.

Mother did not want to go and said,

"I am not going to that jungle!"

In 1937, we departed with the KPM Kaloekoe from

Surabaya to Manokwari on the northeast coast of the *Vogelkop* (Bird's Head). I did not know at that time that I would never see my mother again. She decided to stay behind in Java.

• *KPM Kaloekoe*

Manokwari was situated between a beautiful bay, a tropical forest, and the Arfak mountains. The settlers who landed were shocked that they needed to get off the boat and had to sit in small *prauws* (canoes) from the Papuans. This also meant that for me as a six year old, I had to descend on a rope from the ship into a small canoe.

When we reached the beach by Wosi, a short distance from the government house, local Papuan carriers put me on their shoulders. Strong men with a facial expression that I never had seen before.

We crossed three fast moving rivers before they dropped me off at Uncle Richard's home.

My father, who left before me in 1934, together with a group of forty other colonists, did not have a house yet.

As a rule, big families with children were given that opportunity first.

To prepare the land for farming, the settlers had to use simple tools such as axes, hand saws, and spades. Every square meter had to be plowed.

The colonists were totally self-sufficient. The crops they harvested were just enough to survive on with their own families.

Products like *bajem* (spinach), *ketella* (potato), and *kool* (cabbage) were shared with other families or sold to Chinese merchants who had established themselves many years before.

I also helped with fishing in the small *kali* (small river). It was easy as only a line and a hook were needed. I always had success.

Uncle Richard was expecting another child and that meant that I spend more time away with other families.

Finally, my father, who worked hard on his own farmland in Maroeni, was ready to take me back in. He placed me with good friends, and they became my foster parents. Beforehand, I was not aware of that arrangement.

As is common in our Indo culture, a facial expression or a hand movement to the children was enough to let us know to stay out of the conversation between adults. We did not even want to try to understand the conversation.

One day in my European elementary school in Manokwari, I heard about the attack by Germany in Holland. I had no idea what the word 'war' really meant.

A couple of weeks later, a first unexpected confrontation happened.

A special team of police officers arrived from Java and proudly paraded with pride a group of settlers from German descent in town. These so-called "traitors" on their walk to the boats in the bay received several slaps to the face.

Without any reason, it felt like the people were just waiting for a public beating.

After the attack on Pearl Harbor, the atmosphere in Manokwari changed a lot. The call for mobilization demanded that my father and uncle had to exchange their farm tools for rifles and daily exercises with the KNIL.

Also, my foster brother, Hubert, was one of the mature men who was called for duty. With his gas mask, his battered glasses, and strange mouthpiece, he scared me all the time.

Because travel between the islands was not safe anymore, the KPM could not bring new supplies.

We started to get more and more isolated.

The news of Japanese soldiers nearing our island reached my young ears.

But before they arrived, we were treated first with a heavy bombardment. All the children in school dove under their little desks. It felt like the bombs made the earth tremble.

On that Sunday in April 1942, our bay was full of strange vessels. On the warships, we did see the flags which looked like a red sun with stripes like sunrays...*

---

*The Rising Sun Flag (Kyokujitsu-ki) symbolizes the sun as the Japanese national flag does. This design has been widely used in Japan for a long time. The design of the Rising Sun Flag is seen in numerous scenes in daily life of Japan, such as in fishermen's banners hoisted to signify large catch of fish, flags to celebrate childbirth, and in flags for seasonal festivities. It was originally used by feudal warlords in Japan during the Edo period (1603–1868 CE).

On May 15, 1870, as a policy of the Meiji government, it was adopted as the war flag of the Imperial Japanese Army, and on October 7, 1889, it was adopted as the naval ensign of the

*I*mperial Japanese Navy. A modified flag is flown by the Japan Maritime Self-Defense Force and a different version is flown by the Japan Self-Defense Forces and the Japan Ground Self-Defense Force.

Left: War flag of the Imperial Japanese Army (1870–1945)
Right: Naval ensign, flown by ships of the
Imperial Japanese Navy (1889–1945)

The flag of Japan and the Rising Sun had symbolic meaning since the early 7th century in the Asuka period (538–710 CE). The Japanese archipelago is east of the Asian mainland and is thus where the Sun "rises."

In 607 CE, an official correspondence that began with "from the Emperor of the rising sun" was sent to Chinese Emperor Yang of Sui. Japan is often referred to as "the land of the rising sun." In the 12th-century work, *The Tale of the Heike*, it was written that different samurai carried drawings of the Sun on their fans.

As the flag was used by the Imperial Japanese military during Japan's actions during World War Two, it is regarded as offensive by some in East Asia, particularly in South Korea (which was ruled by Japan) and China. This symbol is often associated with Japanese imperialism in the early 20th century in these two countries.

The Japanese government's basic position on the Rising Sun Flag: "Claims that the flag is an expression of political assertions or a symbol of militarism are absolutely false."

A history professor at the University of Connecticut, Alexis Dudden, however, pointed out that "Too few survivors of Japan's wartime atrocities remain alive to fill the Olympic stadium and explain the meaning of this symbol and the International Olympic Committee must learn from history instead ... countless Japanese historians, activists and regular citizens have resisted the efforts of their own government to deny Japanese history, by continuing to dig up bones and government documents, and recording the oral testimonies of those who suffered during Japan's imperial occupations and wars and their work gives solid accounting to what happened under the rising sun flag."

• Japanese Navy destroyer Amatsukaze
On 6 April 1945, the ship was attacked by USAAF B-25s, six miles east of Amoy. Her crew managed to beach the ship; salvage attempts were abandoned on 8 April. On 10 April, the ship was scuttled by charges placed on the ship.

• The Japanese A6M Zero, also known as the terror of the Pacific

Jean Victor de Bruijn:
Working and Living with the Papuans. White Piglets

5

Jean Victor de Bruijn, Captain of the Netherlands East Indies Army was a District Officer in Central New Guinea. His interactions with the local Papuan population adds a great insight into the daily living of indigenous tribes in that area as does his personal experiences of the events before and after the invasion of Japanese troops in New Guinea.

Jean Victor de Bruijn, was a *Sunday child*, and was born with a *helm* (caul) over his head. Both these things were good omens.

A *Sunday child* is supposed to be lucky, and amongst English people, to be born with a caul is also thought to bring good fortune and is supposed to protect against drowning. In the East Indies, it is believed to give one the power to see into the future.

The boy, one of a family of eight children, was born of Dutch parents, in 1913, at the sugar plantation at Mertojoedan, near Magalang, Java.

Jean Victor de Bruijn (1913 – 1979) was a Dutch district officer, soldier, explorer, ethnologist and writer. He gained fame for holding out with native Papuan soldiers in the mountainous interior of Western New Guinea against overwhelming Japanese forces as part of Operation Oaktree (see Chapter 20), maintaining one of the last Dutch-controlled outposts in the Dutch East Indies during World War Two.

His father was manager of the plantation.

From the secondary school in Semarang in 1931, he enrolled into the University at Leiden, where he took an education for a career in the civil administrative service of the Netherlands East Indies.

It was a five-year course, but de Bruijn finished his studies in four years.

At the age of twenty-four, he was ready to go to Netherlands New Guinea. The discovery that time of the Wissel Lakes, in the interior of that little-known country, had made him more eager. The government thought him to be too young for that responsible nature of work (anthropologist, ethnologist).

Two or three-years' experience was deemed necessary before an officer could be considered capable of filling such a position.

Unexpectedly, after only ten months in the service, de Bruijn got his opportunity.

In 1939, the government sent him an urgent telegram to fly to Amboina. From there, he was to proceed and take charge at the base at the newly-found Wissel Lakes. His big chance had come.

One day in October 1936, Flying Officer Naval Lieutenant-Commander F.J. Wissel, in the service of the Netherlands New Guinea Petroleum Company, made a survey flight from Seroei on the island of Japen, north of the Geelvink Bay, to Aika, east of Timoeka, situated on the southern coast of New Guinea.

Flying low over the central mountains between the two great coastal ranges north and south in Netherlands New Guinea, he noticed a glare in the valley. Officer Wissel took a dive with his plane for a closer look.

He was amazed to see a large body of water beneath him. He turned his around plane and dived again, this time flying very low over this large lake. He did not know at that time what excitement he caused.

There were several Papuan canoes on the lake, and Wissel was surprised to see the people jump overboard and swim for the shore.

Without him knowing, the plane's aerial had become detached, and with a piece of copper at the end of it was swinging dangerously low over the water.

This was too much for the fishermen, who, in any event, had never seen a plane before.

It so happened, that the Papuans in their village by the shore were preparing to celebrate a pig feast.

Three years later, they told De Bruijn that they had been so terrified when the plane flew over that they thought some awful thing was about to happen to them. In their fear, they abandoned the feast, threw the pigs into the lake, and ran into the jungle to hide.

This large region of Netherlands New Guinea and the numerous surrounding islands came under the government of *The Great East*, with a governor residing in Macassar (Celebes).

The Great East was divided into four residencies each directed by a Resident Magistrate. Divisions of these residencies were formed, each controlled by an Assistant Resident Magistrate. These divisions were split up again into subdivisions, each one to be in charge of a *Controller* (District Officer).

Still smaller districts came under a *Bestuursassistent*, who had to report to his controller.

The *Wissel Lakes* (Three Lakes), were given the Papuan names of Paniai, Tage and Tigi from north to south, respectively.

In May 1938, Commissioner of Police J.P.K. van Eechoud* used the trail from the coast, with about forty carriers and leaving another 380 carriers to follow with supplies.

Of these about 365 deserted.

Lieutenant-Colonel van Eechoud, later became Resident Magistrate of Netherlands New Guinea

They were people from the coastal tribes, unaccustomed to walk in the mountain and the cold climate.

Van Eechoud pushed ahead with his forty men, and eventually arrived at Lake Paniai, where, at Enarotali, he established the first Dutch administration outpost in the central mountains of Netherlands New Guinea.

The base at Enarotali was staffed by the District Officer and a doctor, a radio operator, about twenty native police, one hundred and twenty Papuan coolies who worked between different posts and twenty Javanese convicts.

This post consisted of one hut forty meters in length, a kitchen, a hut for the coolies, and one for the convicts, and there was also a small hospital, the Bernhard Hospital, named after Princess Juliana's husband.

All the huts were made of bamboo, with a thatched roof, and the entire party lived within this simple compound.

In the valleys, between the mountains, were several villages of Papuans of the Ekari tribe.

All these Papuans, of the central ranges of Netherlands New Guinea, had lived in complete isolation until 1936.

They are, perhaps, the most primitive people on earth, and in every respect still belong to the Stone Age.

They did not have any contact with the coastal tribes. Their environment was entirely of their own making, without any outside influence whatsoever.

Their skin is dark, almost black and slight of build, only about five feet high, that is known as a pygmoid type.

They have kinky hair and very flat feet. The latter striking evidence of their continuous padding through the marshes and over the mountain trails, which they cover with remarkable agility.

At first it may appear that their life is carefree, but a deeper knowledge of their customs and beliefs shows that this is not so. They live in perpetual fear of evil spirits, and there are numerous tribal differences which keep them on guard and bring inevitable bitter conflict.

Some of their tribal laws must cause considerable anxiety as well. One for example: if a man dies, his wife will be killed as well. Many women live with this knowledge hanging over them.

Their needs are quite simple. They generally have two hot meals a day: morning and evening. In the ordinary family community, the meals are cooked in hot ashes, but for a larger number of people, they usually cook the food under hot stones.

This method is as follows, a primitive oven is made by digging a hole in the ground. Into this is placed a layer of hot stones covered with banana leaves. Next more stones, another layer of leaves, then vegetables also wrapped, and more hot stones on top. And so on, layer upon layer of hot stones, food, and more hot stones.

Normally in their gardens, they grow sweet potatoes, yams, taro, a kind of cucumber, bananas, *pawpaw* (a fruit tasting like a combination of banana, pineapple, and mango), and the long bean such as *ketjipir* (green vegetable), also ginger and spinach. One of their special delicacies is raw ginger eaten with salt.

Clothes of any description were unknown to them. The women wore only a grass skirt, and the men *the penis koker* (Dutch for a long, dried, gourd-like penis covering) which is known as a *koteka* in the Ekari language and *gosara* in the Migani.

Though healthy, fifty years appeared to be their average lifespan.

Into this region, and to live amongst the people, at twenty-five years of age, and after only ten months experience in the administrative service, came District Officer Dr. J.B. de Bruijn.

One wonders if the *helm* (caul) of his birth gave him the power to see what the next five years were to bring – exploration and discoveries of the greatest importance. His life and adventures with the Papuans, sickness, hardship, and endurance. The utter loneliness after the Japanese occupation of the East Indies. The loss of his only brother, who died in an internment camp in Singapore. The agony of his country under the Japanese yoke. The invasion of Netherlands New Guinea and his commando raid on an enemy coastal position.

De Bruijn entered a land where time stood still.

He knew neither the country nor the people and knew nothing of their language and tribal customs.

There were, however, some things he did know: one was the importance of first contacts.

"If first contact with the people is not good," De Bruijn said, "the opportunity is never recovered. Once it is made it will always be safe."

De Bruijn gained their confidence. They visited his hut; sometimes they would just stand quietly watching him at work or would squat on the earthen floor and chat.

Often they brought him presents, and even stayed for lunch, and some remained to spend the night by his fire.

They were always welcome to visit.

It is noticeable that de Bruijn never refers to them as "the natives"; to him, they were always "the people."

He watched them lazily bobbing up and down in the breeze on the lake. He could see the women in the canoes handling the big nets full of crayfish and pulling them into the canoe.

On one of the canoes, a roof of grass had been erected as protection against heavy rain. From other canoes, plumes of smoke could be seen rising and floating towards him.

The Papuan people light fires in their canoes and cook their meals as they fish. Sometimes the men dive, and remain under water for two minutes or more, and when they come to the top, they make a whistling noise that can be heard some distance away.

During one of his expeditions, De Bruijn visited the Moni tribe of Papuans. The chief called Soalekigi said to him: "I am your friend. Welcome ame."

64

The chief called his people together and told them that the new *Kontolulle* had come (to them, the Controller was known as the Kontolulle, their nearest approach to the correct pronunciation). After the introduction, they all danced for about half an hour and a great feast of welcome was prepared.

De Bruijn never encouraged the Papuans to wear clothes. They believed that dirty, tattered garments were unhealthy and added nothing to their beauty or dignity. He was to find later that several Papuan tribes regarded clothing, even as worn by the white people, as a prelude of disease.

All Papuans are very superstitious, and probably their greatest fear is of ghosts. Many things that are mystic, or at any rate without substance, are presented in their language by a common term *Aja*. They seek protection from ghosts during their daily life by wearing, in their woven armlets, the strongly camphor-scented leaves of the Dako plant. The evil spirit they fear most is the *Mado*.

To everyone's satisfaction, all the imported animals had proved to be a welcome addition. Especially the pigs. Little white piglets were plentiful, for their mothers had delivered litters of seven and nine at a time.

The people took great care of them. At night, they kept them in their own huts, at the far end and beyond the central fireplace. The women took the little piglets and slept with them to keep them warm.

They did not, however, suckle them, as the coastal people in Manokwari will do, but gave them every other attention. Pig-breeding is one of the most important things in their village life and trade. They would rather possess one pig than two goats. From the many animals De Bruijn had received as presents, he selected some for himself and gave the others away.

All his own pigs, with a devilish humor that might not have been appreciated in some quarters, he named after his former girlfriends. There were quite a number, and the animals answered to their given names.

One was called Thea, and she loved to be petted. It became Thea's habit, whenever she wanted a little attention, to come to De Bruijn's hut.

With a fore-leg knock at the door, it was opened to her. She would come in and lie on the floor at his feet to have her back scratched.

Thea knew no greater joy than this, unless it was, perhaps, the sweet potato with which she was rewarded before she went home.

Suddenly one day, Thea did not come. De Bruijn went out and called her, but there was no response.

No one had seen Thea all day. They concluded that she must have heard the call of the wild and was an abandoned female.

After a couple of weeks, there was a knock on his door.

"Come in," De Bruijn said.

No one came in, but the knocking was repeated.

"Come in, " he repeated again.

Still no response, and still the knocking. De Bruijn got up and opened the door.

And there stood Thea, with nine little white piglets all asking for food. It was a lovely sight.

They all came into his hut, and Thea had her back scratched. He gave her some sweet potatoes, after which she and her family departed.

On the 6th of December 1941, Resident Magistrate J.H. Janssen, in a private letter to De Bruijn, wrote from Amboina: "Whatever happens at the Post, maintain your position in the central mountains."

Two days later the Netherlands East Indies declared war on Japan.

De Bruijn, however, had already written to Amboina volunteering to stay with the Police in the interior, and did not wanted to stop the work of exploration, as had been done in the previous years.

In answer to this letter, Janssen send a radio message.

It was dated Christmas Day, the 25th of December 1941: "The Netherlands flag will continue to fly in Dutch New Guinea. I know that under all circumstances, you will be brave."

After the last KNILM supply flight came in, began, as De Bruijn described it "a long dark night that lasted for half a year."

On the 29th January 1942, Amboina was occupied, and two weeks later Resident Magistrate Janssen died in a concentration camp.

The only communication with the west was Fak Fak.

On the morning of the 8th of March 1942, they heard of Java's plight:

"Dutchmen in these territories. We have fought shoulder to shoulder with our Indonesian friends; we have won and lost battles with them. The white inhabitants of the Indies never left their domiciles, thus proving to the world that we Netherlanders – no matter what race or color – are inextricably bound up without Indies Territory."

All day, restless and sad at heart, they hovered about the radio hut, waiting, hoping, but also knowing their last hope was gone.

At 10:30, while the crisp silent night lay about the little mountain hut, they were still listening, and they heard that Bandoeng had capitulated – and the last message:

"We are now closing down.

Good-bye until better times.

Long live the Queen."

De Bruijn: "I was laying in bed and was thinking of that day on the 3rd of July 1596, when the Dutch first landed in Java. All night I followed the course of our history in Indonesia through those three hundred and fifty years."

*• KNILM Augustus 1940 announcement of flights
starting to depart from Batavia (Java) to Ambon*

• 1940s KNILM DC2 ready for take-off

68

Manokwari 1936:
Life of the Settlers. The War Is Near

6

In 1936, back in Manokwari, a military presence was established. There were ninety Indonesians under a European command. Most of the military men were married and brought their wives and children with them.

An airline service for transport of mail and passengers was started with seaplanes from the KNILM *(Koninklijke Nederlandsch-Indisch Luchtvaart Maatschappij).*

The Marines came to visit regularly on a corvette or a couple of Dornier seaplanes. Activity picked up in Manokwari.

In 1937, the Government started a rubber plantation in Ransiki at the Geelvink Bay. The first administrator brought the first car, but he needed to make driveable roads before he could use the car in New Guinea.

Kokkeling: "In 1939 Mr. J., my benefactor died. His widow and daughters shifted to Manokwari, and his son - now a grown man - stayed with me on Mangoapi to continue the business."

In the same year a Japanese marine trainingship with officers and cadets visited Manokwari. This beautiful ship stayed in Dorey Bay for three days.

The crew walked undisturbed, took pictures, and made notes and maps. The Japanese were very polite and interested in every detail about the area. They even visited many of the settler businesses.

The settlers were trusting and believed that they came to learn and were pleased by their interest in their farms and businesses. The Japanese ship travelled from Manokwari to

Momi, to visit the Japanese cotton plantation. They stayed for only a couple of days, but later the people in Manokwari heard that they left one of their officers behind. Probably not to take care of his health!

In 1939, there was a long drought that lasted for nine months. This had never happened before. The wells that had always supplied a fresh stream of water diminished to a small trickle that was caught with utmost care. Taking a bath or washing clothes was not possible. The settlers even had to kill their pigs as they did not have enough water for them.

But it was the land that suffered the most. The dry earth split open like after an earthquake, all the vegetables rotted away and planting for new crop did not make much sense. It was a disaster and for local farmers a huge catastrophe.

In the beginning of the 1940s, the first news about the war reached the colonists, but nobody believed that they would be taking part.

They thought that if the world would get into a war, the Netherlands would be spared, just as it was in the First World War.

They were shocked when they heard on the radio what had happened in Europe: the German invasion, the bombing of the city of Rotterdam, the Dutch Royal Family fleeing to England and Canada.

By order of the Government all men, women and children of German descent were to be picked up in New Guinea, guarded and placed in a Government ship bound for Java.

The colonists still thought that they would not be part of a confrontation in New Guinea or the war in Europe.

The commanding officer of the KNIL garrison in Manokwari, Captain Willemsz.-Geeroms, thought it would be better to take certain precautions.

All people able to take up arms were called to report for duty. They each received a military uniform and a rifle, and went through the same drills that some of them had done during their time in the military service in Java.

After fourteen days, the militia was sent home again, but had to check in every week for a couple of hours to undertake more preparations and perform military drills.

They received six and a quarter cents per hour, and they deposited the money into a container for the little Spitfire fund that was standing on the table in the canteen.

This did not help the usual routine of the settlers. There was a lot of negativity, but at the same time they thought of their fellow men in the Netherlands who had it much worse. They still enjoyed their freedom, and it was worth the sacrifice of these military drills.

The news about the war was contradictory and confusing. They all believed that eventually their side would win.

In addition to the messages received through the radio, they read the newspapers which were a couple of weeks old before they arrived in Manokwari.

They read about negotiations with Japan, and they were proud of the Dutch Indonesian Government who fought against demands to surrender.

During all this time they did not believe that Japan would escalate from words to military action.

Then suddenly Pearl Harbor was attacked.

The last newspapers received wrote about the work that was done in Java to prepare for a defense against an invasion. They read about the landing of American and Australian troops who brought with them large quantities of war materials.

Above all they trusted the Government, the army, navy, air force, and the Allies.

On the sixth of March, Radio Bandoeng announced the capitulation of Java, and then stayed silent.

With that final announcement, any connection was broken, not only with the Netherlands, but with the rest of Netherlands Indies, and the rest of the world.

Now they were totally committed to defend themselves. Did they lose faith?

71

No!

Kokkelink just finished planting a part of his land and one of his pigs just had given birth to piglets when he received the order to report for duty.

He understood he would possibly be gone for a long time. It could be the end of eight years of hard labor on his farm with his animals.

He did not earn much money, but he respected what he had and loved his animals. It was difficult to let go of what he had built from the ground up, but he was not the only one.

Many settlers had to do the same.

Kokkelink opened the cages and hoped that Mother Nature would take care of the animals.

Now he was a soldier again. He did had not enjoyed his previous military duty in Java and had not seen the benefit of learning something he would never use in real life. Now this was a different situation.

They were under attack by an enemy who did not care about other people, who ignored conventions and treaties and used them like pieces of scrap paper. It was a deadly attack on freedom of life and ideals.

With that understanding, he was a proud soldier and ready to do anything necessary.

In December 1941, Theodoor Beynon was also asked to become a member of the militia to protect the group of Eurasian settlers.

The militia was part of the KNIL division in Manokwari under the command of KNIL Captain Willemsz.-Geeroms.

Following the news of the attack by the Japanese on Pearl Harbor which drew the USA into the conflict and the subsequent declaration of war by the Dutch Government, evacuation plans were finalized. They directed Theodoor Beynon, KNIL Sergeant Zeelt and a small group of other troops, to protect a large group of women, children, and older men, and escort them to the military evacuation camp in Oransbari which had been prepared earlier.

 Theodoor Beynon was asked because by that time he had a large family (eight children), and was well-known by the tribal chiefs of the Papuan population. He employed many Papuan people to work on his property and he understood their dialect very well. He was seen as a great 'chief' or 'governor' in the Manokwari area and well-respected. He had a large mustache and was recognized everywhere. He had often been asked to be a mediator in conflicts between settlers and the Papuan people.

The journey to Oransbari was done by boat and continued thereafter on foot.

On one of the days before the Japanese invasion, they were called back in the camp when KNIL Captain Geeroms called a special meeting. He explained the imminent invasion but at the same time said he believed that New Guinea would not be part of the war as it was so far away from other territories.

He told them with a strong voice to be ready, no matter what. Be prepared as if the war is in front of our doorstep.

"I understand that this is asking you to make sacrifices, but we have a duty and responsibility for our Queen and Nation and put our personal interests aside."

His speech made a big impression. The troops felt part of his vision, and they needed to trust his command and be part of the mission to defend themselves.

After the commander finished his speech, they were joking again and Kokkelink had to take it on the chin. Rightfully so, as he looked like a scarecrow with his uniform that was three sizes too big. "When the Japanese soldiers see you, they will get so scared they will run away," one of the guys said with a smile.

The professional soldiers made fun of the colonists' unmilitary ways of responding to action. You cannot make a perfect soldier from a settler immediately.

A couple of days before the invasion, all Japanese people were picked up from the cotton factory in Momi and brought to Manokwari, including about fifty women and children. They did not take their capture seriously and were feeling happy, as if they were going on a picnic. They did have guns, but they did not fight the small number of militia men that came and arrested them.

The troops were perplexed to see the homes of the Japanese workers, with modern equipment etc., compared to their own.

Of the three motorboats that the Japanese cotton factory owned, only the *Daito Maru* was anchored in the bay. But, they did find another small speedboat.

The Dutch militia took control of the boats and the Japanese crew was ordered to bring them to Manokwari. More important was the modern telephone installation of which they could make good use.

Mr. Saito, head of the Nanyo Kohatsu Kaisha in Manokwari was taken prisoner. It was a difficult decision, as he was a well-respected man in the community.

During his arrest he was joyful and courteous but had a cynical smile on his face.

A short while later, the interned Japanese people were taken to Ambon, with exception of a heavily pregnant woman who on doctor's advice had to stay behind.

In the middle of January 1942, suddenly a Japanese airplane arrived above Manokwari, dropped four bombs, dove low over the military base, and sprayed it with machine gun fire. It was a miracle that there was no real damage; only a dog lost his life.

The colonists were more surprised than scared because, until that moment, nobody believed that they would be part of the Pacific War.

They were grateful as it shattered their belief that they would not be part of it.

As a military target, strategic or otherwise, they did not think that Manokwari or even New Guinea was an important target for the Japanese troops.

It was crazy for the Japanese to send a military airplane thousands of miles to kill a couple of people.

From the viewpoint of the Japanese, they could imagine an attack on Java would help them with supplies of oil, rubber, tin, and other important military materials.

But why would they waste their time and military power on this jungle? That is what the colonists believed.

Although they did not understand Japan's motives, they understood that this Japanese pilot was not conducting a pleasure flight. There would be more to follow.

The militia also understood that with a *klewang* (machete) and a rifle – their only weapons – you could not bring down any airplanes.

The commanding officer told the troops to dig and prepare trenches. There should be room enough for the total population of Manokwari. Even women and children helped with the digging of the trenches.

At a different part on the island and on top of a hill close to the base, they placed a reconnaissance post in which they used the Japanese captured telephone network to connect the camp with the home of the commanding officer.

Personnel manning the post were instructed to report anything suspicious. Outside the home of the commanding officer a large bell was hung to provide air raid warnings. At the sound of the bell, everyone needed to get into the trenches.

The military had to take their arms, flasks for water, and their field bags with provisions enough for four days.

Now that the colonists were disconnected from the rest of the world, they had to survive on what the land provided. That also meant requisition and distribution.

All the farm animals like cows, pigs, and chickens which

the settlers had left behind were assembled and placed in an enclosure close to the base camp.

As most of the colonists were mobilized, there was now less fresh fruit and vegetables available. To make matters worse, the local Papuans had fled into the mountains after the first bombardment, and the colonists did not get food delivered from their plantations anymore, such as pork, turtle meat, turtle eggs, fish, fruit, and sweet potatoes.

The main staple, rice, had not yet been planted, and they only had a limited supply available. Baking flour was in short supply, and the rations of bread were cut by half. In the end, there was no more bread left.

Although in the beginning the food supply was not critical, shortages came soon. A cup of coffee for a settler is like an alcoholic drink for somebody working on a ship.

Even worse is that the *weduwe* (Van Nelle strong tobacco) was running out. A quick replacement is not found, because the flavor of Van Nelle tobacco was irreplaceable. No other means of smoking were available now. But people accepted that without too much negativity. To keep the food supplies at a reasonable level, everyone spent more time fishing.

It was amusing to see young boys and girls fishing in the bay with a long bamboo stick, a worm, and a short thin rope. Fortunately they did not understand the predicament and emotional roller coaster that was about to happen.

Japan Attacks the United States

7

When Japanese bombers appeared in the skies over Pearl Harbor on the morning of December 7, 1941, the U.S. military was unprepared for the devastating surprise attack, which dramatically altered the course of World War Two, especially in the Pacific theater.

There were several key reasons for the bombing that, in hindsight, made it seem almost inevitable.

Before the attack, tensions between Japan and the United States had been mounting for the better part of a decade.

The island nation of Japan, isolated from the rest of the world for much of its history, embarked on a period of aggressive expansion near the turn of the 20th century.

Two successful wars, one with China in 1894-95 and the Russo-Japanese War in 1904-05, fueled their ambitions, as did Japan's successful participation in World War One (1914-18) alongside the Allies.

During the Great Depression of the 1930s, Japan sought to solve its economic and demographic woes by forcing its way into China, starting in 1931 with an invasion of Manchuria. When a commission appointed by the League of Nations condemned the invasion, Japan withdrew from the international organization.

It would occupy Manchuria until 1945.

In July 1937, a clash at Beijing's Marco Polo Bridge began another Sino-Japanese war. That December, after Japanese forces captured *Nanjing* (Nanking), the capital of the Chinese Nationalist Party, or *Guomindang* (Kuomintang), they proceeded to carry out six weeks of mass killings and rapes now known as the *Nanjing Massacre.*

In light of such atrocities, the United States began imposing economic sanctions against Japan, including trade embargoes on aircraft exports, oil and scrap metal, among other key goods, and gave economic support to Guomindang forces.

In September 1940, Japan signed the *Tripartite Pact* with Germany and Italy, the two fascist regimes then at war with the Allies.

Tokyo and Washington negotiated for months leading up to the Pearl Harbor attack, without success. While the United States hoped embargoes on oil and other key goods would lead Japan to halt its expansionism, the sanctions and other penalties actually convinced Japan to stand its ground, and stirred up the anger of its people against continued Western interference in Asian affairs.

To Japan, war with the United States had begun to seem inevitable, in order to defend its status as a major world power. Because the odds were stacked against the Japanese, their only chance was the element of surprise.

In May 1940, the United States had made Pearl Harbor the main base for its Pacific Fleet. As Americans didn't expect the Japanese to attack first in Hawaii, some 4,000 miles away from the Japanese mainland, the base at Pearl Harbor was left relatively undefended, making it an easy target.

Admiral Yamamoto Isoroku spent months planning an attack that aimed to destroy the Pacific Fleet and destroy morale in the U.S. navy, so that it would not be able to fight back as Japanese forces began to advance on targets across the South Pacific.

Japan's surprise attack on Pearl Harbor would drive the

United States out of neutrality and into World War Two. A conflict that ended with Japan's surrender after the devastating U.S. nuclear bombing of Hiroshima and Nagasaki in August 1945.

At first, however, the Pearl Harbor attack looked like a success for Japan. Its bombers hit all eight U.S. battleships, sinking four and damaging four others, destroyed or damaged more than three hundred aircraft and killed some 2,400 Americans at Pearl Harbor.

Japanese forces went on to capture a string of current and former Western colonial possessions by early 1942 including Burma (now Myanmar), British Malaya (Malaysia and Singapore), the Dutch East Indies (Indonesia), and the Philippines 'giving them access to these islands' plentiful natural resources, including oil and rubber.

But the Pearl Harbor attack had failed in its objective to completely destroy the Pacific Fleet. The Japanese bombers missed oil tanks, ammunition sites, and repair facilities, and not a single U.S. aircraft carrier was in the vicinity during the attack.

In June 1942, this failure came to haunt the Japanese, as U.S. forces scored a major victory in the Battle of Midway, decisively turning the tide of war.

• *Battle of Midway. The Mikuma before sinking.*
It was one of four carriers of the Japanese that sunk.

On January 11, 1942, the Japanese declared war on the Royal Dutch government and invaded Borneo and the Island of Celebes. The date marked the beginning of the end of the Dutch presence in the East Indies.

79

• The Curtiss P-40 Warhawk is an American single-engined, single-seat, all-metal fighter and ground-attack aircraft that first flew in 1938. The Warhawk was used by most Allied powers during World War Two, and remained in frontline service until the end of the war.

• The North American B-25 Mitchell is a medium bomber that was introduced in 1941 and named in honor of Major General William "Billy" Mitchell, a pioneer of U.S. military aviation. Used by many Allied air forces, the B-25 served in every theater of World War Two, and after the war, many remained in service, operating across four decades.

The Netherlands Declares War On Japan

8

On December 8th 1941, the day after the Japanese attack on Pearl Harbor, Queen Wilhelmina of the Netherlands issued the following proclamation:

"The Kingdom of the Netherlands considers itself in a state of war with Japan.

While negotiations which were in progress between the governments of the United States and Japan were not yet completed, and while President Roosevelt exhibited the greatest patience and did his utmost to preserve peace in the Pacific, and while an appeal which President Roosevelt had sent to the Emperor of Japan still remained unanswered, Japanese forces attacked American and British territory without a declaration of war.

This war has been forced on the United States and the British Empire. You know how Germany, in the same manner that Japan now emulates in Asia, attacked many countries in Europe, one after another. Japan, motivated by the same spirit of aggression and the same disregard of law, follows in the footsteps of her German Axis partner.

Neither the safety of the territories of our Kingdom in the Far East, nor the ties which bind us to our British Allies, nor the special relations which exist between the Netherlands and the United States allow the Government of the Kingdom to look on passively.

The Kingdom of the Netherlands considers itself in a state of war with Japan because the aggression-which seeks to put out of action, one by one, the countries which desire peace can only be halted through a strong coalition.

Now that the American and British peoples, with whom we are closely bound in friendship, are attacked, the Kingdom of the Netherlands places all its armed forces and resources at the disposal of the allied war effort.

The development of our Kingdom for centuries has been guided by a unified destiny. In the hurricane which threatens this development, it rises with resolute unity to maintain its place in the world. The Netherlands did not hesitate to defend herself immediately, with courage, when she was viciously attacked in Europe. The Netherlands East Indies will not waver now that she is menaced by a similar attack.

The Indies stood with the Netherlands in her hour of trial. The Netherlands and our West Indies will stand with the East Indies now that the Indies are resisting aggression. I rely on the Navy, the Army and the Air Force, the authorities and the civilian services.

I and all my subjects rely on the courage, resolution and determination of all those in the Indies. Trusting in God, whom all my subjects desire to serve in freedom and who know that our cause is righteous and our conscience clear, we accept the challenge together with our powerful allies.

We will triumph and our Kingdom, beset but at the same time purified, steeled and standing with inviolable pride will survive stronger than ever to live under our free banner in a world free from aggression."

In the Indies, Governor General Van Starkenborgh Stachouwer made the following declaration by radio to the population of the Netherlands East Indies:

"People of the Netherlands East Indies: In its unexpected attack on American and British territories while diplomatic negotiations were still in progress, the Japanese empire has consciously adopted a course of aggression. These attacks, which have thrown the United States of America and the British empire into active war on the side of already-fighting China, have as their object the establishment of Japanese supremacy in the whole of east and southeast Asia. These aggressions also menace the Netherlands East Indies in no small measure. The Netherlands government accepts the challenge and takes up arms against the Japanese empire."

Dutch naval ships joined forces with the Allies to form the American-British-Dutch-Australian (ABDA) Fleet, commanded by Dutch rear admiral Karel Doorman.

On February 27-28, 1942, Admiral Doorman was ordered to take the offensive against the Imperial Japanese Navy. His objections on the matter were overruled. The ABDA fleet finally encountered the Japanese surface fleet and which Doorman gave the order to engage. This came to be known as *The Battle of the Java Sea.*

The Allied fleet suffered heavy losses. The Dutch cruisers *Java* and *De Ruyter* were lost, together with the destroyer *Kortenaer.*

The other Allied cruisers, the Australian *Perth*, the British

Exeter, and the American *Houston*, tried to disengage but they were spotted by the Japanese in the following days and eventually all were destroyed.

Numerous ABDA destroyers were also lost. According to legend, Admiral Doorman's attack order was *Ik val aan, volg mij!* ("I am attacking, follow me!"); in reality, the order was *"All ships follow me!"*

After Japanese troops landed on Java and the KNIL had been unsuccessful in stopping their advance (due to the Japanese ability to occupy a relatively unguarded airstrip), the Dutch forces on Java surrendered on 7 March 1942.

Some 42,000 Dutch soldiers were taken prisoner and interned in labor camps, though some were executed on the spot. Later all Dutch civilians (some 100,000 in total), were arrested and interned in camps, and some were deported to Japan or sent to work on the Thai-Burma Railway.

During the Japanese occupation between four and ten million Javanese were forced to work for the Japanese war effort. Some 270,000 Javanese were taken to other parts of Southeast Asia; only 52,000 of those survived.

A Dutch government study described how the Japanese military forcibly recruited women as prostitutes in the Dutch East Indies. It concluded that among those 200 to 300 European women were working in Japanese military brothels.

Others, faced with starvation in the refugee camps, agreed to offers of food and payment for work, the nature of which was not completely revealed to them.

The Dutch submarines escaped and resumed hostilities with the Allies from bases in Australia such as Fremantle. As a part of the Allied forces, they were on the hunt for Japanese tankers on their way to Japan and the movement of Japanese troops and weapons to other sites of battle (including New Guinea). Because of the significant number of Dutch submarines active in this theater of the war, the Dutch were named the *Fourth Ally* in the theatre along with the Australians, Americans, and New Zealanders.

Many Dutch army and navy airmen escaped and, with airplanes provided by the U.S., formed the Royal Australian Air Force's Nos. 18 and 120 (Netherlands East Indies) Squadrons, equipped with B-25 Mitchell bombers and P-40 Kittyhawk fighters, respectively.

No. 18 Squadron conducted bombing raids from Australia to the Dutch East Indies, and both squadrons eventually also participated in their recapture.

The Dutch government finally ended all resistance to the superior Japanese forces on March 8, surrendering on Java.

• *Illegal salvagers looking for scrap metal, have plundered at least six World War Two shipwrecks near Indonesia. The damaged wrecks include three Dutch and two British warships sunk by Japanese forces after the Battle of the Java Sea in February 1942, and the American submarine USS Perch, which sank in the Java Sea in March 1942 after being damaged in an attack on Japanese destroyers. The scale of damage to the historic shipwrecks was discovered by an international team of divers and underwater survey specialists, sponsored by a Dutch naval memorial society, the Karel Doorman Fund. The fund had hoped to capture video footage of the Dutch shipwrecks in preparation for the 75th anniversary of the Battle of the Java Sea. The Dutch wrecks were almost intact when they were rediscovered by amateur divers in 2002, but the latest expedition found only holes in the seabed where many of the wrecks once lay. "It was shocking," Jacques Brandt, president of the Karel Doorman Fund, told Live Science. "As the representative organization of the next-of-kin of the ships' crews, it was a big blow to us, as we considered those ships as being war graves under the sea and they clearly should not be tampered with."*

The survey team reported that the wrecks of two of the Dutch warships - the HNLMS De Ruyter and the HNLMS Java - are missing. A large part of a third wreck - the HNLMS Kortenaer - is also missing. They also reported that two British war wrecks in the area - the HMS Exeter and the HMS Encounter - have been almost entirely scavenged for scrap metal, and that the wreck of the USS Perch has "completely vanished."

• Japan invades New Guinea.

Japan Invades New Guinea

9

 The Japanese invasion of Australian and Dutch New Guinea lasted from November 1941 until April 1942.

The takeover happened in record time because there were few battalions of the Royal Dutch Army in the East Indies (KNIL) in New Guinea at the time.

The Imperial Japanese Naval Force, which occupied the Dutch New Guinea territories, was called the N Expeditionary Force and was assembled at Ambon Island at the end of March 1942. It departed from Ambon Island in the night of March 29, 1942.

The Order of Battle of the N Expeditionary Force, led by Rear-Admiral Ruitaro Fujita was as follows: The 11th Carrier Division with seaplane carrier *Chitose* and the 3rd Section of 16th Cruiser Squadron with light cruiser *Kinu*. The 1st Section of 16th Destroyer Division with destroyers *Yukikaze* and *Tokitsukaze*, torpedo boats *Tomozuru, Hatsukari* and patrol boats. The 54th Submarine-chaser Division with submarine-chasers *Shonan Maru #5, Shonan Maru #17, Fukuei Maru #15* plus assorted smaller craft.

The Naval Landing Force (NLF) was under the command of Captain S. Shibuya which included the 4th Guard Unit (a battalion) and the 24th Special Base Unit (500 men).

The NLF troops were under Captain S. Shibuya's command, and subordinated to the 24th Special Base Force then on Ambon Island. The 24th Special Base Force moved to

Endeh, Flores Island on November 15th, 1943. Transport Force: 2nd Gunboat Division with gunboats *Manyo Maru, Taiko Maru* and *Okuyo Maru* and oil tanker *Seian Maru* and transport ship *Hokuriku Maru*.

On 5 March, Imperial General Headquarters by Navy Directive No.62 ordered Commander-in-Chief, Combined Fleet, upon completion of the Java operation, to annihilate the remaining enemy forces in Dutch New Guinea and to occupy strategic points of that territory.

The objectives were to survey the countryside for possible sites for air bases, anchorages, and oilfields, and to secure a good communication and supply line with British New Guinea.

Plans involved called for landings at Fakfak, Babo, Sorong, Manokwari, Moemi, Nabire, Seroei, Sarmi, and Hollandia with the garrisoning of troops in the Fakfak and Manokwari areas.

The force used was to touch down at Boela (Ceram Island) to investigate the condition of an oilfield known to be there. To carry out these operations the 2nd Southern Expeditionary Fleet organized the Dutch New Guinea Invasion Force under command of Rear-Admiral Ruitaro Fujita at Ambon on 15 March 1942.

The Japanese invasion fleet left Ambon Island on the night of March 29, 1942 and arrived at the town of Boela, Ceram Island, on 31 March 1942. They found the town deserted and decided to divide their forces into two detachments. The 1st Detachment occupied the town of Fakfak on 1 April 1942. The small KNIL garrison surrendered without a fight.

A Dutch garrison of about 200 KNIL soldiers was stationed in Babo. The airfield was still under construction. The town was important because of its nearby rich oilfields. Babo was raided by the Japanese planes for the first time on 30 December 1941, and was considered as a substitute base in case Laha and Namlea became inoperable. Three Hudson bombers were sent there to act as 'fighters,' a temporary duty was regarded to defend against four engined enemy flying boats.

The Dutch garrison at Babo was hard at work improving defenses and clearing for a second runway. The Japanese 2nd Detachment arrived in Babo on 2 April 1942, landed their NLF unit and occupied the town. Most KNIL soldiers managed to escape to Australia.

The Dutch Naval Air Group GVT-2 was stationed at Sorong, with three flying boats Dornier Do-24K under the command of Lieutenant 2nd Class W.J. Reynierse plus a support ship, the seaplane tender Arend.

During a reconnaissance mission northwest of Vogelkop Peninsula, on December 8th 1941 (the first day of the war), the crew of the Dutch flying boat X-12 (Lieutenant A. Höfelt) spotted a group of Japanese fishing vessels and a big schooner located in the Straight of Bougainville, between the islands of Sajang and Waigeo trying to make a run for home. Bombs were dropped, but resulted in only one near miss.

The next day, two other Dutch flying boats attacked the Japanese schooner setting it on fire. On Tuesday, December 16th the seaplane tender Arend was attacked by a Japanese flying boat Kawanishi H6K5 type 97 Mavis, but did not score any hits.

The Kawanishi attacked again the following day. Three bombs exploded behind the accelerating X-11. The two other Do-24K-1's who were already airborne tried to intercept the Kawanishi, but failed.

The 1st Detachment arrived in Sorong on 4 April 1942, landed their NLF unit and occupied the town. The town's small KNIL garrison surrendered after a short skirmish.

The elements of the Japanese 5th *(Amphibious)* Infantry Division arrived at Sorong in December 1942 in order to garrison the town and nearby vicinity for awhile.

In Ternate (situated on a small island near Halmahera Island) Dutch Naval Air Group GVT-5 with three flying boats Dornier Do-24K was stationed.

Ternate was raided by the Japanese planes for the first time on 17 December. The 2nd Detachment arrived in Ternate on 7 April 1942, landed NLF and bombarded the enemy positions.

The KNIL garrison soon surrendered and Japanese managed to capture approximately 150 Dutch civilians. Both, 1st and 2nd Detachments, met in Ternate harbor.

On 8 April 1942, the Japanese forces landed and occupied the town of Djailolo on Halmahera Island without a fight.

The reunited N Expeditionary Force arrived in Manokwari on 12 April 1942, landed and quickly occupied the town. Approximately 150 Dutch KNIL troops were reported to be at Manokwari, but at the time of the landing, there they had fled to the mountains.

To counter any possible action by these troops, a detachment (192 men) of the 4th Japanese Guard Unit remained in Manokwari.

The Dutch garrison commander, KNIL Captain J.B.H. Willemsz.-Geeroms, took the command of approximately sixty Dutch militiamen and seventeen native soldiers and retreated into the jungle to fight a guerrilla war against the Japanese troops.

On April 18th, 1944, sick and exhausted Captain Geeroms fell into enemy hands and was executed by the Japanese in Manokwari in May 1944.

The remnants of the KNIL troops, now under command of KNIL Sergeant Mauretz Christiaan Kokkelink, retreated inland and continued with the guerrilla warfare until October 1944 when they made contact with the American troops at Sansapor.

They were eventually evacuated to Australia.

In pre-war times the small town of Moemi (situated south of Ransiki) was a post for the civil administration of the area. There were also several plantations those times which were run by Japanese citizens.

As Moemi was absolutely unimportant in a military sense

(no harbor, no garrisons, no airfield), it might be that the Japanese plantations were the reason for their landing in the small town.

The 2nd Detachment arrived in Moemi on 15 April 1942, landed his NLF unit and occupied the town without a fight.

The 1st Detachment arrived in Seroei, Japen Island, on 16 April 1942 and occupied the town. There were no KNIL troops on the island.

Biak Island was not occupied until December 25th, 1943 when the elements of the Japanese 36th Infantry Division landed on the island and began the airfield construction.

In the prewar days, the Japanese had a forestry concession in Nabire. The 2nd Detachment arrived in the town of Nabire on 17 April 1942. The NLF unit landed and occupied the town after a short fight with the local KNIL military outpost.

The 2nd Detachment then arrived in the town of Sarmi on 19 April 1942, landed the NLF unit and occupied the town after a short fight with the KNIL soldiers.

The Japanese left a small garrison in Sarmi of about sixty-eight NLF troops until the Army units relieved them until late 1942. The 1st Detachment arrived in the town of Hollandia on 19 April 1942, landed their NLF unit and after a short fight overran town's KNIL garrison.

The invasion force left a small garrison of NLF troops in Hollandia until the Army units relieved them in July 1942.

The N Expeditionary Force assembled at Manokwari on 21 April 1942 and as a result of having met so little resistance, the force was dissolved, with all the participating units returning to Ambon Island. There were (by Japanese reports) no casualties during the campaign.

After the expedition, they established seven garrisons with guard units. They all belonged to the 24th Special Base Unit. The garrisons were as follows: Manokwari (207 men), Fakfak (67 men), Ternate (79 men) near Halmahera Island, Boela (76 men) on Ceram Island, Babo (86 men), Hollandia, Nabire, Sarmi, and Sorong.

During the Dutch New Guinea operation, it often happened that the Japanese had no army units available for landings or various garrison duties, so they formed special units, assembled from the ship's crews.

They were used for a temporary service on shore as garrison troops. Light Cruisers contributed one platoon (forty-five men) for each operation. The Heavy Cruisers, provided one company (usually ninety men).

After the occupation of New Guinea, Japan planned to go across to Australia, but they did not advance further than *Frederik Hendrik Island*.

The Japanese did not attach any importance to Merauke on the southeast coast. This settlement was the only unoccupied territory for the duration of the war, and the Dutch flag continued to fly there.

• *Japanese troops in the jungle*

Manokwari 1942:
Hans Fuhri Captured and Beheaded

10

The KNIL *(Royal Netherlands East Indies Army)* garrison at Manokwari, New Guinea lost contact with KNIL HQ in Java at the beginning of March 1942.

On April 12th, the Japan invasion fleet arrived at Dorey Bay in Manokwari, situated north of the Vogelkop area. and approximately four thousand troops landed.

There were only about 150 Dutch soldiers stationed there with their commander KNIL Captain J.B.H Willemsz.-Geeroms.

At the beginning of 1942, the troops included a number

of civilian reservists and home guards *(landstorm)* who had been called for service.

As the KNIL ground force had no chance of successfully engaging the Japanese invasion force; it withdrew to the interior of Dutch New Guinea and initiated guerrilla warfare.

The garrison commander had already established a number of hidden food and weapons depots deep in the jungle

---

Hans Herbert Moritz Fuhri 1915 - 1942
Hans Herbert Moritz Fuhri was born on May 30 1915, at Malang. Hans had one brother: Erwin Joyce Fuhri. His occupation was Luitenant AR 3 of the Royal Dutch Navy. He was awarded the Bronze Lion of the Netherlands Military. He is buried at Dutch Ereveld Kembang Kuning in Surabaya, Java.

of the Vogelkop (Bird's Head). These would allow the KNIL force to operate for months without resupply.

The only Dutch naval presence in Manokwari was the small Dutch Marine patrol boat *Anna* under the command of 2nd Officer Hans Fuhri.

While a Japanese torpedo boat docked, Fuhri ordered his crew to open the seacocks of the *Anna* and burn the ship to prevent her capture as a Japanese destroyer moved in.

He and his wife tried to escape upriver into the interior in a small sloop while the burning ship sank in the bay. All valuables and food supplies had been taken off the ship and were shared with the crew.

Fuhri and his wife were soon caught and sent to an internment camp with the rest of the European population.

For sinking the *Anna*, the Japanese sentenced three crewmen to death. They were tied to a tree in front of the military detachment.

Fuhri asked the Japanese soldiers to release the prisoners and told them he was the only one guilty of the sinking of the *Anna*. The prisoners were released, and he was tied to a tree.

Fuhri said that he was still acting under Royal Navy orders, although Java had fallen and the Royal Navy command structure in the Netherlands East Indies had been dissolved six weeks earlier.

He was put on trial by the Japanese. During the interrogation, he behaved bravely despite being kicked and beaten repeatedly.

He continued to give the Japanese interrogators the same message: "It was my duty to destroy the ship, as this was an order from the commanding officer of the navy. I am a Dutch marine officer, and I will always stay a Dutch officer."

The Japanese maintained that with the fall of Java, all Fuhri's orders were null and void since he could no longer take orders from a command structure that no longer existed.

Hans Fuhri was condemned to death.

He was tied to a tree in the blazing sun for more than

twenty-four hours. In the evening and during the night, he was beaten by the Japanese soldiers. One, named Mahoon, kicked him in the head so hard that all his teeth broke.

On April 2 at 7:00 p.m., he was dragged to a space behind the military compound.

They put a Dutch flag on the ground and demanded Fuhri to stand on top of it.

He refused.

It was still for a moment, but the officers surrounding the group made a decision.

Hans had to dig a hole.

But it was not fast enough for the Japanese.

With angry eyes, they looked at Hans' wife, who was white as a ghost. She watched her husband dig and probably did not realize what was going to happen next.

The earth was dry and hard. The spade was not sharp.

In the distance bombs were exploding. Grenades made sharp sounds. They were irregular, like lightning strikes which usually warned that there was a weather change on this tropical island.

Hans Fuhri stood in the hole up to his knees.

The Japanese soldiers became nervous as things grew to a climax.

Hans was blindfolded and forced to his knees with his hands tied behind his back.

Hans' wife was dragged close to the spot where he was kneeling.

Several other prisoners of war were made to watch.

The executioner delivered a single stroke, decapiting Fuhri. His head and body both fell into the hole with a thump.

The earth ran red with his blood.

His young wife fainted.

When the executioner did the same to one of the native sailors, the Japanese soldiers looked disappointed.

They found it unfortunate that the white woman was not executed as well.

The Japanese soldiers left the scene and the he prisoners were taken back to the old military post of the KNIL.

Hans Fuhri's remains were buried so poorly that some of his body parts were sticking above ground and the flies were invading these parts *(See Reburial ceremony in Chapter 32)*.

After several bombing raids on Manokwari, the Japanese set up a command base there.

All the Europeans were taken off and interned on Ambon.

Before the invasion in Manokwari, some of the Dutch infantry *(KNIL)*, sixty-two Dutch soldiers and seventeen indigenous Papuans *(Meja-Arfakkers)* disappeared into the jungle and fought a guerrilla warfare against the Japanese for the remainder of the war.

The following account of an unrelated
beheading of a prisoner reflects the
Japanese view of Bushido

"On March 29, 1943 - All four of us - Kurokawa, Nishiguchi, Yawate and myself - assembled in front of Headquarters at 1500 hrs ... The "Tai'" commander Komai, who came to the observation post today, told us personally that in accordance with the compassionate sentiments of Japanese *Bushido*, he was going to kill the prisoner himself, with his favourite sword. So we gathered to observe this.

After we had waited a little more than ten minutes, the truck came along. The prisoner, at the side of the guard house, is given his last drink of water. The surgeon, Major Komai, and Headquarters Platoon Commander came out of the Officers Mess, wearing their military swords. The time had come.

The prisoner, with his arms bound and his long hair now cropped short, tottered forward. He probably suspected what was going to happen next, but he was more composed than I thought he would be. Without much ado, he was put on the truck and we set out for our destination.

I sat next to the surgeon. Approximately ten guards rode with us. To the pleasant rumble of the engine, we run swiftly along the road in the growing twilight. The glowing sun has set behind the western hills. Gigantic clouds rose before us and dusk was falling all around. It will not last long now. As I pictured the scene we were about to witness, my heart beat faster.

I glanced at the prisoner. He had probably found peace within himself. As though saying farewell to the world, he looked about as he sat in the truck, at the hills the sea, and seemed deep in thought. I felt a surge of pity and turned my eyes away. The truck ran along the seashore. We left the Navy guard behind us and came into the Army sector. Here and there, we saw sentries in the grassy fields, and I thanked them in my heart for their toil, as we drove on. They must have 'got it' in the bombing the night before last. There were great gaping holes by the side of the road, full of rain water. In a little over twenty minutes, we arrived at our destination and got out of the truck.

Major Komai stood up and said to the prisoner: "We are going to kill you." Then he told the prisoner that in accordance with Japanese *Bushido*, he would be killed with a Japanese sword and that we would have two or three minutes grace; he listened with a bowed head. He said a few words in a low voice.

He was an officer, probably a flight lieutenant. Apparently, he wanted to be killed with one stroke of the sword. I heard him say the word "one." The major's face became tense as he replied: "Yes."

Now the time had come and the prisoner was made to kneel on the bank of a bomb crater, filled with water. He was apparently tense. Precautions were taken, guards with fixed bayonets surrounded him, but he remained calm. He even stretched his neck out. He was a very brave man indeed.

When I put myself in the prisoners place and thought that in one minute it would be good-bye to this world, although the daily bombings filled me with hate, ordinary human feelings make me pity him.

The major drew his favorite sword. It is the famous *masamune* sword, which he had shown us at the observation stations. It glitterred in the light and sent a cold shiver down my spine. He tapped the prisoner's neck lightly with the back of the blade, then raised it above his head with both arms and brought it down with a powerful sweep. I had been standing with muscles tensed, but in that moment I closed my eyes.

A hissing sound - it must have been the sound of spurting blood, spurting from the arteries: the body fell forward. It was amazing - he had killed him with one stroke.

The onlookers pushed forward. The head, detached from the trunk, rolled forward in front of it. Dark blood gushed out. It was all over. The head was dead white, like a doll.

The savageness, which I felt only a little while ago is gone, and now I felt nothing but the true compassion of Japanese *Bushido*.

A corporal laughed: "Well, he will be entering Nirvana now." A seaman of the medical unit takes the surgeon's sword and, intent on paying off old scores, turned the headless body over on its back and cut the abdomen open with one clean stroke. They are thick-skinned, these *keto* (hairy foreigner - term of opprobrium for a white man); even the skin of their bellies was thick. Not a drop of blood came out of the body. It was pushed into the crater at once and buried.

The wind blew mournfully, and I saw the scene again in my mind's eye. We got on the truck again and started back. It was dark now. We got off in front of headquarters. I said good-bye to the major and climbed up the hill with technician Kurokawa. This would be something to remember all my life. If I ever got back alive, it would make a good story to tell; so I wrote it down."

Japan Trained Papuans to Become Spies

11

Undercover activities (remember that navy officer who stayed behind in Moni after his ship visited Manokwari) of the Japanese in New Guinea differed according to the location of the Japanese, the extent to which the occupation was in an area previously settled by the Japanese, and the distance from the Allied advance.

In general, garrisons in Dutch New Guinea were established where there had been a strong pre-war presence of the Japanese, usually by the South Seas Development Company, and the focus was then on long-term work with the natives.

In the east of the island, the Japanese had no strong presence pre-war and with the inevitability of battle there, the focus was on stemming the Allied advance. There were coast watching and observation posts set up on the north coast to monitor the presence of Allied aircraft.

The Japanese occupied several settlements particularly on the northern coast of the island where they established or expanded facilities such as ports and airstrips as well as setting up garrison units.

The Japanese utilized the so-called *Naval Minseibu Civil System* for administering New Guinea, along with the actions of the feared Kempeitai; the coordinating 8th Navy Development Department was installed at Wewak by February 1943 and Hollandia by March 1944.

Natives were involved in their administration, in setting up schools, being recruited into the militia unit known as the Native Police Force, and in the utilization of the native hierarchy in pacifying or controlling the community.

Garrisons were established in the west at Manokwari, Fakfak, Babo, Nabire, Hollandia, and Sorong. It is likely there was a *kikan* (nucleous) or at least a *Kempeitai* unit established in the Manokwari area and the far west of the island from the time the Japanese first landed there.

Nakano (name of school for spies) agents undertook four main activities: training the natives in military activities; establishing spying operations; guerrilla operations; and establishing special agencies in Dutch New Guinea.

Natives were being used by the Japanese from the early months of the war, not only in standard military training but for undercover purposes. One report said: "In 1942 there existed at Manokwari, Dutch New Guinea, a special training school known as *Hirata Tai*, after its commanding officer, Hirata".

In September 1943, this school was transferred to Kaimana (also in Dutch New Guinea). The school trained Papuans in secret police methods. Graduates were to ascertain the allegiances among the natives, whether they were passing Allied pamphlets, spreading false rumors, and so on.

There were other Allied reports that indicated the military use of the natives. One Allied report of 6 December 1943 said that "The enemy is reported to train Papuans in the use of rifles at Iworep village" (that is, near Dobo, the largest settlement in the Aroe Islands off the west coast of Dutch New Guinea).

Lieutenant G.B. Black, sent on the Inter-Allied Services Department (ISD) Locust mission from Bena Bena to Aitape, wrote in his diary on December 9, 1943: "Natives being trained at Aitape in the use of firearms, grenades etc." The latter suggests that similar training exercises might have been quite widespread, extending into the eastern part of the island.

Where possible, the Japanese incorporated the natives into a spy system, regardless of whether it was in the east or west of the island. In part, the controversial activities were oriented to this, and the natives were urged to help the Japanese forces to bring in any downed airmen and let the soldiers know of any useful intelligence. As one Allied intelligence report said, the "Japanese have organized an extensive native intelligence system for reconnaissance and espionage purposes." Where the Nakano agents were not active, it was the Kempeitai that operated the spy system. Schools for potential spies were set up and one report noted that "at present there about one hundred receiving education" at Lae.

Spies were paid for their services. The total number of paid spies is not known, although natives bringing advice were likely to have been compensated so the potential number might have been in the thousands. Certainly, the life of Allied troops or patrols was made difficult and many were betrayed by willing natives (The guerrilla fighters under Captain Geeroms were always unsure of who to trust.) Even if the natives did not betray their presence, the likelihood of food or shelter being given to an Allied soldier was markedly reduced.

With a multitude of spies and helpers, the Japanese were able to cover a large amount of territory at any given time, thus: "Native spies were sent out to investigate the conditions in the vicinity of the Nako River ... Spy squads in about three groups (organized with a CO who is an officer competent to gather intelligence and some NCOs plus natives) will infiltrate into villages and gather intelligence ..." An uncorroborated report suggests on the possibility of agents being active far from base during the Kokoda operations.

References to guerrilla tactics occur frequently in the Japanese writings on New Guinea, and it was the agents of the Nakano School who created an effective fighting force. There were four stages of development. Standard guerrilla activities were used in Guadalcanal and New Guinea.

In December 1942, at a time of desperation at Buna, infiltration tactics were recognized as being the only means of silencing American artillery. Volunteers were split into groups of twenty; the units penetrated the lines around Soputa in December 1942 and January 1943, blowing up at least one twenty-five pounder but failing to silence the guns.

Realizing the potential impact of such activities, there was a second stage training of special units to undertake infiltration and guerrilla activities. Some fifteen Nakano agents were sent to eastern New Guinea in early 1943 to teach. A training camp was established fifty kilometers east of Lae.

The two hundred recruits were from the Takasago tribes of Formosa, and these men distinguished themselves in all subsequent actions. Nakano squad leaders provided instruction in means of attack, topography, as well as in the pacification of natives. Known as the Saito Unit, the initial team left in early September to attack an Australian camp in the Kainantu area in the Eastern Highlands Province.

Their role was to destroy installations using special incendiary devices (capable of producing heat of over 2,000 degrees Celsius) developed by the Noborita Institute. The first raid resulted in over sixty Australian casualties. Considerable arms and material were confiscated, and much of the camp destroyed. This success was followed by over sixty raids on Allied positions, notably in the Ramu Valley, at the Driniumor, and an attack on Dagua airfield.

The third stage was a tribute to the work of the Nakano agents. Because of the perceived value of their work, a commitment from Imperial General Headquarters in Tokyo that more irregular forces were required. This led to the opening of a section of the Nakano School devoted to guerrilla training, the Futamata branch accepted its first intake on 1 September 1944. So, the Nakano impact in eastern New Guinea was significant not only on tactics but future training of Nakano agents.

The final stage occurred in early 1945 when the 18th Army realized that it could no longer operate as a normal fighting force. A decision was made to launch wide-scale guerrilla actions.

The original Saito unit was broken up and dispersed throughout other units with the aim of instructing the 18th

Army generally in the performance of infiltration activities with Nakano agents assisting in the instruction.

Special Agencies in Dutch New Guinea

The final area of Nakano activity concerns the use of the special service agencies in Dutch New Guinea. The 8th Naval Construction Department landed at Wewak and established its headquarters and a field branch of the *Kempeitai* was established. In February 1943, Captain Michiaki of the Japanese Navy oversaw the unit that set about the development of military and agricultural projects, working with civilian firms, Mitsui, and the South Seas Development Company. Numerous Nakano agents were attached to this unit.

The Department was divided into four sections: General Affairs, Development (agricultural projects), Intendance (supply), and Medical. General Affairs concerned itself with investigation of political conditions, morale and the loyalty of the natives, propaganda, and recruitment of laborers. Any disciplinary actions were turned over to the Kempeitai, and important findings were sent to the Naval Special Service Department in Surabaya. The latter location was the home of the Kana Kikan under Naval Captain Hanada and was the headquarters for western New Guinea operations.

Several small agencies or kikans were established in the area from Hollandia (near the border of Dutch New Guinea) west, under the cloak of the 8th Naval Construction Department. They were known by different names, including Kikans, Agencies or Agents, Pacification Units, and Construction Agencies. They covered the north and west of the country with some presence in the north central area.

• *Asmat Papuan village*

104

Evacuation to Camp Oransbari:
Captain Geeroms Takes Troops Into the Jungle

12

Two months prior to the invasion of Manokwari, a large group of Dutch women and children under the guidance of several men appointed by KNIL Captain J.B.H. Willemsz.- Geeroms, and under the direction of Sergeant Zeelt, evacuated to Camp Oransbari.

Sergeant Kokkelink:
"On the eighteenth of January 1942, our women and children, about 150 people total, under the guidance of twelve mobilized settlers were evacuated to Oransbari, a small village not far from Ransiki. The Daito Maru, a boat captured from the Japanese cotton company at Ransiki, was used.

Saying goodbye was not easy, but we all realized it had to be done. We held back our tears and hoped to meet again in better times. Some women refused to leave, like the wife of the commanding officer with her little son and the wife of assistant resident Linck.

Oransbari is about sixty kilometers to the south of Manokwari and connected to a beautiful bay with a background of high mountains. There was a small settlement of settlers there and now arrived we quickly built additional shelter facilities for the evacuated. The evacuation came just in time."

Suze van Geenen (daughter of Theodoor Beynon):
"When the war started, we had to leave the city and hide in the jungle to get away from the Japanese invaders.

My father was asked by Sergeant Zeelt to help with this task. We could not bring many clothes but in the rush of leaving some of us girls did not wear any underwear.

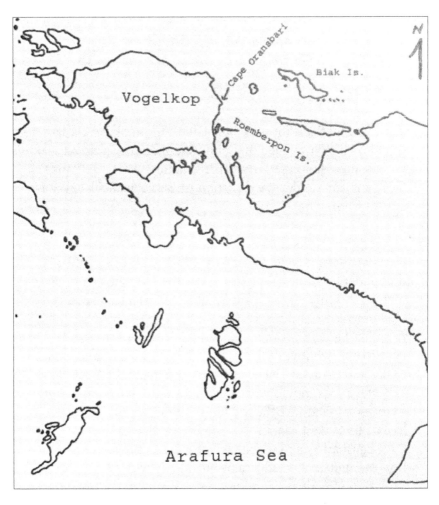

• *Western area of New Guinea, including de Vogelkop and Cape Oransbari, the place of the internment camp*

We had to climb the stairs to get on board the ship. Sailors standing on land could look up our skirts. Mom found a quick solution and sewed the bottom of our dresses together. I still remember that moment and it made us smile."

Paula Mellenbergh:
"To feel a bit more protected, my foster parents gathered with other families in the area. mostly women. It meant that I got less time to spend outside, sometimes just around the small house so as not to attract any special attention.

Eventually we were placed in an internment camp just outside the city of Manokwari. More than likely to force the men that fought in the jungle to surrender."

Sergeant Kokkelink:
"A few days after the departure of our women and children the Japanese returned for the second time. Now two airplanes. They threw six bombs and aimed another salvo of machine gun fire over our heads. One of the bombs hit our prison. Luckily, all prisoners, and all conscripts who came over with the military from Java, were working outside and no one was hit. The jail was reduced to rubble. The air siren sounded after the airplanes were right above us. They came not over sea this time but were flying just above the mountains from the south.

Because we only had so many men available, there was no post situated there. But now our commanding officer sent two men there immediately. My first command!

With a *klewang* (machete), my comrade and I chopped our way through the jungle to reach that location close to the mountain. It was a fight with the jungle and deadly tiring.

When we reached the foot of the mountain, we saw a steep straight mountain side that gave us heart palpitations.

We tied our guns with vines and climbed on hands and feet to the top and arrived with many cuts and bruises.

Through the air, the distance to our camp was no more than two kilometers, but it took us six hours to get there. As a reward, we had a spectacular view over the Bay, but that was all.

The other side of the mountain was not as steep, and the descent to the bottom was quite easy. In the valley, we found a little stream with clear cold water. Drinking, bathing, and cooking would be no problem as there was also a lot of firewood available.

There was nothing to protect us from the elements, so rain, wind and cold air was attacking us. Especially at night, we were shivering from the cold.

We carried a large red flag. My resourceful partner discovered a bamboo area in the distance, and without my permission he walked over there and about an hour later came back with a long piece of bamboo.

We attached the flag to the stick and attached it between a small opening in the mountain. I raised the flag, to make sure it would work.

"Are you crazy?" my buddy screamed at me, and a bit embarrassed, I pulled the post down as it would indicate a false air attack. But it was too late.

In Manokwari, where everyone was swimming at that time of day, my signal was taken as serious and everyone ran into the trenches for cover. I had to listen to many complaints after I was relieved from my post on that mountainside. The relief took a long time to get to us.

After the four days of waiting, we wanted to see if the new watch would be there. We were worried as the night before it was raining hard. We did not dare to go back of our own accord, but our food supply was getting low. We were happy to finally see our guys show up after six days.

Back in base, Captain Geeroms first gave me a tongue lashing about the false air raid signal. Then he told us that because a lot of the troops got sick, there was a shortage of men and no more troops were going to be sent to the top of the mountain.

Nothing really happened in the next couple of days.

Suddenly a third attack came, and of course, the planes flew straight over that mountain. We were really upset by that attack.

Fortunately nobody was injured during the attack.

In the end, it was only one airplane that circled around Manokwari but did not drop any bombs. Probably a reconnaissance plane.

With a lot of anxiety, some of our troops shot at the plane without creating any damage. Our commanding officer told us to stop immediately.

About a week later, we received a radio message from the Japanese commander on Ternate, which was captured by the Japanese troops. We were told to surrender.

Captain Geeroms answered the Japanese with a strong message: 'That is not going to happen, sir.'

It was now clear what we could expect in a matter of days. The captain called us together and told us about the ultimatum and the answer he had given to the Japanese.

'I believe the Japanese are not going to talk about this, and we can expect some action soon,' the captain said. 'I am expecting an invasion soon. With just a handful of men, there is nothing we can do to defend ourselves. We would only help the Japanese as they would have the opportunity to destroy us in one major blow. But there is something else we could do. We will fight using guerrilla warfare. That is my decision. It will be a bitter struggle, and I expect your commitment to defend and attack when we can. I have complete faith in our troops. I am asking you to trust and follow me wherever I am going.'

We loudly applauded and all swore to follow him no matter what would happen to us.

A large section was immediately deployed to make obstacles for the expected landing, and the rest were ordered to pack provisions in soldered tins for one hundred men for six months: Rice, salt fish, corned beef, *katjang idjoe* (type of green bean), *sambal badjak* (sweet hot sauce), tea, sugar, salt plus thousands of cartridges, medical supplies, and a radio receiver with extra batteries.

Four Papuan police men transported convicts and Papuans to three hiding places: Wasirawi, Tjosi, and Testega, 100, 150, and 180 kilometers southwest of Manokwari in highly mountainous terrain.

In Tjosi, a Menadonese man was given a written order to look after these goods and to wait for our eventual arrival. Now we had to wait for further instructions.

We practiced with three short marches into the mountain each day, crossing rivers, stalking and attacking, constructing bivouacs with bamboo, leaves and twigs, hiding our tracks; everything that is necessary for jungle fighting.

We got instructions from the European physician, Koppeschaar, in the management of illnesses and wounds, and also instruction in botany so that we would know what plants were not suitable for consumption. Our Captain was everywhere at once; nothing was too much for him; his energy was endless.

Then, suddenly, but not unexpectedly, the attack came. On Sunday, April 12, 1942, just after sunrise, one of the coast guards telephoned that a large number of ships had come into the bay. As none of the ships were flying flags, he was not sure about their nationality, but he feared the worst. The commandant of the watch raised the alarm immediately.

As it was a Sunday, most of us were still asleep. We crawled out of our beds, hastily dressed and ran to the trenches with our weapons. Thinking this was another practice, we left all kinds of equipment behind. We would suffer severely for that mistake later.

I was up early that morning and went over to my friend, the cook, who was preparing *nasi goreng* (fried rice). The nasi goreng was a feast. So when the alarm sounded, I had already started. I wanted to start my day early with a good breakfast.

I ran to my camp, grabbed my stuff and raced into the trench. Captain Geeroms came running: 'Bloody hell, the Japanese are here! Get out at once and follow me!' he screamed. 'Sergeant-Major, you will form the rearguard and make sure everyone links up properly.'

On top of the hill, we stopped under cover to rest. When I looked around, I only saw a small troop. The captain asked, 'Where are the rest?' There was no answer.

We could see Manokwari below. The Japanese were busy landing troops. They were about eight hundred meters from our previous camp, obviously their first target. We weren't a minute too soon getting out of there.

Our own war, the fight in the jungle, was beginning. The captain did a quick roll call. This now was our total strength: KNIL Captain Geeroms, KNIL Sergeant-Major Maas, Quartermaster de Beaufort, Militia Sergeant Kapteyn *(a settler)*, Militia Sergeant van der Muur *(a teacher),* and fifty-three settlers.

We were strengthened by the KNIL Timorese Corporal Mandala, and three lower-ranked men who had formed an observation post. There were also seventeen conscripts, appointed by the Captain of the police corps, under the command of the Commissioner of Police 2nd class H., only one lower-ranked had joined.

For those who stayed, we harbored deep contempt. We thought that we only have a place for good men. We could do without cowards.

'Forward!' the captain said, and the column began to move. Our war in the jungle was about to begin."

• *Native boatmen transport Allied supplies by water.*
Image courtesy of the Library of Congress

• *The Korowai, also called the Kolufo, are the people who live in south-*
eastern West Papua close to the border with Papua New Guinea.
Until the late 1970s, the Korowai were unaware of the existence of
any peoples other than themselves.

Pieter de Kock Guides His Team
Into the Jungle

13

Petrus Pieter de Kock (1918-) is a surviving member of the guerrilla fighters of Captain Geeroms and together with Sergeant Kokkelink liberated an internment camp in the area of the Prafi River. The following are some of his memories from the War in the Pacific.

The Japanese invaded Manokwari on Sunday the 12th of April, 1942 with more than a hundred warships.

Our two command posts who would have a perfect view of the Dorey Bay probably missed that exact moment when the ships entered the Bay. We just did not see this happen in time.

The Japanese fleet was able to get very close before finally the alarm sounded.

It was early in the morning, 5:30 a.m.

It was a preferred time for the Japanese to attack.

Many places were attacked simultaneously:

Ambang, Wosi, and Manokwari.

Enemy fighting planes circled above the city, unhindered by air raid guns, because none were available. We also did not have that material available for us.

It looked like a fun airshow. There was nothing we could do, just accept it as it was happening.

We did hear some alarming news before, but we did not believe anybody at that time. It must have been the same as in 1940 when the German troops invaded Holland.

We could not believe it, and above all, we were far away from any support from other KNIL armories.

The four of us fled into the jungle.

While climbing up the hills, we saw that our radio station was bombed and in flames.

Captain Geeroms was with the larger military unit ahead of us, and we followed with Sergeant Mellenbergh in the lead.

We were not sure about which direction to travel and in a bit of a panic. Our training had not prepared us for a situation like this.

Most of the population in Manokwari had already left their homes.

On a higher point in the hills, we could see Manokwari and the blue ocean was full of uninvited ships.

It was clear to us how this gigantic Japanese military power was able to concur South East Asiain about four months.

The dark clouds of bombs and fires turned daylight into darkness. Our troops burned all the dossiers so they would not fall into enemy hands. Night fell.

At last, New Guinea was captured by this enemy who had imitated the German strategy of warfare called *Blitzkrieg.*

Sergeant Mellenbergh picked some oranges from the garden of a colonist who had fled, and we searched for a safe campground.

The Japanese soldiers installed troops with machine guns on both sides of the road. They would point and shoot at anything that moved or made a sound.

Occasionally, we heard recognizable commands, which were typical for Japanese soldiers. It sounded like they were always upset about something.

We could not remove the heavy foliage and branches in the jungle without making noise. The Japanese heard our struggles and started shooting in our direction.

Bullets were flying over our heads, as they tried to find a way to kill us.

Although we were quiet and lay flat on our bellies, could it be that our heartbeats were the reason that they heard us?

We travelled deeper in the jungle.

I spent the night with an old professional cook.

It was raining hard, but I did not realize it. Exhausted, I fell asleep beside a tree. My uniform stuck to my body, and I was longing for food. The oranges were not enough.

The old cook told me about the *nasi goreng* (fried rice) he would be making, and how to prepare the rice and the addition of herbs and spices and the making of *sambal* (hot peppers). He told me he learned the recipe from another cook when he was working in the home of a military officer.

My saliva was running in my mouth.

That *nasi goreng* from the day before was a distant memory.

We heard gun shots in the distance. We listened to these sounds as if we had been part of this war for several months already. The sound of heavier canon blasts followed.

Did the Allies attack the Japanese?

With this thought we strengthened our hearts and forgot about hunger for a moment.

The next day we heard that the Japanese fired some warning shots in front of the second government boat in the bay.

We marched in the direction of Wosi and saw women and children in the distance. It was colonist families who went back home to take care of their gardens.

They thought that they would not be a threat to the Japanese but also told us that some of the female family members of the Dutch government were hiding behind Wosi.

More refugees returned and went back to return to as it was before. They told us that a group of soldiers passed just before us.

After a couple of hours, we found the three Koch brothers. With the additional troops, we felt that we were ready for the fight.

Shortly after we reached a settlement of Papuans and

wanted to spend the night there. They told us that Captain Geeroms had passed their village with a large group of soldiers earlier.

We were finally able to connect with the main group and exchanged our experiences. It felt like we had been in this war for a long time.

We now totalled thirty-six men. The oldest was Mr. Werdmuller von Elgg who was about fifty years old. The youngest was his nephew, Johnny who was only seventeen.

The next day the captain called us together.

"We have a difficult task in front of us," he said.

"We need to stay fighting till the end, or at least until the Allies will arrive to help us."

He could not tell us how long this would take.

"It will be a difficult fight," he said.

Many of us had wives and children. The captain said: "You can leave the group if you wish, but you have to leave your guns and ammunition with us."

The next day, no one had left our group.

We marched for four days.

We finally arrived in Isrods, a main district area of Wasirawi.

Mr. Nuhawae, who was in charge in this district, his wife, and his sixteen-year-old cousin, Coosje Ayal, welcomed us with open arms. He had heard about the beginning of the war, but he did not know any details.

He had never seen such a large group of soldiers in his life.

Coosje Ayal:
Vivid Memories of Her Time With the Guerrilla Fighters

14

Coosje Ayal (1926-2015), the only surviving female member of the guerrilla fighters who fought with Captain Geeroms was interviewed many times about her memories of the 'fight in the jungle' against the Japanese invaders.

After the war, she was honored with five awards for her time in the jungle. The first was the *Cross of Merit* "for courageous and discreet" action against the enemy. She was awarded this in Brisbane, Australia, where she was trained as a nurse. She also became a corporal in the Women's Military Corps. "From the airplane stairs I saw a guard of honor of women's corps. A red carpet had been laid out for me. General Van Mook presented me with the *Cross of Merit*." In the Netherlands, she received the *Resistance Memorial Cross* pinned by Prince Bernhard, the *Badge of Honor for Order and Peace*, *the Mobilization War Cross,* and *the War Wound Badge.*

Coosje Ayal tells her story: "When the Japanese invaded Manokwari on April 1942, I was living with my aunt and uncle, Seth Nahuwae, who worked for the government.

Like a pearl in the immeasurable blue sea, hidden between the larger islands of the Moluccan archipelago lies the small island of Nusalant. On that island, I was born on April 15, 1926. My childhood was like that of all other children on the island. The population lived on fishing and the proceeds

117

of cloves and nutmeg. Many islanders, therefore, moved away from the island to work on the larger islands. So was my uncle, Seth Nahuway, who worked as an administrative officer in New Guinea.

During one of his vacations on Nusalant, it was decided that I would return to New Guinea with him and his wife as a family, as his marriage had remained childless. I was very happy with my uncle and aunt. Because of his job, my uncle was often transferred.

It was in the year 1940 that there were more and more rumors about an imminent Japanese invasion. My uncle, as an administrative officer, had meanwhile been ordered to stockpile food supplies in various places in the jungle in case it was decided to fight the Japanese guerrilla.

Three months before the raid on April 12, 1942, my uncle, along with his wife and I, had already moved to the *kampong* (village) Nasi-rawe.

After we heard about the atrocities of the Japanese soldiers against the population, my uncle and aunt connected with a guerrilla fighter group of the KNIL with Captain Geeroms. We were asked to join this group through the jungle and over top the mountains on the north side of New Guinea, also know as the *Vogelkop* (Bird's Head).

With pistol and rifle, we fought against the Japanese soldiers sometimes with the help of the local Papuans. I received, as a sixteen-year-old girl, a rifle and a knife.

In the beginning, we were with sixty-two people, and my aunt and I were the only women in the group. Sergeant Kokkelink told the men from the beginning: "The person who touches Coosje is going to get it." I always felt protected.

My task was the same as for the men: Try to kill as many Japanese as possible. In the same time, I supported the group with repairs to clothing and took care of the wounded.

Day and night, we marched through the jungle. During the journey, we had many encounters with Japanese soldiers. I received shrapnel from a hand-grenade just above my

118

eye. We had to suffer many challenges which included hunger and diseases.

When it rained, we captured the water to drink with our own hands. To make sure the Japanese soldiers could not kill us as a group we split up and created separate camps.

The enemy became more and more active and sent more troops on land. Their mission was to capture and kill the "pesty' guerrilla fighters.

On the side of the Aroepi-river, Sergeant Kokkelink moved our camp to the top of a hill with a better view over the valley. He was always looking for opportunities to prepare to ambush and attack the Japanese troops by surprise.

A couple of days later, three soldiers from another guerrilla group joined us. They got caught in a fight with a Japanese patrol and killed several Japanese soldiers who were bathing in the river. You knew there would be revenge by the Japanese.

On 18 April 1944, I was with my uncle by the river where we used to bathe and wash our clothes. We heard a big commotion, and while hiding in thick grass, we saw Japanese soldiers peeking out above the hill. Captain Geeroms wanted to grab his rifle, but he was too late.

During this attack by the Japanese, many of our troops were killed and our camp was set ablaze. They took Captain Geeroms and my aunt. Later we heard that they were tortured and executed (beheaded) by the *Kempetai* in Manokwari.

A Papuan messenger brought us a letter from our captain; evidently he was forced to write in captivity. He told us to surrender.

Nobody in the group wanted to follow that order.

Sergeant Kokkelink answered him in a letter that we would ignore his orders because he was in captivity and that we would fight till the bitter end.

After the Japanese attack, my uncle sent me to our other camp at the Aroepi river, to warn the other men in our group.

After six days, sometimes running but mostly walking

through the heavy terrain, I met a Papuan boy. He asked me: "Tell me where your group is. I will bring you to them!" I was afraid and did not trust him because a lot of Papuan people were bribed by the Japanese soldiers. I answered: "You go to that camp, tell them I am here, and then return to me!"

One of our guerrilla fighters came back with him, to meet up with me, and escorted me to their camp. We dismantled the second camp and moved away quickly to stay ahead of the fast approaching Japanese soldiers.

From our group of sixty-two, only seventeen remained.

Sergeant Kokkelink decided to go into the eastern part of the Vogelkop, hoping to find a safer area. After a week, we did find a perfect hiding place at the Adjai-river.

Occasionally the Japanese soldiers and us camped on opposite sides of a river. We did not shoot at each other as we were all trying to save on ammunition.

We searched for food to eat from gardens of the local Papuan tribes. We picked young bananas and vegetables.

One day I found in the jungle a large apricot-looking fruit. I picked it and brought it for the men but did not eat it myself. The next day I was shocked to see that the fruits I picked were poisonous. Everyone had swollen lips, a bloated face, and a stomach ache. Luckily nobody blamed me for this mistake.

During the night, we really did not sleep very well. There was always the fear of being surprised and captured by the Japs.

I placed my bible under my 'pillow' of leaves. Every morning and evening I prayed for strength.

Suddenly, I must have had all tropical diseases at one time. I was dealing with dysentery, malaria, and beri-beri. All the strength in my body was gone

Prior to my illness, it was agreed that we would not take seriously injured or sick people with us. Anyone who, for whatever reason, could not continue, was shot. The safety of the fighting group as a whole took precedence, as the Japanese could torture a captured combatant in such a way that he could betray the group's hideout. So it happened that at some point, I got tropical sores on the inner side of my thighs. When I walked, I got excruciating pains, and in the end, I couldn't take a step. As a result, the combat group could not move quickly enough, which is essential for a guerrilla battle to ensure the safety of the group as a whole.

A council of war was held, and the verdict was "execution!" The execution crew was appointed. At that point, my uncle, Seth Nahuwaye, asked if he could be alone with me for a while. He carried me a little way into the forest and asked me to pray with him. With tears in his eyes, he begged the Lord for strength. He took me in his arms and said, "Coosje, don't give up! God will help us, don't be afraid. He won't abandon us."

I don't know what happened to me then. Superhuman strength flowed through my body. Arm-in-arm, we walked out of the forest to meet the group. There were cheers and laughter! For a moment, we had forgotten all misery. After that, the fight went on again.

With the help of three loyal Papuan tribal leaders, we survived the jungle. The Papuans protected us and supported us in our battle to the very end. We carried the Dutch flag with us in a hollow piece of bamboo.

Suddenly, we received a message from a Papuan messenger. Sergeant Kokkelink was afraid to open the message that came in a piece of bamboo. He was afraid it was a boobytrap, and there could be explosives.

After carefully opening it, he found a letter from Lieutenant Abdul Rasak who wrote: "Dear guerrilla fighters. We are part of the Dutch-Indonesian forces and have landed on the Kebar-area. We have been given the task to find you and to make contact. With this letter there is a Dutch flag as a sign of our intention."

Nobody recognized his name, and could it be another trick to capture us?

In the end, it was a true message.

• Japanese soldiers crossing a river in New Guinea

122

Pieter Petrus de Kock:
Shots Fired. Sergeant Kokkelink Takes Command

15

The night in the tropics closed as a dark curtain in the jungle. The animals started their biological duties.

I saw a *tjitjak* (gecko) draw a line across a wall at the front of the home. He was looking for love.

The lines he was drawing looked like rivers on a map.

The night vibrated.

You could hear sounds everywhere. Someone shouting, crickets and other night animals, but you did not see them.

The sounds in the jungle have been there forever.

I slowly fell asleep and started to think back about my life experiences up to this moment.

Would everything in life have a purpose? Is everything pre-destined or is everything based on luck? Does luck really exists?

Was it a coincidence that a soccer game created a different change of direction in my life? I am in the jungle of New Guinea in between tribes and some of them still live in the Stone Ages.

It seemed like the world was giving me a chance to start my life over.

I was getting confused about the thoughts that entered my mind, and I did not know how to sort them.

Many times I had heard and experienced how a meeting with someone new created an opportunity for a change in your career. With some difficulty I obtained a job at the office of a commander of the artillery in Amboina (a port in the Moluccas, the capital of Ambon on Amboina Island.)

The soccer club of our area was called *Bintang Timoer* (Star from the East). It was known over the years that a soccer game without someone getting injured was a game for girls.

If incidents did not happen during the game, they would happen right after.

It was a regular occurrence and the spectators were part of a large fight. The result might be a draw as there were as many injured on the one side as on the other.

The common agreement was that there had to be a fight for one of the teams to be declared a winner.

One of the corporals of our team told me that the guys in the artillery would want to take revenge on our area.

I told my friends to be aware and be prepared.

We told everyone not to leave the house in the evening and the younger people were also called in to defend our district. We all liked the excitement a lot.

Playing wargames.

We had conventional arms: fists, catapults, and rocks.

Sometimes a person would bring a boxing ring.

The artillery troops arrived in our area in army trucks: more than one hundred troops with corporals and some lower-level officers.

Our catapults and rocks were enough to keep them away from our district.

They got angry as they could not get close enough to do their preferred hand to hand combat. To release some of their aggression, they damaged some houses. The fight lasted for several hours.

In the meantime, local authorities became aware of this scuffle, and they sent military police and other armed troops to clear the streets. The guys from the artillery said I was a "traitor," and that they would eventually "get" me.

The next day, I resigned from my post, and Captain Hanssen, told my commanding officer. He was not happy and told me that he should have known about this conflict before.

A couple of weeks later, I was appointed to be an office worker in a government office in New Guinea.

I will never forget the arrival of our government boat in Sorong Bay. It was pitch dark and with unfamiliar sounds, to be honest, I was a bit scared.

Suddenly there were a couple of Papuans right beside me. They were only wearing a penis protector.

They came to the boat with the head of the district to pick up my luggage. They loaded everything in a small canoe. It was an unreal experience.

Small, slim, dark ghosts that moved against a sinister background. They brought me to the government building which did not have any furniture or lights.

There was three of us and we went to lay on our field beds, a size not larger than one hundred and eighty centimeters by eighty centimeters. It was a new place where thoughts, feelings, and memories were trying to find their place.

I finally fell asleep early in the morning.

The next morning, we had a meeting with the head of the government in Sorong who, much to our surprise, was wearing shorts and an unbuttoned shirt.

He looked at us with an espression of mistrust and made statements that we are all very typical young men looking for a new adventure.

He talked about the dangers of the jungle and believed that only the strong could survive.

He said with a grin, it would surprise him to see "who of you will survive this way of life in the jungle for a long period of time."

To start our training we were to take a trip with the task to meet all the local Papuan tribal leaders. We were told that it would take a couple of months.

I was assigned to J. Maitmoe, a young intelligence officer. We had to buy food and supplies for a period of about three months. Everything was prepared.

The *barang* (luggage) was carried onto the government ship that would take us sixty-five miles to the east. It seemed to be all very peaceful.

The ship sputtered through the water, leaving behind a large V-sign. Would that be a special sign?

My mind was jumping up and down, looking for truth, security, and strength to help me to pursue this adventure. Finally the boat arrived at our destination and dropped the anker.

Papuans with *prauws* (canoes) got close to the ship to pick us up together with our luggage. I never imagined you could easily get-on and get-off a ship without a quay.

Another challenge was to get into a small boat without getting wet. I suspected the Papuans did this on purpose to see if they could get the *tuan besar* (mister) to fall in the water.

My known civility was now a distant memory. I did not recognize that we had gone back centuries to the Stone Ages again.

With twenty bearers we marched for two days through the jungle to my new post, Sainkedoek. My body was in pain as I was not used to marching for so long through this type of terrain.

My feet were swollen, probably from heat and sweat. My socks were so wet they looked like I walked through a puddle.

The Papuan bearers made monotone sounds, which had the same effect as when a group of Papuans, banging on their drums, would be dancing in trance.

We settled in an area in the jungle that had been cleared of trees. There were three houses: one for the commanding officer; one government home where I would stay for a period of time, and another home for the rest of the people.

The sun was burning hard on this spot that from the sky would look like the top of a priest's head.

The Dutch flag, our proud symbol, was hanging there

without any movement. Suddenly with a bit of warm breeze, it started to move more until the night fell.

The pain in my feet was almost unbearable. It felt like I had walked on burning coils.

First I washed them in cold water and elevated them on a cushion to improve blood flow to my legs.

I felt peaceful and did think about what the governor told us before we left. He believed that we would not survive in the jungle.

From a short distance away, I heard voices and the smell of burning flesh. A group of Papuans returned from hunting in the jungle and were preparing a meal.

My initial two-day march eventually proved to be just a preview of what was to follow. Next we would head out for a longer trip. During this fourteen-day journey, it rained quite hard. We travelled on hands and feet, twenty Papuans and twelve agents, through an area that was only travelled before by local indigenous people.

We slipped more and more as if we had ice under our feet, instead of mud and leaves.

I suffered from back and muscle pain. Had cuts on my hands and legs, and a nasty cut from a vine on my face.

The Dutch *cadaster* (land registry) people travelled to meet up with a few registered villages in the hope that they could give us more information about other tribes that were unregistered.

We travelled through the jungle for forty days. I realized that I could count my ribs, but at the same time I felt like a cat with nine lives.

My legs developed muscles like an athlete. I started to walk upright with my chin held high.

In comparison to three colleagues who had given up the challenge, I was, together with two others, the only survivors on this trip. Finally, we were given residency posts around the coast in small villages with regular inhabitants..

There were Chinese grocery stores in these villages. That

was a great surprise for me. I was the only one in a small village doing this pioneer work.

It was in the middle of December when some of us, during the heat of the day, travelled back to Sorong in a small boat to celebrate Christmas and New Year.

It was a trip back to the city.

A place where we could use our regular money.

Life was looking up again.

Suddenly, a Japanese bullet passed by my ears.

The guerrilla war called me back from my thoughts.

I did not know where the bullet came from. It struck some wooden branches behind me.

We realized that the Japanese were able to bribe some of the Papuans with gifts, such as shells, rice, and so on.

The Papuans were ordered to spy on us and tell the Japanese where our camps were located in the jungle.

My nerves were stretched to the limit. I expected that the bullets were not only going to hit the trees in the jungle. Our group was stuck here, and we did not move for about an hour.

Finally we were satisfied that the enemy had left. We thought about preparing food again.

It was difficult to coordinate food rationing and the dividing of ammunition between the groups. No rice was brought to us from Manokwari.

With our fourteen troops, including Sergeant-Major Maas and militia soldier I. Koch, we were sent to Hattam to pick up military supplies and ammunition.

When the war is over, I thought, I would be back in charge of my former duty as a government employee.

Two extra guerrilla teams of three troops each were joining us on our trip to Hattam. They were to go to the posts of Testega and Sensenemes to protect the supplies and ammunition. Militia soldiers L. Attinger and T. van Genderen were part of these groups.

The arrival in Tjosi, three days after we departed, was a

128

great event. The Dutch flag was raised to show that the head of the district was back.

Another nice surprise was that we met up with father and son Tuinenburg and Mr. Griet.

Sergeant-Major Maas sent them to Wasirawi the next day to report to Captain Geeroms for duty.

The Japanese tried several times to destroy our supplies of food and ammunition. These areas were so well-covered that we had to assume that policeman Pantouw must have told the Japanese about these locations.

Policeman and translator, Manikabar Mandatjan, came to our location armed with a rifle. He took over Pantouw's position.

A couple of small groups went on reconnaissance. It was hot as hell in the jungle.

The women and children of our guerrilla troops, who were across the coast in an internment camp in Oransbari, had been told to move more inland.

We realized that we had to bring more supplies there to help them survive this war.

The women of the group did not like the change of location and the quarrels between the women and men became like a small internal war.

The tiniest disagreements escalated to something bigger, and I wondered if these women really understood what situation we were in.

We were informed by militia soldiers Griet and Soentpiet, who had left us two weeks earlier, that in Ransiki and Oransbari, additional detachments of Japanese soldiers had taken position.

The police commissioner, Mr. Roborgh, arrived from the area of Wandamen. He told us that Mr. Van Eechoud and J. de Bruyn had stayed near the Wissel Lakes.

He was sent to the Wandamen area to pick up *sago* cakes for us. But the Japanese troops had also arrived there.

Luckily, he was able to find his way back to us. At the

same time, militia soldier Kokkelink had contacted a group fighters from Ambonia, loyal to the Dutch, who were able to tell us about additional Japanese troop movements.

The commander of this guerrilla group was Mr. Latumahina. He told us that, at one time, a large group of Japanese soldiers had got close to the Ambonese. They, in turn, set up a trap and all the Japanese were killed.

• *KNIL (Ambonese) recruits being trained in Ambon*

Paula Mellenbergh:
Leaving Manokwari to an Internment Camp

16

When KNIL commander Captain Geeroms gave the order to start the guerrilla war against the Japanese invaders, my father and Uncle Richard went to locations, where before the war started, supplies were brought for survival in the jungle.

The Japanese military police force in Manokwari started immediately with interrogations. I was told that they were hard interrogations.

Family members and friends of the men who left to fight the guerrilla war were getting questioned harshly.

During that time, I was overwhelmed with fear.

The soldiers of the Japanese Royal Army, in their olive-green uniforms and hats with a flap in the back to protect against the sun, landed in greater numbers.

They took control of all the buildings in town, forced people to prepare defenses in the streets, and took control of our vegetable gardens.

The few cows of the settlers were also taken.

American planes suddenly appeared in the sky and dropped their bombs. The sound of the bombs dropping and the anti-aircraft machine guns made a huge noise.

Until late in the evening, the search lights from the Japanese swept in the sky for more planes.

Manokwari was in rubble.

I wondered if the Americans knew about our existence in the city and the trenches we were hiding in. The Japanese soldiers took cover in the hills.

After a couple of years, the liberators finally came close to our internment camp.

The Japanese guards hurried us to march faster, through the difficult jungle. A deserted Papuan village beside the Prafi River was going to be our destination.

I remember the feeling of hopelessness in this area that contained small primitive huts. How I felt every day, with a handful of rice or *sago* and some tender vegetable leaves.

My clothes slowly, but surely, rotted away, and I struggled against *koetoe maleo*, an insect that makes your skin itch like crazy.

It became more devastating when the group (about one hundred and fifty people) died of exhaustion and typhus. I saw a young girl in her bed who was very restless, and a couple of hours later, she was stiff and lifeless.

I learned to take care of the dead, including my foster parents.

• Women prisoners in Singapore, circa 1945
They were required to bow to their Japanese captors
during daily roll call.

Meity Kneefel:
My Parents' Memories in a Japanese Internment Camp

17

Meity Kneefel (1947-2010) the sister of Roy Kneefel, after the war, talked to her parents about their experiences in an internment camp outside Manokwari. The parents names are Albert Kneefel and Johanna de Mey. They got married inside the camp in November 1942.

Albert Kneefel and Johanna de Mey recall: Our area was regularly attacked by aerial bombardments. For the Japanese and their prisoners, there was nothing else to do for safety but go to the trenches.

At the entrances to the trenches, daredevils were able to follow the air strikes, as well as the attempts of the Japanese to shoot the allied aircraft out of the sky.

Especially in the evening, when the moon was shining brightly, the battles offered a fascinating sight.

The image of small silver objects sequencing against a moonlit sky, haunted by Japanese searchlights, was almost a fairytale.

The roar of the airplane engines and the explosions around the people watching from these shelters, on the other hand, were sobering. It was an overwhelming fireworks display of lights and thunderous bangs.

A spectacle so captivating that you would almost forget the bitter gravity of the situation.

As the occupation continued in Manokwari, people were captured for various reasons. Europeans and their sympathizers, in particular, had to pay a heavy price for their culture.

It was clear that the Japanese intention was to systematically eradicate this Eurasian population.

Families whose fathers had joined the resistance took it extra hard. They were monitored continuously, even though they had no idea of the present situation or the whereabouts of their husband and fathers in hiding.

The family members would have liked to know how the men were doing, but for their own safety, had to remain in the dark.

During sporadic and hasty encounters of the guerrilla fighters with the Papuans, they were told only the most important message: "They were doing well and that they should not be worried about them."

It was believed that this was the best way to protect those who were left behind. This was also the reason why their affiliation with the resistance had quietly stopped.

Yet, the Japanese invaders did not give up.

As an example, one day, they forced anyone suspected of ties to the resistance to spend Christmas in prison.

The Japanese knew that Christmas was an important family celebration, and their hope was to catch guerrilla fighters who may have wanted to liberate their families this way.

The Japanese soldiers expected that they would take great risks to contact their relatives to celebrate Christmas. If they tried to enter the camp, they could be arrested without any problems.

The enemy was wrong. No resistance fighter showed up.

Papuans, who worked as informants for the guerrilla fighters, had taken notes of the Japanese preparations at the prison. They had seen that security had been strengthened and advised the men to refrain from any attempt to approach the prison.

Fiercely disgruntled, but determined to learn more about the resistance movement, the occupiers took a different approach.

They started with cruel interrogations of the un-willing prisoners. The Japanese torture chambers have been able to prove their usefulness. Hair-raising practices must have taken place during that period.

My poor grandfather experienced this firsthand. He talked to us about the details of his tortures. I believe they are too gruesome for me to talk about it.

I want you to know that this kind man, who once played the violin very well, could not bend his wrists, after a ten-day stay in a cell.

Electrical cables were used to hang him from his wrists. They did their work well. All because he did not want to betray his son. Although he said that he did not know the location of his son, he was not believed.

Because my father was not seen as a family member, he was excluded from captivity. *Opa* (grandfather) would have preferred to go with him. He missed his wife terribly and lived in constant anxiety and fear about her fate.

It also happened that there were Japanese guards who were not completely harsh towards us. When they were on guard, they would allow the two lovers (my mom and dad) to meet secretly in the evening.

Opa was able to smuggle Meity's parent's notes in and out of the camp, which was a risky undertaking. They allowed Mama and Papa to arrange a space and time to see each other.

One of the notes was that she kept a small diary. A notebook in which even the smallest things were written down. But also dates and times of bombings.

Things she had heard or seen or what could or could not be done.

In that diary, she kept track of the events of everyday life as accurately as possible. Such a find, however, could be fatal.

Also fatal for my father, who didn't even know about its existence. The dairy always had to be tucked away quickly and carefully. Then Mama just hoped that there was no betrayal in the home and that it would end well again.

Dad also didn't make it easy for her by often telling the the truth about the injustice the Japanese were guilty of. Surprisingly, he was never taken into custody for that.

The days, the weeks in which one even became somewhat accustomed to the bombing, the constant fear of treason, the risk of being rightly or wrongly punished for something, the lack of food and supplies, and the very limited freedom, continued until some of the prisoners once again were summoned.

With the increase of Allied air strikes, the situation for the Japanese became more precarious. For their own protection they were forced to move into the jungle together with their prisoners. They had prepared other camps for that reason.

Avoiding the bombing by the Allies was not the only reason to go into the jungle. The planned extermination of the Europeans and their siblings could also be carried out more quickly and effectively.

The camps in the forest could be reached via two paths. The prisoners were divided into two groups.

The two smaller groups were easier to control. They would follow a path and get back together at the end of the march through the jungle. This split, unfortunately, marked the final separation of my parents and my mother's family.

They were not placed in the same group and did not see each other gain. Missing your loved ones during a time of imprisonment must have been devastating.

The uncertainty and thoughts of whether they're still alive would continue to haunt you. The impossibility of giving them a final resting place created a big knot in your stomach.

You never lose the pain of the missed goodbye. You erase that memory.

What we have experienced, with my mother in particular, is that for many years she has cherished the hope of seeing her family one day.

Any news that Eurasians had been spotted in the jungle revived that hope.

"Would they be?" was her recurring question.

It was only when we settled in the Netherlands that Mama accepted the fact that her family died in the jungle.

It was very difficult because there was no evidence to be found. Sometimes, she let her imagination run wild about where they might lie.

Her mother always had a premonition to die on one of New Guinea's dry and sharp coral coasts. We'll probably never know.

The only memories Mama has kept is her childhood. Those remains like stories, which she tells us regularly when we visit her.

The march to the camps was hard to endure. In the scorching heat and the pouring rain, we went through dense, barely passable, muddy jungle, and over beaches in which the sand seemed to suck you in, which made moving fast almost impossible.

Sharp and slippery rocks had to be climbed, where each wrong step could have painful or even fatal consequences.

At the same time, we had to remain aware of continued Allied air strikes. No matter how sick and weak one felt, we had to march on.

Mama once proudly told us that her group must have broken the record by covering the distance in four and a half days. "Was it possible because there were no children walking with us?" she added. As painful as that action was for my father, it was the only way to spare himself and the others a gruesome spectacle.

After the war, my father ran into fellow internees a few times. Each time, they embraced my father, telling bystanders that "this man saved my life!"

What about my father? He has always been against the need for heavy-handed intervention. In the first months, they were placed into barracks in the first camp.

The food supply was not really a problem during that stay because all the men from the group worked together and everyone got a share of the supplies.

When the forced movement was made to the top of the hill, times were considerably more difficult. The food rations distributed before departure were very small.

For example, my parents had to survive with about five hundred grams of rice. It was not clear to my father if the distribution was according to the size of the families.

A separation by the Japanese on the base of ethnic background put an end to the collective gathering of food.

Each group had to do that separately. Soon nothing was left of the rice in storage.

Climbing and transporting the sick had taken a lot out of the stronger among them. To make matters worse, the new area on the hill had to be mined. Pure madness, but probably the intent for the eventual extermination of the prisoners.

The small group of Eurasians could no longer count on the help of others to arrange shelters. Vastly outnumbered, as they were with only a handful of men, it became a difficult task.

First, we had to start providing the necessary shelter from the bright sun and tropical rain showers. This had to done immediately and with everyone helping out.

The desolate wasteland consisted largely of weeds and vicious scrub, which made the collection of building material quite a challenge.

Exhaustion and lack of food began to take their toll.

Despite all efforts, only a few pathetic huts could be set up: roofs of coconut leaves, supported by wooden poles. Walls were missing.

In order not to lie directly on the ground, an elevated wooden floor was built between a rectangle of poles pushed into the ground. This consisted of a framework containing a row of branches and planks nailed together. They slept on that, because mattresses were not available.

Such shelters can be seen in commercials. They stand at a beautiful beach with sunny weather and smiling people; however, the huts in this camp had nothing to do with a commercial because under the roofs were a lot of sick, hungry people.

Even my mother was forced, sometimes in vain, to beg the other groups for food. Because of the hunger, but also because of missing her family, she became very ill over time.

A few times, during the forced labor of mining, she had her legs cut open to thorns and other prickly stuff. She suffered from dysentery.

The chance of recovery was low due to lack of medication. Finally, the wounds became so infected that Mama could hardly walk.

And any food she ate she almost immediately lost. She had no energy at all.

It was so bad at one point that Papa, in his desperation, sneaked into the occupier's storage shed in search of a cure for his wife.

Anything was better than being a bystander.

All he could find at the time was a few grains of rice lying on the ground among garbage and dust.

He washed the grains as well as he could and then roasted them. We can't really call this a cure, but it helped my mother.

Within a few days, the dysentery was gone. It was remarkable that Daddy was able to brew something out of trash for Mama.

The Japanese meanwhile, continued their degrading practices. Despite the lack of basic facilities, the forced hard labor had to be done. This all while the prisoners had little energy left.

My father always talked about "the road to the grave," by which he meant that particular place.

Hunger became so desperate that my father and a friend felt the need to provide extra food for the rest of the community.

They decided to walk back to their previous location at the bottom of the hill. There they were able to harvest a few wild sago palms.

The extraction of flour from the palms became a long and difficult task. It would require extra energy.

The back-and-forth, as mentioned earlier, lasted one day in each direction. The descent to the ground below was easier, but at the same time, they had to be constantly wary of not slipping or falling.

Reaching their destination, a *sago* palm had to be cut down first and then cut open. The fibers then had to be broken and crushed to release the nutrients.

This time-consuming and gruelling work was called knocking. It demanded a lot of physical energy.

Finally the moist flour extracted from the fibers was laid to dry for a few days in the sun. During that time, the men were able to rest and return to the camp after all that effort.

But wild sago palms only give a small amount of flour.

The meager harvest had to be transported up the hill towards the camp. All that was done with an empty stomach.

The men left hungry and often came back even hungrier.

They didn't bring any food with them. If they were lucky, they found a snake or an iguana. The animal was killed without hesitation, chopped into pieces, roasted and eaten.

This was definitely not a school excursion or boy scout event. But every time they returned to the camp with their loot after a few days, they were met with enthusiasm.

The joy on the emaciated faces of the waiting, especially the children, gave the two exhausted men satisfaction and motivation to go back and forth up and down the hill.

They were aware that their efforts had not been in vain, and it was greatly appreciated.

From the sago flour dough, a kind of hard, dry roll was baked.

They were laid on a fire in wooden molds.

Unfortunately, the children did not digest this food very

well. It made them severily constipated. A cure for this condition was not available in the camp.

Powerless, my parents had to see how much their skinny children's bodies suffered from the only edible thing that was available at the time. They desperately needed food in whatever form.

When the Japanese managed to lay hands on a batch of canned fish, some of it was given to the prisoners.

It was the very last thing that was handed out.

The fish was placed on the batter for the sago buns and baked with it. As a change from the tasteless dry buns it was a treat everyone enjoyed. After that, they really got nothing.

Everything is relative, but if you literally have to tighten your belt to get rid of a hungry feeling, it's a deadly and nasty situation to live in.

If you have to beg others for two measly pieces of an iguana tail you are really desperate. I just can't believe how they were able to survive this hell.

There were no fruit trees. No edible crops either. Bushes were robbed of their leaves. No leaf was spared.

Often they fed on mushrooms and did not think for a moment that they could be poisonous. Prisoners chewed on pieces of wood. And all this to satisfy hunger as much as possible.

No one could be trusted anymore. Everyone was watching everyone else in case they happened to have something to eat.

Once the women, under the supervision of a Papuan guard, took a bath in a river near the camp. The man sat on a higher elevation, to make sure no one tried to escape.

My dad sat down with him and looked at my mother. Watching how skinny his wife had become, he burst into tears. He decided to make a deal with the Papuan.

He offered his watch, that was still in good condition, in exchange for some rice. This offer was accepted by the Papuan.

In the evening, my mother felt a hand slide under her pillow, while a voice in the dark said, "Rest assured. It's so good. It's already settled." The Papuan turned out to have put rice under her pillow in a sock as agreed.

The intention was to cook that rice secretly the next day. However, the people who were in an adjoining hut had heard what had been said to my mother.

What Mama received was not known to them. But undoubtedly it had to do with food. Something else was hardly conceivable.

The next day they went looking for my parents and could find them easily. At a small shelter, where Mom and Dad thought they could cook the rice unnoticed, they were betrayed by the sound of it simmering.

My parents insisted on giving up a part of the little bit of rice. It was a wise decision. Otherwise the people would most likely tell on them.

Their Papuan savior was not heard from again.

It was hoped that his act did not bring him trouble. The hopeless situation made Papa sometimes despair. Especially when he saw the abundance clearly present among the invaders.

On the way to and from the sago forest, he passed through the Japanese huts. He could see how women in the kitchen were preparing food. Women from the camp had joined the kitchen workers. They had surrendered to the enemy.

They simply couldn't stand the hunger and misery anymore. In addition, so much was cooked that some of it could easily be handed over to the internees.

Papa has always told us not to be picky about food. He could enjoy the smallest and simplest snacks himself.

I remember as a kid observing him as he was enjoying a slice of bread with some lettuce, slices of tomato, cucumber, and some canned tuna.

Because he didn't like to eat alone, he tried to persuade me to at least taste some of it.

Although the combination didn't appeal to me at the time, he got me to take a piece of it, I now make tuna sandwiches myself.

It is mainly the way in which he savors his snacks, a talent for arousing a certain appetite in people. Even though they are satisfied and there is no crumb left.

When we have something to celebrate, there is always a large variety of dishes. Because no one should be short of anything, there must certainly be some of the dishes which are liked by everyone.

Enjoying food together is very important to him.

I have taken his reverence and love of food to heart. I try to enjoy it consciously, preferably with appropriate company.

The careless disposal of leftovers will almost never be seen in my kitchen. I have to admit that, much to the annoyance of my family members, I sometimes exaggerate a little. But I'm sure I got this trait from my father.

Besides being miserable, life in the camp on top of the hill was also monotonous and hopeless.

With the little energy they had left, the women tried to re-engage daily on the household tasks and gardening. The group of men in the forest mainly worked together in the search for food.

There were no more interrogations. Everyone was too weakened or too sick.

Reconnaissance aircraft of the Allies, which had been flying over regularly, could only be checked if you desired.

Waving or attracting any form of attention was strictly forbidden.

What they would have liked to shout it out loud:

"Come free us! Get us out of this madhouse!"

But their potential rescuers continued to fly high up in the sky, unsuspecting of the drama unfolding on the high plain slipping by, beneath their powerful machines.

143

• *Thanks to Ronald and his son Gilbert Ang who live in Manokwari,
Louise Beynon, Ferry Boum Bletterman and I visited the beach
of Oransbari a couple of years ago.*
*We took several pictures, but this one taken by A. Mixie on Flickr
shows the difficulty of landing that the liberation team of the Alamo
Scouts encountered during the rescue of Camp Oransbari.*

Sergeant Zeelt Report of Internment Camp Oransbari.
Women and Children of Guerilla Fighters
Were Imprisoned Here.

18

On July 29, 1947 landstorm Sergeant Joop Zeelt wrote a report that was sent to The Military Conduct Commission (C.G.) Cabinet of the Army Commander in Batavia.

Sergeant Zeelt: "In response to your request to write a report on my experiences as a member of the protection brigade for women and children of soldiers of the War Detachment Manokwari (military evacuation camp in Oransbari) during the war years, I have the honor to inform your Commission the following.

On December 8, 1941, our four militia and landstorm brigades were called into active duty. The following day we were stationed in the SIKNG passanggrahan in Manokwari.

After several aerial bombardments by the Japanese, bivouacs were set up in the woods behind the military compound at Manokwari. This for the benefit of the military personnel and their families.

In January 1942 it was decided to set up a military evacuation camp for women and children in the jungle in Oransbari, about eighty kilometers to the south of Manokwari and six kilometers off the coast.

On February 2, 1942 Sergeant Pongo was sent there with a few men to prepare the camp. After a few weeks, the construction had advanced so that the first team of women and children could be directed there.

The evacuation then took place.

On February 19, 1942, Captain J.B.H. Willemsz.-Geeroms put me in charge of the administration of the evacuation camp Oransbari, and I received the following orders:

(1) Leave for Oransbari that same night with the last group of women and children; (2) In addition to administrative work, ensure the correct distribution of food and pocket money; (3) In the event of a possible Japanese invasion, try to protect the women and children first and take necessary measures about food supplies in cooperation with Sergeant Pongo; (4) Under no circumstances were we to engage in a fight with the Japanese to avoid reprisals against the women and children; (5) Under no circumstances to leave the camp, unless ordered to do so. Points 4 and 5 also applied to Sergeant Pongo, under whose command the protection brigade was constructed. From time-to-time Captain Geeroms would try to get in touch with us.

On 20 February 1942, I arrived in Oransbari with the last group of women and children. In total, the camp had about 250 women and children and the protection brigade. Until the date of the Japanese invasion of Manokwari, 12 April 1942, the daily routine in camp continued.

On March 30, 1942, I asked my friend, landstorm soldier Theodoor Beynon to come to the camp with his family.

On April 12, 1942 around 5:00 a.m., several warships were seen close to the bay of Oransbari, and we recognized them as Japanese. Later we heard that this small fleet turned out to be the rearguard of the Japanese fleet which invaded Manokwari that day.

Together with three militia soldiers, Sergeant Nikijuluw, who had returned to camp two days earlier with the mail from Manokwari, wanted to go back. I warned them not to leave as they would take a risk to be captured by the enemy.

Despite our advice and warnings, they left. The result was that they were captured by a Japanese warship near Maroni.

We immediately tried to move the camp further inland, but were unsuccessful due to the panicked mood of the women and children and lack of transport availability. We began to prepare land for planting crops as our supplies would not be enough.

Sergeant van Lochem, who visited Oransbari with orders to transport cattle for slaughter from Ransiki to Manokwari, was unable to carry out that task due to the Japanese invasion. He was picked up and taken by the Japanese to Manokwari. Also soldier Deeken and his wife, who were heading the European primary school in Manokwari before the outbreak of the war, were taken.

Suze, Nancy, and Olga: *We had to hide in the jungle where there was no sunshine. My father created a place for us to sleep and we used burlap bags for blankets. My mother knew what was edible in the jungle. She knew how to avoid sickness and what could be used as medicine. My parents, had valuable experience in jungle living and hygiene measures needed to avoid disease. In the forest my mother and father would find roots, herbs, and leaves, which we would cook to prepare an edible meal. In the kali (small river) near the camp, we found small fish and shrimp when we dove to the bottom. We learned how to catch them from Papuans. One edible and healthy plant we found in the jungle was jambu kloetoek (guave) tree. The leaves were very bitter, but can be brewed to a tea that was used for diarrhea. Many people did not know that. My mother explained this to the others in our camp. Sergeant Zeelt, who stayed with our family during the internment, was married (just for safety and not legal) in our camp to my older sister Nini. This was to keep the Japanese soldiers from taking my sisters as comfort women for personal pleasure. Carla, my youngest sister at that time, was called Nini's daughter.*

On 6 May 1942, a Japanese detachment invaded the camp. After inspection and a speech by the Japanese commander informing us of the supreme power of the Japanese in Asia, they left. They took with them the wives and children of Sergeant Maas and Quartermaster Beaufort.

On 9 May, thirty soldiers, who had surrendered at Manokwari, arrived in the camp. They said they were sent there by

147

the Japanese. They immediately proclaimed that everyone in camp was equal to the other, there was no rank or position. We let them talk and carried on with our business.

Suze, Nancy, and Olga: *When the Japanese soldiers came into our camp, we were always prepared. My father kept a close watch on us girls, and we were only allowed outside when he gave the order. We were forebidden to speak Dutch outside our hut, so we used the local Papuan dialect. We did not receive much rice as we had little contact with the Japanese soldiers. We survived on the vegetables we grew in our small garden: cassava, sweet potatoes, and some other vegetables. That was how our parents kept us alive in the internment camp. The Japanese soldiers were always looking for some young girls for personal pleasure. We were prepared. As soon as Japanese soldiers came close to our area, we whistled a certain melody, so our older sisters knew they had to hide. We dug a hole under my parents bed, big enough to keep my older sisters out of sight. We covered them up with burlap and leaves. The Japanese never knew we had older sisters and only saw the younger kids play outside.*

A few days later, we received a visit from another Japanese detachment. In the usual speech, the speaker indicated that since the Japanese had some difficulties with food supplies, we had to be responsible for ourselves.

To prevent disorder on the part of Minakari's former soldiers and a possible capture by the Japanese, I decided, after speaking with Sergeant Pongo, to distribute the food on hand to the camp inhabitants.

Since these ex-soldiers were mainly targeting Pongo, and most of the men of the initial protection brigade could no longer be trusted, I would take on the task of dividing the food and Pongo would stay out of it.

Despite attempts by the former soldiers to cause disturbances, I managed, faithfully assisted by the landstorm soldier Theodoor Beynon, to ensure that everyone received his/her rightful share.

Another group of Japanese visitors, this time from the civilian side, a so-called *Manseibu of Manokwari*, seized the cash still present in the hands of Sergeant Pongo. Some Indigenous police officers were left in the camp.

At the beginning of June 1942, we were informed that two soldiers from Captain Geeroms unit were hiding near settler R. Somokil's house. They were the militia soldiers Griët and Soempiet. We met in secret and provided them with the necessary information.

The success of this was largely due to R. Somokil, who as a non-military man could move more freely. He showed a lot of courage and cleverness. Griët informed us that Captain Geeroms was worried about the fate of the camp and had therefore sent them both.

The group did well under the circumstances. Due to the river drying up, we were forced to move downhill. The move was completed by the end of June.

In the first half of July 1942, the militia soldier Griët came to visit us again. However behind the barrack where Beynon and I stayed, he was seen by a few ex-soldiers who mistook him for landstorm soldier von Bila. In the evening we managed to have a meeting with Griët, where we had hidden him inside a hollow tree behind our barrack.

Pongo, Somokil, and Beynon were present at the meeting. Griët brought orders from Captain Geeroms which included taking the best possible care of the women and children and not to leave the camp without his orders.

The requested information was provided to Griët to transfer to Captain Geeroms. Griët was provided with the necessary food for his journey back by the family Beynon.

A report was submitted by the indigenous police to the Japanese about the arrival at Oransbari of the landstorm soldier von Bila. This mistake would later turn out to be our salvation.

At the end of August 1942, the Japanese HPB of Manokwari came under military escort in Oransbari. Pongo and I were called to come forward. The Japanese informed us that, since we did not work for them, he considered us the enemy and had to behead us all. However, he did not want to do so at this time. He told us that he did not intend to provide us with any food.

Those who wished to go back to Manokwari would receive food, work, money, and housing. Unfortunately, the Japanese bird catcher had a lot of success. That day, eight families of indigenous soldiers left for Manokwari, partly lured to do so by the example of most ex-soldiers who did not like the farm work and had left earlier.

On September 6, 1942, the Japanese civil administration transferred Sergeants Pongo and Zeelt, the landstorm soldier Beynon and the settler Somokil to Manokwari. We were housed in the police barracks and placed under strict surveillance. We were accused of having a hand in the creation of a blacklist, now in Captain Geerom's possession.

We were also charged with housing and feeding the militia soldier Griët. Since we were certain that there was no evidence against us, we denied all the charges, referring to the fact that the police had flagged the landstorm soldier von Bila and not Griët.

After several interrogations, in which we maintained our position of not knowing anything, taking care not to contradict each other, we were separated. Pongo and Beynon were placed in a pontoon boat while Somokil and I remained under surveillance at the police barracks.

After two weeks without any further questioning, Somokil and I were released, mainly with the help of Tanamal, formerly a *mandoer* (chief worker) on a pontoon boat, and now forced by the Japanese to act as police chief.

We returned to Oransbari. Pongo and Beynon seemed to have been forgotten. It was late January 1943 that the Japanese were reminded of them with the result that they too were released.

On 30 January 1943, they were back with us.

By now, the protection brigade had shrunk to eight men: the Sergeants Pongo and Zeelt, landstorm soldier Beynon, Javanese fusilier Sober, Sangit, Setoe, Legiman, and Noya. The others had left their posts and had gone back to Manokwari. I did not hear from them again.

Remembering the captain's orders I suggested the men to build a community garden and to work in it for three hours a day with the main food crops, such as corn, cassava, and sweet potatoes. The rest of the day, we would each plant vegetables, tobacco, *pisang* (bananas), sugar cane etc. in our own gardens. The area of the community garden and the areas to be planted periodically would depend on the number of inhabitants of the camp. The harvests would be distributed to all the families.

The settler R. Somokil made his entire plot available for all. Everyone agreed with the proposal and work started. Joint hunting trips were later established. Two men every night from 6:00 p.m. to 6:00 a.m., protected our crops from the pig infestation.

The proof that the system was effective was demonstrated by the fact that until February 1942, none of the camp inhabitants suffered, even though we were never provided with food from the Japanese.

At the end of October 1942, the cattle still present in the camp were taken away by the Japanese. The cattle were requested by Captain Geeroms when setting up the camp for the settlers; the equivalent would later be repaid to them.

The rightful owners were the families Schuylenburg and Koch, ten cows, Mrs. Ang. two and G. Waajenberg four cows. Since we did not receive any additional soldiers pay, Somokil and I supported the women who no longer owned anything from their

• *Dutch Indonesian money*

151

own resources, partly with cash, partly with purchased items, such as coconuts, coconut oil, etc., which we could occasionally buy from the local Papuan population. We had not complied with the summons of the Japanese to hand in our personal savings and safely stored the small amount we had.

On 18 December 1942 a Japanese detachment came to transfer some families to Manokwari: a total of twenty-four people, comprised of the Mellenberg, Shuylenburg, Fauser, von Bila, Arents, van Genderen ladies and the entire Koch family including children. They were families of soldiers who had served with Captain Geeroms. Later we heard that these people plus those at Manokwari, plus the men and/or sons who had joined Captain Geeroms were gathered in Manokwari and were taken to internment camps.

By doing so, the Japanese hoped to persuade the soldiers to surrender. This did not happen; internment was lifted after approximately two months. Because of rumours, we were very concerned about the fate of the captured families. Somokil volunteered to go to Manokwari with a small motor boat. We realised very well that he risked a great deal, his freedom, perhaps even his life. However, I relied on his steady, daring composure and ingenuity and accepted his offer.

We gathered 150 Dutch guilders to give to the interned ladies to meet their immediate needs. He secretly left in the evening, alone in a small boat. Over the next few days, I hoped for his speedy return. On the fifth day, he happily checked in. He told me that he had managed to get through to those incarcerated and even talked to them, thanks to a Japanese guard. The funds that he brought could be handed over to the ladies. They were well. The children had not lost their courage despite everything. The conversation with Somokil had done them a great deal of good and gave them confidence in their situation.

During 1943, groups of Japanese came from different companies, exploring the region and left after a few days in the area. We avoided them as much as possible and continued our work. These constant visits by Japanese got on our nerves because we never knew what they were up to. We occasionally heard some news of our captain and comrades from the Papuans who could travel without hindrence. However, we had to be very careful, because hardly anyone could be trusted. A few times a month, an American four-engine plane appeared with a red-white-blue emblem, apparently for photographic shots. This gave the citizens courage.

Suze, Olga, Nancy: *We know that our father gave valuable information of our camp to the Papuans (He knew their dialect.) Papa found out later that he was betrayed by Pongo (Menadonese) and that was the reason he was taken prisoner by the Japanese. Papa was tortured and imprisoned for months. After his return to camp, he did not trust anyone from Menadonese background.*

Eddy Beynon: *It was a very difficult time for everyone in the camp, and I truly hope you will not experience such a negative feeling of hopelessness in your life. We had nothing and our parents' stress must have been extremely high (Eddy was asked by his son Bert to tell him a little about the time in the prison camp.)*

In May 1943 suddenly from the south several American B-24 Liberators appeared, flying in the direction of Manokwari. A few minutes after their passing, we heard dull explosions. We realized that Manokwari was being bombed. During the following days, these bombings were repeated by squadrons of six to ten B-24 Liberators, all of whom came from the same direction and returned there as well. However, our expectations and hope that now the great attack had been launched and the liberation would not be long, went up in smoke when after about two weeks, the bombing suddenly stopped.

The Japanese probably regained their composure, because

at the beginning of December 1943 another group arrived in Oransbari. They announced that the Japanese company NKK was going to establish itself in Oransbari. They began to parcel up the open areas but left our plantations untouched. They suggested we plant vegetables and sell them to the NKK, in other words, work for the Japanese. They also said we were good workers, but we were the only eight men who did not work for Japanese. Since we did not feel like working for them, we replied that we could not accept their proposal, since we had to use all our time available for our own food supply. The Japanese did not comment further. The fact that they did not forget this discussion and finally blamed us for our refusal would be experienced later.

On 11 February 1944 a group of Japanese suddenly appeared in Oransbari. The next morning, a division of the infamous Japanese *Kempeitai* secret police walked in our camp. We were immediately handcuffed, and we were also paired together with ropes. They accused us of secretly working with Captain Geeroms. In a locked room of the barracks they inhabited, we were left under heavy armed guard while the rest of the Japanese soldiers went on a intensive search.

The women were ordered to take care of our food while we were in captivity. Nothing was provided to us by the Japanese. The soldiers (Sobor, Sangit, Legiman, and later Setoe) were released after a short interrogation, while Noya was permitted to continue his work as a nurse. So, it was clear that it was all about us four: Pongo, Beynon, Somokil, and me. Every day we were each subjected to cross-examination, which sometimes lasted for hours. Fortunately, Somokil, and I still had the opportunity to exchange views with each other so that our statements did not contradict each other. We were accused of supplying Captain Geeroms and his guerrilla fighters with salt and food, following our saltmaking (boiling out of seawater). Our guard fires were said to be signal fires.

We followed the same tactics as we used earlier in 1942: "We know nothing!" Since the search did not yield any evidence, nor did the interrogations, Pongo, Somokil, and I were later taken to Manokwari. All those days and nights, we had been lying on the ground handcuffed. Beynon, who had a severe attack of malaria stayed behind; in his place, his seventeen-year-old son Nono was taken hostage. To our chagrin, we saw that the soldiers Sobor and Sangit and their families, were also on board the ship. They would certainly have been frightened by the rough treatment that was done to us. The Arents, Mandala, Kalempo and Tilengboelan ladies were also taken to Manokwari. In my opinion forcibly. On board we were locked in a small room, locks on all sides, always handcuffed, and left without food or drink until the arrival in Manokwari. We arrived in the afternoon and were taken to the kempeitai's baracks in Fanindi, where we arrived at the evening.

We slept on the floor of the office while we were paired again with handcuffs and ropes. During the day we were moved under the house, still with handcuffs and ropes, and always under armed guard. Talking was strictly forbidden while the food consisted of one ball of rice, mixed with corn kernels each day. Meanwhile, interrogations continued about the same allegations. They tried in all sorts of ways to prove that we were spies, and from time to time we were promised the lovely prospect of being beheaded. However, we insisted that we knew nothing, knowing that this was the only way out of the impasse unless we were betrayed.

This lasted about two weeks, after which the shackles were removed and we were told we were free and could sleep under the house. After two days, we were locked up again, now on a pontoon boat, which had just been completed, following the arrival of the commanding officer of the Kempeitai. In this small room of three by three meters we stayed for eight days together with sixteen other prisoners. The ration was increased to two rice balls mixed with corn kernels. After the departure of the police chief, we were released again, but were not allowed to leave the yard. We expected to be locked up again. The wait was very nerve-wracking. Pongo occasionally had a breakdown, so Somokil and I had to give him a pep talk every time. Young Beynon got it a little bit easier. Since no accusations had been brought against him, he was not handcuffed, but had to help the *heiho's* (Indonesian soldier working with the Japanese) in the kitchen.

Finally, on March 21, 1944, we were able to return to Oransbari with a motorboat from the NKK. Back 'home' it was clear to us what a search by the *Kempeitai* meant. Anything of value or useful had been appropriated. Papers and books were destroyed. Our plantations had been confiscated by the NKK, on behalf of the *Kempeitai*. This was a tough blow for us. However, we did not lose our courage and immediately got the camp back into shape and went back to intensive planting. The consequences of the accommodation by the *Kempeitai* did not last. We were badly beaten and were not worth much in the first few weeks. I was particularly affected by beriberi and from leg and foot injuries, for which there was no cure.

In early May 1944, three *Kempeitais* of Momi settled in Oransbari, according to them to protect the indigenous people, followed the next month by about twenty Japanese soldiers, who had a radio device with them. Meanwhile, the bombardment of Manokwari had started again. This time it did not suddenly stop, but continued and increased in intensity every week. At the end of June 1944, the NKK company left in the middle of the night.

At the beginning of July 1944, American aircraft began bombing and shelling Oransbari, Ransiki, Momi, and other coastal towns. We decided to go deeper into the woods. A few miles inland we found a few suitable spots under big trees close to the Moari River, after which soon the *pondoks* (temporary place to stay) were set up.

On July 7, 1944, a squadron of airplanes appeared over Oransbari. They were shooting at us. Our barrack and Somokils were riddled with bullets. Fortunately, we had all, including the children, left the houses a few minutes before and were on the field at work, so that we could take cover in time. For safety, we moved to the new accommodations the same day. There we were relatively safe and quite far from the Japanese. We had to take food from our gardens every day, which was not only heavy, but also dangerous work in view of the airstrikes, which took place regularly every day. We were beginning to weaken, since we had not much food to eat since April.

In July, the Japanese exodus from Manokwari to Mond and on to Babo began. Japanese troops in the hundreds passed us, many appeared exhausted. Some had thrown away their weapons and dragged themselves on with the help of sticks. A large number died on this journey, partly due to exhaustion, partly affected by the aircraft and PT boats, which attacked the columns day and night. As a rule, they stayed overnight in Oransbari and continued the next morning. As a result, within a few days everything edible disappeared from our gardens.

By now the food issue began to get dire. Our menu consisted mainly of various leaves and young *pisang* (banana), papaya, and *zuurzak* (soursop), as far as they could still be found. We had not had salt, sugar, coffee, and tea in a long time. We reserved the little *djagoeng* (corn) of the last harvest for the children.

At the beginning of August, the Japanese settled in our vicinity, as their barracks had been hit by airstrikes, and they had already lost a few men. In addition to the daytime airstrikes, the coast was now also bombed overnight by PT boats. The bullets sometimes struck the wood near our pondoks; fortunately, no one was injured. A pair of lost Heihos, a Javanese, and a Sumatran, four ex-KNIL soldiers then came to us completely exhausted, and we were able to hide them for a week. Rest and some food allowed them to move on. They no longer wanted to stay for fear of being found by the Japanese. That is how the days went by. Unfortunately, the

157

news of an American landing, which we expected at any moment had not happened.

The lack of food was widespread and undermined our forces. Strange that despite all that misery, most of us remained healthy. The *Kempeitai* also expected that the Americans would be landing soon, and in early September, they forced us to settle in a triangle around their barracks.

The Japanese soldiers lived opposite them, separated by an offshoot of the Moari River. They wanted to keep an eye on us and take cover behind us in the event of an attack. As a result, our situation became extremely precarious, as the search for food was made more difficult. We received a lot of help from the Arfakkers of Oransbari, who were always on our side of this war and brought us pisang, cassava and sweet potatoes from time to time. They also provided us with news about the movements of the Japanese. The Japanese were afraid of them and avoided the Arfakkers as much as possible especially after a Japanese was found in the forest with a machete cut over his face. He died soon after.

One day, Somokil informed me that he had met a well-known Papuan on the beach, from Ransiki, who informed him that the Americans had occupied Biak, Noemfoor, and Roemberpon and that he himself was in their service as a spy. As evidence, he showed Somokil a handful of white rice and a colt revolver. We were very pleased with this good news and discussed the possibility of the Americans coming soon. We agreed that Somokil would visit the Papuan in question again and make efforts to get help from Roemberpon. If he did not return, I would know that he had managed to go to Roemberpon. We agreed not to make our intentions known so that everyone could safely declare that they knew nothing about his disappearance. We risked discovery of his escape. We had to take reprisals from the Japanese side, for unless the Americans arrived, we would all be doomed to death.

The next day, Somokil did not return from a foraging trip to the beach. He stayed away the following days. I knew then that our comrade had managed to make it to Roemberpon. The Japanese, especially the *Kempeitai*, were very angry about Somokil's disappearance and threatened us all with beheadings. They were especially after Beynon and me. They searched for Somokil everywhere in the vicinity, to no avail. They questioned us one by one. The Arfakkers and Papuans were also questioned, but of course no one knew anything about his disappearance.

The obvious explanation of his disappearance was that he had died in an airstrike, since all his belongings remained in his hut. The Japanese seemed to believe that, at least the threat against us was not carried out.

Every night I expected Somokil's return with auxiliary troops, but day after day passed without anything happening. The situation became unbearable. We hardly had food, our few clothes were worn to threads, and our physical condition was getting worse.

Finally, on 4 October 1944, at 4:00 a.m. we suddenly heard machine gun fire and the explosion of hand grenades coming from the direction of the Japanese barracks. Not long after that we saw the flames rising from it. I saw some Japanese tumbling down like cones. To our great delight, we heard English and Dutch language. It was finally our comrade Somokil, who had managed to bring salvation in the form of a team of Alamo Scouts with Lieutenant Rapmund as a guide.

Suze, Nancy, Olga: *We remember that night very well. Papa was awakened by Somokil, who used to live with us in the camp but escaped to get help. Somokil whispering, "Beynon, Beynon, quietly wake the children. We are going to get you out of here. Wait for my signal." My father told us to hide under the bed. Loud explosions followed, and when it became quiet, we were finally taken from our imprisonment.*

The attack worked brilliantly. Within minutes all Japanese, I believe twenty-four men, were down, while the Japanese guards, consisting of three men, were also shot. In view of the possibility of the presence of Japanese deployments in the vicinity, we marched to the beach as soon as possible. There we embarked in PT boats that sail a long way back and forth from the coast. Everyone was very pleased with the happy ending of the expedition. On board we were welcomed by the Americans with soup, sandwiches and especially cigarettes, the taste of which we almost had forgotten.

Suze, Nancy, Olga: *The American soldiers together with Rapmund and Somokil guided us through the jungle till we arrived at the beach. We were put in PT boats and brought to Noemfoer. We arrived at a camp where people were welcomed, and the sick were taken care of immediately. There was a field hospital. Our family stayed with Dutch military officers. We remember the long barracks with beds side by side. My mother started to work in the hospital kitchen right away. We were so happy to finally have a regular meal. Many of us would never forget what the American soldiers had done for us.*

In the afternoon we arrived at Bosnik, where, after I first reported to Captain Bannink, was admitted to the field hospital. The others were housed in tents and sent to Noemfoor ten days later. I requested to be relocated immediately after release.

On 7 November 1944 I was sent to Hollandia, where I was assigned to the former Papuan Battalion, later called the 1st Battalion auxiliary troops, and put in charge of its administration. Beynon was granted leave by the army commander. He arrived in Hollandia on 1 January 1945 and was employed there as an electrician.

After a short stay in Hollandia, Somokil was sent to Australia and enlisted as a *milicien* (conscript) at the KNIL. I heard that he was later assigned to the NEFIS and promoted to Militia Sergeant at Pontianak.

He must have distinguished himself.

Pongo was sent to Merauke via Noemfoor and Hollandia.

After that, I lost track of him. I heard that Setoe was given a pension for completing his service.

Of the 250 souls originally in the evacuation camp, only thirty-one remained: six men, four women and twenty-one children and arrived at Biak. Of the others who had left the camp, some voluntarily, but most transferred by the Japanese to Manokwari, only a few survived.

Most of them died in of the the three Japanese camps on the Pravi River due to exhaustion and hardship or were murdered by the Japanese and the Hattam people. I have tried to carry out the tasks assigned to me and to comply with the orders given promptly, even under the most difficult circumstances.

This report shows your Commission that the Militia Sergeant R. Somokil made himself deserving. It is thanks to his determination and courage that we were finally liberated. Because of his knowledge of the region and the people living there, he was able to do the camp a great service. As a citizen, he was able to move more freely, which circumstance he exploited conveniently and with courage to serve us.

He was always willing to do a dangerous job. With land storm soldier Theodoor Beynon, we formed one solid unit. Sergeant Pongo has always remained loyal. Although in our opinion, he was too timid towards the Japanese and showed too much submissiveness and was too careful in our opinion. He was not accepted as a commander by his men. I could not say for sure what caused this. It is probably in his earlier performance.

As a landstorm, of course, I am not very familiar with the professional soldiers. He has done what needed to be done and in his way did his best to serve the good cause. The guerrilla troops of the late Captain Geeroms were all endowed with the *Bronze Cross*.

I have been continuously employed since 8 December 1941 and have only taken a short three-week leave in all these years, which was spent in Manokwari, mainly to take a pulse at the state of our agricultural plot. For your information, people that should be mentioned are also the landstorm soldier Theodoor Beynon and Militia Sergeant R. Somokil.

Before the war, they had small farms and were in possession of agricultural plots in the vicinity of Manokwari. We would very much appreciate it, now that demobilization is imminent, to be eligible as soon as possible to be given the opportunity to resume our old profession. I can certainly say this for Mr. Kokkelink, Mr. Jacquard, Mr. Beynon, Mr. Koch, Mr. Somokil, and Mr. Zeelt.

I hope to have fulfilled your request through the above report.

J. Zeelt, landstorm Sergeant-Major Administration
1e Bat. Hulp trpn. Gen. stbnr, 13094 Manokwari (Nw. Guinea).

NKK Corporation

NKK Corporation, until 1988 Nippon Kōkan Kk, was a major Japanese industrial company and one of the country's largest steelmakers. Headquarters were Tokyo. Nippon Kōkan KK was founded in 1912 to make products using the steel from Japan's first steel mills. The company's innovative seamless steel pipe proved superior to conventional welded pipe, and Nippon Kōkan eventually also began producing raw steel from iron ore. Nippon Kōkan expanded greatly in the decades after World War Two, with large steelmaking complexes at Fukuyama (in Hiroshima prefecture) and at Kawasaki and Yokohama (the Keihin Steel Works, near Tokyo). In the late 1970s the company expanded its Keihin complex by building an ultramodern steelworks on man-made Ōgi Island in Tokyo Bay. The NKK Corporation is the second largest steelmaker in Japan (after the Nippon Steel Corporation). In addition to producing a great array of finished and semi-finished steel products, the company designs and builds industrial plants, ships, and other large-scale steel structures; produces specialty metals, ceramics, plastics, and chemicals; and makes computer hardware and software.

19

The Alamo Scouts (U.S. 6th Army Special Reconnaissance Unit) was a reconnaissance unit of the Sixth United States Army in the Pacific Theater of Operations during World War Two.

The unit is best known for its role in liberating American prisoners of war (POWs) from the Japanese Cabanatuan POW camp near Cabanatuan, Nueva Ecija, Philippines in January 1945.

The Scouts were organized on Fergusson Island, New Guinea, on 28 November 1943. Their purpose was to conduct reconnaissance and undertake raids in the Southwest Pacific Theater. The Scouts operated deep behind Japanese lines.

They were under the personal command of Lieutenant General Walter Krueger, Commanding General of the U.S. Sixth Army.

General Krueger wanted a unit that could provide timely vital intelligence on the enemy's troop numbers, unit types, and locations to the Sixth Army.

General Krueger had previously received faulty intelligence reports from other sources outside of Sixth Army.

• *General Krueger*

Krueger sought to create an all-volunteer elite unit consisting of small teams which could operate deep behind enemy lines. Their primary mission was to gather intelligence for the Sixth Army.

The Alamo Scouts were so-named because Alamo Force was the name given to Krueger's command (and Sixth Army in particular) by General Douglas MacArthur, Supreme Allied Commander of the South-West Pacific.

(MacArthur deliberately created the Alamo Force to give himself direct control of U.S. army units, as a parallel structure to the official Allied Ground Forces command, under Australian General Sir Thomas Blamey.)

In addition, Krueger had personal links to San Antonio, Texas, location of the Alamo Mission and had a personal interest in the Battle of the Alamo.

In the Scouts' two years of operation, they were credited with liberating 197 Allied prisoners in New Guinea.

During the New Guinea Campaign, Alamo Scout missions normally lasted from one to three days and were mostly reconnaissance and intelligence gathering in nature, but as the Allies advanced into the Philippines the unit's mission expanded dramatically, with some missions lasting two months or longer.

Furthermore, the unit assumed a central role in organizing large-scale guerrilla operations, establishing road watch stations, attempting to locate and capture or kill *Japanese flag officers* (commissioned officers in the armed forces), and performing direct action missions, such as the Cabanatuan POW Camp Liberation.

In January 1945, the Scouts were teamed with elements of the 6th Ranger Battalion and Filipino guerrilla units to liberate 513 POWs in a daring night attack.

The Scouts provided reconnaissance and tactical support for the 6th Ranger Battalion during the raid of the Cabanatuan Prison Camp.

The Scouts performed advance reconnaissance of the POW camp prior to the 6th Rangers' raid on the camp.

Prior to the raid, two of the Scouts dressed themselves as local Filipino rice farm workers.

These two Scouts then set up a covert observation post

inside a shack in the rice fields that surrounded the POW camp.

This hidden observation post was located within a few hundred yards of Japanese Army guard posts at the camp's fence line.

The Scouts were never discovered by the Japanese during this reconnaissance.

The Scouts were credited with the capture of eighty-four Japanese prisoners of war, and only two Scouts were wounded in the mission.

While not on missions, Alamo Scout teams were assigned as bodyguards for General Krueger and had specific instructions to kill the general if capture was imminent.

• *Alamo Scouts training center in Hollandia*

Near the end of the war, Alamo Scout teams were preparing for the invasion of Japan, where they were slated to conduct pre-invasion reconnaissance of Kyushu as part of *Operation Downfall*, but the war ended.

The Alamo Scouts performed 110 known missions behind enemy lines, mainly in New Guinea and the Philippines, without losing a single man. The unit was disbanded at Kyoto, Japan, in November 1945.

In 1988, the soldiers of the Alamo Scouts were awarded the *Special Forces Tab* in recognition for their services in World War Two, including them in the lineage of the current United States Army Special Forces.

The Raid at Cabanatuan, carried out by a combined team of Alamo Scouts, Rangers, and Filipino guerrillas, has been depicted in feature films.

Edward Dmytryk's 1945 film *Back to Bataan* opens by retelling the story of the raid on the Cabanatuan POW Camp, including real life film of the POW survivors.

The 2005 John Dahl film *The Great Raid*, based on the books *The Great Raid on Cabanatuan* and *Ghost Soldiers*, focused on the raid.

In 1950, the Philippine army named their special forces unit the *Scout Ranger Regiment* in honor of the Alamo Scouts and the U.S. Army Rangers.

Former Alamo Scout Sergeant Major Kittleson founded the *Alamo Scouts*, a local Venture Scouting unit, in his hometown area Toeterville, Iowa after his retirement from the military.

The organization offers a military-style training environment for local youth.

Troop 253 in East Grand Rapids, Michigan has an Alamo Scouts patrol, named in honor of the original unit. Its patrol motto is "Remember!" and the patrol patch was adapted from the World War Two unit logo.

Operation Oaktree 1942-1944:
Jean Victor de Bruijn Fought Against the Japs
With Papuans

20

Operation Oaktree was a Dutch military operation in
Dutch New Guinea during World War Two. Under the
command of Captain Jean Victor de Bruijn (center of
picture below), some forty soldiers operated in the
highland region of Western New Guinea for more than two
years between December 1942 and July 1944, handled
by the Netherlands East Indies Forces Intelligence
Service, with Australian assistance.

The Wissel Lakes region was not known outside New
Guinea until 1937. In order to assert Dutch control over the
area, a Christian mission and a radio-equipped government
post were established at Enarotali in May 1938.

Most of the Dutch East Indies was invaded by the Japanese in early 1942, followed in April 1942 by Dutch New Guinea, thus isolating the post from the coast. Enarotali maintained contacts, albeit loose ones, with Merauke (the last remaining Dutch stronghold in the Dutch East Indies) and with Australia due to liaison seaplanes landing on Paniai Lake.

Dutch and Australian governments considered evacuating the post, but its district officer, Jean Victor de Bruijn, was determined to stay and fight in order to keep the little of the Dutch East Indies that remained.

In July de Bruijn went to Australia to plead his case. At that time, all the planes in Australia were restricted either by General Douglas MacArthur or the Australian government to fight in Eastern New Guinea and the Solomon Islands. This made it impossible for de Bruijn to receive reinforcement. It was agreed that he would return to the highlands with rifles and ammunition, but that no further help could be immediately provided. On the morning of 5 November 1942, a plane flew him from Merauke to Enarotali.

When de Bruijn came back to the highlands, he found out that because of his departure, the natives had been convinced by the Japanese to report directly to their headquarters in Fakfak, which they had occupied in April 1942. The following month, in December, he was made aware that the Japanese had sent two destroyers along the coast south of Enarotali.

He managed to reach the coast, raid the village of Oeta and disarm the sleeping Papuan policemen who had sided with the Japanese. While interrogating the natives, he discovered that the Japanese had landed 450 marines at Timoeka near Kaukenau, who were constructing an airfield and a base there.

He and his men withdrew from the coast and headed for the mountains, destroying bridges along the way to slow the Japanese. De Bruijn did not know until he reached the post that the Japanese, angered by his raid on Oeta, had sent Zero fighters and floatplanes on reconnaissance flights over the lake in order to show their awareness of his presence there.

Owing to Japanese's sheer numerical superiority, de Bruijn decided to limit his operations to intelligence work on Japanese troop movements. However, in early 1943, Japanese reconnaissance aircraft were making long passes over the lakes, often flying below 150 feet, taking photographs for a planned occupation. On 11 May a mountain Papuan brought in a report indicating that a party of sixty Japanese were coming inland.

A few days later, a plane with Rear-Admiral Pieter Koenraad on board, Commander-in-Chief of the Royal Netherlands Navy in Australia, landed on the lake. Koenraad pressed him to evacuate, but de Bruijn was determined to stay.

On 26 May 1943 the Japanese reached the lakes, only to realize that Enarotali had been torched by de Bruijn and his men during their retreat to safety in the surrounding valleys. While there, de Bruijn met with Joseph, a young Papuan who had guided the Japanese and escaped as soon as they reached the lake.

The previous year, he had been convinced by the Japanese to go to Fakfak, and was disgusted by what he had seen there. Joseph provided important information about Japanese forces stationed at Ambon, Seran, and Timika.

De Bruijn subsequently radioed the (NEFIS) Netherlands East Indies Forces Intelligence Service HQ in Australia, which started realizing the importance of his mission in the highlands. Further information about the Japanese airfield at Nabire was also provided. It soon became obvious that the Japanese were staying and intended to guard the lakes in case any plane should attempt a landing on Lake Paniai (one of the Wissel Lakes).

De Bruijn kept a low profile, gathering intelligence and using airdrops of supplies such as ammunition and rifles, while training his men on how to shoot. De Bruijn also called on his HQ to bomb Japanese positions at Enarotali to impress the natives, who were bribed by the Japanese to collaborate with them. From August 1943 onward, the Japanese post was frequently bombarded.

In September 1943, an armed band of four hundred Papuan natives, angered by Japanese exactions who had mistreated or killed neighboring villagers, attacked Enarotali with bows and arrows but were repelled by the soldiers' superior firepower, leaving six Papuans killed. From then on, the Japanese would not go out on patrol unless fully armed.

The Oaktree party was now getting stronger, fortified by new radio sets, food, rifles, and military training, reaching about forty men strong, who were based at Bilorai. It was agreed that they would try to ambush Japanese parties along the trail from the coast to the lakes, which the Japanese had felt safe to use until then. However, the Japanese struck first, forcing them to pull back from Bilorai.

One day, east of Bilorai, the Japanese were ambushed during their sleep by a patrol of two Indonesians and five Papuans, killing fifteen with Thompson submachine guns and hand grenades.

At the same time, native observers reported that more and more Japanese troops were moving toward the mountains, fleeing from their strongholds on the northern coast at Hollandia and Sarmi, which had been invaded by the Americans. To avoid becoming trapped between Japanese troops retreating from the north and those to the west at Enarotali, an evacuation was called. On the morning of 26 July 1944, a Catalina met them on Hagers Lake, ending the mission.

Over a two-year period, this guerrilla force raided and ambushed Japanese positions, pillaged supplies and destroyed ammunition dumps, killing more than thirty Japanese soldiers in the process.

Although they managed to divert some Japanese forces and destroy their supplies, the highland lakes region was of little military importance.

Nevertheless, it did allow the gathering of information on Japanese positions at Nabire, Timika, Fakfak, and further west at Ambon, which proved useful during the Western New Guinea campaign.

It was essentially a symbolic victory, as de Bruijn was portrayed as the irreducible symbol of Dutch resistance in the Dutch East Indies by Allied and Dutch propaganda, waving the flag and maintaining the prestige of the Dutch among the inhabitants of the area, just as Hermann Detzner had done in German New Guinea twenty years before, and who was a source of inspiration for de Bruijn.

Queen Wilhelmina personally awarded Jean Victor de Bruijn with *the Netherlands Cross of Merit, the Netherlands Bronze Cross,* and *the Order of Orange-Nassau.*

• *Papuans carrying a wounded soldier*

171

• Picture of an American B-25 bomber

The bomber was produced in numerous variants; nearly 10,000 B-25s were built. These included several limited models such as the F-10 reconnaissance aircraft, the AT-24 crew trainers, and the United States Marine Corps' PBJ-1 patrol bomber.

Louis Rapmund:
His Heroic Actions Saved Many Lives in New Guinea
Working With the Alamo Scouts

21

During his research on crashed bombers in New Guinea,
and the daring rescue of a B-25 bomber in the
jungle (KAIS), Dutch writer Bas Kreuger, came across
the history of Reserve Second Lieutenant of the Royal
Dutch Indonesian Army, Louis Rapmund. The short life of
this adventurous Navy photographer had many heroic
highlights, but unfortunately had a tragic ending.

How did Louis Rapmund feel when he saw Java disappear on the horizon on the evening of March 3, 1942?

Relief that he had come aboard the MS Tawali in the chaos of the evacuation of Tjilatjap (southern coast of Java)?

Fear for his family left behind in Bandoeng and the uncertain prospects they had under the rule of the Japanese occupiers?

Questions about the journey on the *MS Tawali* and what would await him there?

We don't know, as we know little to nothing about the thoughts, emotions and desires of the thirty-two-year-old navy conscript who just a month before was called into military service as he was ready to flee his homeland.

Had he gone, out of a sense of duty, with the hundreds of

other men from the naval establishment in Surabaya?

Wouldn't he rather have stayed behind to go back to his family?

Probably not, because the opportunity had been available to him in Tjilatjap, where the government quickly crumbled as the battle for Indonesia appeared lost.

It wasn't in his personality as we understood it from his sister-in-law. Louis was an adventurous guy who, she said, wanted to take on the challenge of the unknown.

As an avid amateur photographer, he was always looking for beautiful or exciting images, and the period ahead promised him to bring plenty of images.

During my research on an American bomber that had crashed into the Bird's Head in the summer of 1944 and whose crew had to be rescued from the swamps and jungles of New Guinea, the name Louis Bernardus Jan Rapmund appeared in the written stories.

• *Picture of the rescued crew of the B-25 bomber with
the rescue team of American, Australian, KNIL and
Papuan (rowers). On the far right is Louis Rapmund
Picture courtesy of Louise van den Eikhof*

In the report he prepared on the rescue, I thought that I could read between the lines that he had been an initiative-rich, decisive man with a certain sense of humor.

His pragmatic approach intrigued me enough to see what Rapmund had done more during the war.

This resulted in a nearly two-year investigation into a machinist, photographer, and intelligence officer who at the same time left behind an astonishing amount of material and also nothing at all.

Due to his death shortly after the Japanese capitulation at the beginning of the Bersiap period and the disappearance of his personal belongings before they could be delivered to his family, there are no personal documents to give him a voice other than for some official documents.

On the other hand, there are a few hundred photographs that he took, illustrating important parts of his work and life during the war and which make it possible to view the war somewhat through his eyes.

Born in Surabaya in 1910, Louis Rapmund worked as a supervisor of the signalling system at the Dutch-Indonesian Railway Company until 1940.

In 1936 he had completed his military duty as a machinist in the Royal Navy which on 2 February 1942 resulted in his call of military service in the Naval Barracks Goebeng.

As part of the naval component in Surabaya, he was evacuated to Tjilatjap on March 2 and escaped to Ceylon with the MS Tawali.

He had his Leica camera with him and took pictures aboard the ship during the crossing to Colombo.

On board the old cruiser Hr Ms Sumatra which sailed from Ceylon to England, where he was part of the "black choir" (the engine room staff), Louis took a series of photographics that often show crew members at work.

He had a preference for pictures of ordinary work: peeling potatoes, the cook in the galley, that kind of imagery.

After arriving in England in October 1942, we see the

then thirty-three-year-old Louis in various photographs with his colleagues of the Hr Ms Sumatra in London.

How he managed to be placed as a machinist at the newly established Marine Information Service is not entirely clear. It seems likely that his abilities as a photographer played a role in this.

Until the end of 1943, he worked as the first photographer of the Marine Information Service (MARVO) in England.

In the only surviving photo album, his hand looms a picture of a special life in 1943 England which, given all the risks of war, showed not have been unpleasant.

The navy sent him to various places as a photogapher. Navy divisions, activities and events.

From a state funeral of a Javanese minister to the launch of a new destroyer, from visits to 320 Squadron of the Military Aviation Service to the soccer match Netherlands - Belgium and from an all-ranks party to a visit by Prince Bernhard to the Dutch Motor Torpedo boats in Dover, Louis is everywhere.

There are beautiful photographs he took at the naval headquarters in London; they depict daily life and work in the office of *C&A* (a large well known department store) which was rented by them to the navy for the duration of the war.

The Battle in the Pacific began to change in favor of the Allies in the course of 1943.

After the Japanese defeats at Guadalcanal and in the mountains for Port Moresby in 1942 and early 1943, General Douglas McArthur's army fought slowly along the north-east coast of Papua New Guinea towards Dutch New Guinea and the Philippines (of which McArthur had vowed to return).

Photographs in Louis Rapmund's living room in London show him closely following the War in the Pacific on a map of Southeast Asia with an insert of New Guinea.

The Dutch authorities in Australia had to prepare for an Allied landing on Indonesian territory in New Guinea and the rebuilding of Dutch authority there.

Given the very limited number of Dutch people in Australia (some 1,500 men in 1943) and the need to obtain suitable people for a militarized administration service, Hubertus van Mook turned to the navy, where the largest reservoir of personnel was found.

At first, Admiral Furstner fought tooth and nail against the surrender of naval personnel. He did not object to the argument that during an American invasion there would be no Dutch units present to restore authority.

After lengthy negotiations, it was decided that no professional staff, but only reserve and conscript staff, would be added.

From November 1943 onward, lists were drawn up which included suitable (and preferably Dutch Indonesian) naval personnel.

Louis was put on the list with the highest priority because of his knowledge and experience with the Indonesian railways and the fact that he had worked as a teacher.

Against that designation, his boss, Lieutenant Ter Zee First Class Antoine Kroese, head of MARVO, objected because Louis was an exceptional worker (He had a full list of assignments), and he was the only war photographer in the navy. Regardlesss, Louis was handed over to the Department of Colonies and was transferred to the KNIL as sergeant major.

Van Pelt, head of the National Information Service, wrote to his colleague Huib Quispel, head of the Netherlands Indies Government Information Service (NIGIS), that he might also be able to use Rapmund as a photographer for the NIGIS in a kind of dual function.

It is not known whether that ever happened.

In February 1944, Louis boarded the steamship *Nestor* and sailed in a convoy to Australia where he arrived in Melbourne on May 24.

We know little about the short period after that.

There must have been a hectic pace during his travels,

training at Camp Columbia in Brisbane *(if there has been any training)* and deployment because in June he was added as a NEFIS (Netherlands Forces Intelligence Service) intelligence officer to the NICA detachment that had been stationed in Hollandia since April 1944.

His job was to determine, with the help of the Papuans, where the Japanese were and whether they would pose risks to the Allied forces.

In part one of the film *The Liberation of the Dutch East Indies,* we see Louis talking to three Papuans who point out on a map where the Japanese troops are hiding.

On the north coast of New Guinea, the Alamo Scouts, American commandos working behind Japanese lines, operated and gathered intelligence.

The training centre for the Alamo Scouts was located in Hollandia and due to the nature of their work they frequently worked with the NICA detachments.

On July 5, Louis and a pair of corporals went with a team under the command of Captain Hobbs to the island of Japen where they would pick up the skipper of a small cargo ship that was forced to work for the Japanese.

The mission was completed without any problems.

This action brought Rapmund to the attention of the Americans who, impressed by his decisive action, were more likely to call on him.

They soon did. On July 27, 1944 a B-25 bomber had to make an emergency landing in the middle of the swamps and jungle of the *Vogelkop* (Bird's Head) in Dutch New Guinea. The crew of four survived the crash landing but could not be taken away by a flying boat.

Besides leaving them to their fate (a certain death), there was only one thing left: send a rescue mission into the bush.

The SONICA (Senior Officer NICA) in Hollandia, Colonel Raden Abdulkadir, was asked to transfer Louis Rapmund to the American Air Sea Rescue on Biak for a few days as part of the rescue mission.

This was probably the most spectacular action Louis performed during the war: a three-week mission into the jungle with a team of Australians, American infantrymen, KNIL soldiers from NICA, and Papuan rowers to get First Lieutenant Ira Mason Barnett and his crew out of the swamp.

The report of this mission, prepared by Louis, reads like the script of a Hollywood film, with ambushes of Japanese troops, picking up traitors, bombing villages in which Japanese soldiers were suspected, Japanese prisoners of war trying to storm an American flying boat, and consuming a celebrational rice table while singing the Dutch National Anthem: *Wilhelmus*.

No wonder this mission was an important element in earning Louis a *Bronze Lion* at the end of the New Guinea campaign.

Immediately after completing this assignment, Louis went out with the Alamo Scouts again in early September 1944 on a double mission in the Geelvink Bay.

On the small island of Roemberpon, hundreds of *romushas* (forced laborers), former heihos, and British-Indonesian prisoners of war had been reported as left to their own devices by the Japanese.

With an Alamo Scout team and supported by motor torpedo boats, Louis managed to take these people to Biak and save them from starvation.

During the action, the team received information that an internment camp was situated in the village of Oransbari on the mainland where, among others, a large Dutch Indonesian colonist family of fourteen was held captive *(This was the Beynon family from Manokwari.)*

The Scout team under the command of Lieutenant Tom Rounsville went with Louis and three NICA translators in early October, overran the Japanese guards and managed to free all prisoners unharmed.

179

These are the notes that Louis Rapmund made about the preparations and daring liberation of Camp Oransbari together with a team of the Alamo Scouts:

"During the first days of my stay in Roemberpon, Caspers, an ex-colonist, told me about the existence of an internment camp at Oransbari.

'There, one would likely find some European families,' I was told.

He couldn't tell me anything about the surveillance.

It took some time to find people who knew the area better so I could gather more detailed information.

Eventually, I was able to put a reconnaissance group together, and they left for Oransbari on 12 September 1944.

I gave Hermanis, a Papuan from Biak, whom I found in Jamakani with three other rowers, the assignment to gather as much information and, if possible, to smuggle someone back from the camp.

He needed to be back within a week, because I wanted to take care of the matter as soon as possible so as to not lose the value of the gathered information.

Hermanis carried out his assignment very well.

He promptly returned after six days on 18 September with Somokil, an ex-colonist who lived in this internment camp and gave me all the information I needed.

Hermanis first contacted some Papuans in a nearby village and they, in turn, were able to contact Somokil who, 'without too much hesitation,' agreed to come along to Roemberpon.

Based on the information Somokil gave me, I prepared a plan and presented it to the Alamo Scouts.

Lieutenant Rounsaville, who was stationed with his team of five men at Roemberpon, agreed to help us out right away.

We put together a team of three guides and six soldiers, including Sergeant Papari and five ex-POWs.

Now, we had to wait for the PT boats and Lieutenant Dove, the operations officer for the Scouts at Woendi, who

180

had to approve the plan and arrange the use of the PT boats to bring us to the designated area of attack.

Dove came on Friday, 22 September 1944 and agreed with the plan. However, he said right away that he had to tele-graph the Sixth Army to get permission for this operation, be-cause his men were Scouts and not commandos, and that this would be an unusual operation for them.

Days of anxious waiting followed.

We were hoping that the Sixth Army would give permis-sion, all the more because Somokil gave a sad description of the situation in which especially all the children, who were in the camp, found themselves.

Finally, on Monday, September 25th, Dove came back and told us that he just received a telegram with permission from the Sixth Army.

He promised that the next day at the PT base he would prepare everything and would return on Wednesday afternoon to pick us up for the landing at Oransbari.

Everyone was relieved and happy.

As a big thank you, I promised the Scouts I would take them deer-hunting the next day.

Luck was with us and that night in the moonlight; I shot a beautiful deer which we ate with gusto.

The hindquarter was saved for the PT boats.

Lieutenant Dove arrived on Wednesday afternoon at about 5:00 p.m.

When we boarded, everything went wrong because there was a problem with the radio communication and the boats reached the agreed location too late.

The plan was to use four boats: two for the landing and the evacuation; the other two for cover.

We agreed at that time that we all would go to Woendi and try again the next day.

About 1:00 p.m., we left again and not long after, we were caught in a severe storm. The storm was so heavy that we ar-rived at the landing site hours late.

One of the boats was damaged and many of us, even the sailors were seasick.

Those who were not seasick were dead tired from the tremendous swaying and bouncing up and down caused by the rough sea.

Finally, we decided to postpone the expedition which was very disappointing.

There was just too much risk to continue the operation at this time, considering that we still had hours of walking through the jungle in front of us.

At my request, we changed course and set off for Roemberpon. I already had stayed away too long to my liking and we were dropped off there. The Scouts went back to Woendi.

During the trip everything was discussed with the Scouts again, and Lieutenant Dove felt that it would be better to commit two teams of Alamo Scouts with Sergeant Papari and some guides.

One of the considerations was that if something happened to me, the connection between the Americans and Indonesians and with the Papuan guides would be totally lost. Nobody else could speak Malay and that the six Scouts would be at considerable risk.

Besides, after the trip my ex-POWs were in a bad shape and most became sick. Because of the great exertion and stress, a lot of sickness broke out.

I also had to deal with malaria for some days.

It all worked out for the better because in the next couple of days, it stormed so severely that none of the PT boats could leave port.

On Wednesday, October 4, 1944 Lieutenant Dove finally arrived with two teams of Scouts. At about 3:00 p.m., Sergeant Papari, Somokil, another two guides, Hermanis, and I went on board, and we went full speed to travel the considerable distance to the coast of Oransbari.

The plan for the operation in Oransbari was made: We would land a distance away from Oransbari; from there we would walk to a Papuan village close to the camp to gather the latest information.

At this time, Somokil had been gone for more than two weeks and, if possible, we would try to find more Papuan guides. From there, the teams would be split as follows: Lieutenant Nellist with three Scouts and a guide would attack the machine gun post manned by four Japanese.

Two Scouts from the Nellist team with Hermanis would attack a post of two *Kempeitai*. Finally, Lieutenant Rounsaville, five Scouts, Papari, and I, with Soumokil as guide, would attack a large hut housing about twenty soldiers.

All three places would be attacked at the same time except if Nellist could not find the machine guns. The Japanese machinegun post was set up some distance from the coast and was not always occupied.

Nellist would then, if he did not hear the shots of our fighting, wait until daylight, and if the Japanese were alarmed by the shots, we would wait in ambush on the road to the village to prevent reinforcements from their soldiers. The machine gun post was about four kilometers away from the village.

At about 7:00 p.m., we landed in four rubber boats at a point to the north of Oransbari at least fourteen kilometers from the camp. We started to explore the area.

It took some time to do this, but led by the guides, we were able to find an opening in the jungle.

It was pitch dark.

I had been told that we had to walk for about four hours along a decent pathway.

But we did not find any path.

The ground was too moist, and we had to walk in mud up to our ankles. More than that, it was so dark in the jungle that even our guides got lost.

We couldn't continue this way.

I walked right behind the guides and checked the direction on my compass.

183

Then at some point I discovered that we were walking in a circle. We just had to stop, and I told the officers that we had to use our flashlights.

Half of the team was against it and the other half in favor.

Finally, strongly covered flashlights were used.

It went a little better, but progress was slow.

Then, unexpectedly, around 10:00 p.m., we heard a gunshot.

'Japanese on a pig hunt,' said Somokil.

It was a plausible explanation. We continued on our journey again as carefully as possible.

After walking for another hour, we heard two shots, one after another. They came from straight ahead of us.

Things became very tense at this point, as the hunting Japanese might suddenly encounter us and sound the alarm.

Finally, at about 2:00 a.m. *(We had been walking for about seven hours)*, we arrived at a point that was approximately between the camp and the machine gun post.

Here we rested and deliberated.

Since we were an hour behind schedule, we thought it best not to go to the Papuan village ourselves, but to send out guides who could attempt to bring back other Papuans.

While we were waiting for the return of the two guides, two more shots rang out.

Somokil explained that the Japanese were hunting in the yard of Mr. Pongoh to the east of the camp.

Now that we knew where they were approximately, we were able to prepare ourselves better.

The two Papuan guides came back at about 3:00 a.m. with two others from the village. They confirmed that there were four Japanese with two machine guns at the coast and that there were about twenty soldiers in a hut and two Japanese policemen in another hut.

They also knew the whereabouts of the machine guns. They told us that after Soumokil had been discovered missing, the Japanese had strengthened the guards at the camp.

But later they became less strict and only the coast was patrolled.

The parties were now deployed:

Lieutenant Nellist went to the coast with four Scouts and two Papuan guides.

They had to take a roundabout route to avoid the Japanese who were hunting in Pongoh's yard.

The attack would occur at 4:00 a.m. in the morning.

We synchronized our watches and wished each other good luck and continued our walk through the jungle.

About one kilometer from the camp we split up again.

The two Scouts with Hermanis would crawl to the hut, and upon the signal for the attack *(shooting)*, would enter the hut and eliminate the Japanese or, if possible, take them captive.

Lieutenant Rounsaville with five Scouts, Papari, Somokil, and myself went to the hut were the Japanese soldiers were sleeping.

When we were about thirty meters away (It was a minute before 4:00 a.m.), we saw that the Japanese cook was already awake and had started to cook rice.

This was a problem.

Luckily, the night was dark and there was little moonlight.

But we needed to pass the cook to take our positions.

The hut where we thought the Japanese were sleeping was thoroughly destroyed with all the Japanese in it.

However, on the other side of the hut, there were three Japanese who jumped out and bolted away.

We were able to catch them outside the hut.

Some escaped, unfortunately, however, they were most likely wounded.

After some salvos, we entered the hut and found many interesting papers, which regrettably were lost in a rubber boat when it capsized on our way back.

We also found a cache of weapons in good condition.

At the same time we also heard shooting on the other side

of the river, and we knew that everything went okay there too.

The two Scouts deployed there entered the hut and saw the two Japanese sleeping and shot them dead as they reached for their pistols.

The fight lasted only a half hour at best.

All families were quickly collected.

They were not upset by all the shooting, and at dawn we marched to the coast.

The Scouts were placed up front, on both sides of the group, and some of them in the rear for cover.

When we arrived at Pongoh's yard, we went ahead with a small group and thoroughly inspected the yard.

We met Pongoh in his hut, and he told us that three Japanese had hunted on his property.

When they heard the shots, they went in the direction of the camp; however, for some unknown reason they ran off helter-skelter in the opposite direction.

We arrived by the coast at about 6:30 a.m., about three hundred meters away from the point where Lieutenant Nellist had attacked the machine guns. He seemed to have made radio contact because the four PT boats came full speed toward the beach. They were greeted with great jubilation.

I think I have never seen people so excited to see a ship than these people who, for two long years, had suffered terribly at the hands of the Japanese.

We felt rewarded just seeing all the joyful faces.

Lieutenant Nellist came walking down the beach about fifteen minutes later with a heavy machine gun over his shoulder, while other Scouts carried another machine gun.

They had killed all four Japanese.

At first Nellist could not find the machineguns, as it appeared that the Japanese had moved to another hut.

Luckily, this hut was found and at the right moment when one of the Japanese stood up and lit a cigarette.

Since Nellist didn't hear our shots, he just laid in the grass and waited about thirty meters from the hut.

Luck was with him, because at about 5:00 a.m., he suddenly saw all four Japanese come out of the hut. They were talking to each other in the doorway.

Most likely, they had heard the explosions from the hand grenades we had set off in the Japanese huts. This was the right moment, and Nellist, being one of the best shots in the service, put all four Japanese down.

On board the PT boats, the people who had waited in great suspense, welcomed us with a loud hurray.

The Scouts went out of their way to give all kinds of things, especially to the children, even ice cream. They in return sang *Lang zal ze leven* (Long Shall They Live).

We reached Bosnik around 11:00 a.m., and after thanking everybody with many hugs, we all left the boats.

The next morning, Friday, October 6, Lieutenant Dove came to visit us in Bosnik, and I left the same afternoon with some supplies for Roemberpon.

Finally, I went to thank the PT boats commanders from Woendi, who three times managed to give us four boats, and to thank the Alamo Scouts, especially Lieutenant Dove, who as operations officer of Woendi, went out of his way to Bosnik several times to get supplies and transported them to Roemberpon. And naturally, thanks of course to the officers of the Alamo Scouts, namely Rounsaville and Nellist, without whose teams our work would have been impossible. And finally, to the guides Somokil and Hermanis, who provided vital information for our rescue mission."

This is the end of his notes.

During these months in New Guinea, Louis had apparently contracted malaria, which forced him to recover in Australia. There he was deployed to Camp Columbia to write reports on the Indonesian railways.

During his rescue actions in New Guinea, Louis wrote reports and is recorded for what he has done. That was no longer the case when he returned to normal duties. From reports from the various NICA detachments, we know where he was deployed. He was part of the NICA detachments on Morotai (January 1945), Tarakan (nr XI – from May 1945) and XIII at Balikpapan (Nr XII - July to October 1945).

His role as an intelligence officer slowly changed from intelligence-gathering on Japanese forces and Indonesian auxiliaries to republican and rebellious elements against Dutch authority.

After the capitulation of Japan in August 1945, Louis felt the need to return to his family in Bandoeng with whom he had not been in contact for three-and-a-half years.

In mid-October 1945, he was granted leave and managed to arrange a place on board a flight to Java from Balikpapan.

His friend Nicolaas Jouwe (the later Papuan leader) would tell him not to go, because it would be far too dangerous.

His answer would have been that he came from there and that he would be safe.

At Tjililitan airport, a dozen people gathered who also wanted to go to Bandoeng. They took a truck and passenger car to drive through the mountains to Bandoeng.

• *Nicolaas Jouwe*

The course of this ride is somewhat foggy because there are three different versions of it. It is clear that the men (a diverse group of NICA officers such as Max Horstink and Louis Rapmund, RAPWI officers such as Blanson Henkeman, a doctor and others) were detained near Tjiandjoer by a Republican militant group after they had previously broken through two barricades.

The men were taken to prison in Tjiandjoer, a town about sixty kilometers from Bandoeng. The intention seems to have been to use the prisoners for a trade with the Dutch authorities against Republican prisoners.

188

The final hours of the eleven prisoners are unclear.

Some of them (including Louis Rapmund) were reportedly shot dead a day later in the truck on their way to a Republican camp. But there are also versions in which the men were all turned over to a furious mob, killed, and dismembered. Whatever the story, the result was that the ten men and their driver were killed in Tjiandjoer and left there.

Louis' family waited in vain for him (He apparently informed them that he was on his way.)

A year later, the bodies were found and identified by the ODO (Investigating Service of Deceased) after which they were given a final resting place on the Pandu honor field in Bandoeng.

Louis' wife, Claudine Elze Kleering van Beerenbergh, decided to leave Indonesia in 1950 with her four children.

Upon arrival in Amsterdam, three of the four chests of Louis' personal belongings that were send from Balikpapan were stolen. Four of his photo albums with photographs he had taken during the war remained. There is only one album left; the rest have *mysteriously* disappeared.

The photos tell the story of an enterprising person and talented photographer who was active on two fronts.

Louise Van Den Eikhof who lives in Las Vegas remembers her father: "The last time I saw my father was in 1942 in Java," said Louise. "He was literally running out the back door of our house as the Japanese were coming in the front door. They were looking for him. This information about his heroics in New Guinea and other places has helped heal a wound in my soul that festered for over sixty years. I loved my father. He was a wonderful man."

• How wonderful to see two sisters of the Beynon family,
Suze van Geenen (left) and Nancy van der Hijde (right),
together with Louise van den Eikhof (middle), the daughter of
Louis Rapmund, who was instrumental in the liberation of the camp,
in Las Vegas a couple of years ago.

April 12, 1945
No. 18

In the name of WILHELMINA, with the grace
of God, Queen of the Netherlands,
Princes of Oranje Nassau etc.

On the nomination of Our Minister
of Overseas Realm Parts
of April 6, 1945, No. 1240.010104

To award the *Bronzen Leeuw* (Bronze Lion) to:

L.B.J. RAPMUND
Res. Second Lieutenant of the
Royal Dutch Indonesian Army

*For showing bravery, tactful decisions, and commitment
in Netherlands New Guinea, after an American B25
airplane had to make an emergency landing behind
enemy lines, and together with his military unit
prevented that the Japanese would capture the crew of
this airplane. Also with special bravery and commitment
led an expedition of American troops and volunteers to a
camp of prisoners of war of military and non-military
make-up, in the area of the Bay of Wandamen and
Manokwari, helped to save and evacuate these prisoners
of war and eliminated most of the Japanese soldiers and
guards of this camp.*

London, April 12, 1945

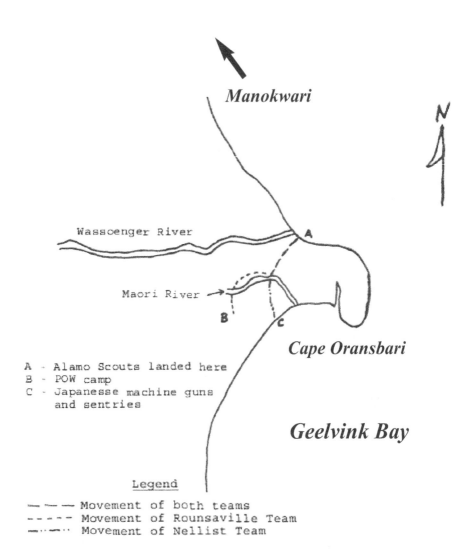

Manokwari

Wassoenger River

Maori River →

A

B

C

Cape Oransbari

A - Alamo Scouts landed here
B - POW camp
C - Japanesse machine guns
    and sentries

Geelvink Bay

<u>Legend</u>

— ·— ·— Movement of both teams
– – – –   Movement of Rounsaville Team
—··—··   Movement of Nellist Team

• This map of the Oransbari area shows the
movement of the two Alamo Scouts
and Rapmund's teams during their rescue
mission of the Japanese POW camp.

Oral History of the Alamo Scouts
Liberating Camp Oransbari

22

My dear friend, Lance Zedric, published a comprehensive
oral history of the Alamo Scouts entitled, "Silent No
More," which included a detailed story of the Liberation
of Camp Oransbari by the Alamo Scouts.
I have, with his permission, taken some of the written
notes of this spectacular mission.

By the end of July 1944, American ground forces had by-passed large concentrations of Japanese troops along the northern coast of New Guinea and were concentrating their efforts on the Vogelkop, the westernmost end of the island.

Codenamed *Operation Globetrotter*, the invasion of the Vogelkop began on 30 July with landings at Cape Opmorai and Middleburg and Amsterdam Islands to the northwest. This was followed the next day with a landing at Sansapor on the western tip of the *Vogelkop*.

The main objective of the landings was to secure areas where large airstrips could be built to support bomber and fighter operations and to bring the Allies one step closer to the Philippines, with a secondary objective of trapping the remaining eighteen thousand enemy troops in the middle of U.S. forces essentially sealing their fate. The operation was an immediate and unqualified success.

In mid-September 1944, the enemy situation in western New Guinea had become increasingly desperate. With food scarce, and facing the realization that supplies and reinforcements from Japan weren't coming, coupled with increasing pressure from the American troops, the Japanese became even more unpredictable.

They began releasing slave laborers and displaced civilians, including Javanese, Indian Sikhs, Papuans, Dutch, and others by the hundreds, into the jungles to fend for themselves. Most civilians were starving, sick, and incapable of working, and the situation was so desperate that the Japanese could spare neither the food to feed them nor the bullets to kill them.

Despite this, the Japanese still maintained a number of internment camps, and word filtered out that a prominent Dutch *governor* and his family (Beynon family) were still being held at a camp on the eastern end of the *Vogelkop*. It was feared that they would soon be killed. Two teams of Alamo Scouts happened to be available.

Although the Alamo Scouts had recovered displaced civilians before, it would be the first time they would assault a guarded compound with the specific mission of killing the guards, capturing enemy prisoners, and liberating an undetermined number of internees. Thus far, the Alamo Scouts had primarily been utilized as a reconnaissance force to gather information and to occasionally capture enemy prisoners, not to conduct raider type operations—although they were formed and trained for such a purpose.

The job fell to two newly-graduated teams, each commanded by audacious young airborne officers and comprised of rugged and capable men who were quick on their feet. The mission at Oransbari would prove to be an unparalleled success, and would remove the veil of secrecy over the Alamo Scouts catapulting them into national prominence. But more important, it would be an invaluable training ground for bigger things yet to come.

Sgt. Gilbert J. Cox (Nellist Team): "We were all at Woendi. I'm not sure how we got the information, but I think it was from those people going back and forth from the New Guinea mainland to the island of Roemberpon. Louis Rapmund, a Dutch officer, gave me a shotgun that I carried on the Oransbari mission. After careful planning, two teams, ours and

Stud's [Rounsaville Team], went in by PT at Cape Oransbari, N.G., killed eighteen Nips and brought out sixty-six prisoners of war.

While we were [on Roemberpon], we got word from one of the escapees that the Japs were holding a bunch of Dutch women and Javanese women in a camp on up the line there. So we were sent in by PT to pick them up. It was quite an ordeal."

• *Nellist and Rounsaville*

Lt. Tom J. "Stud" Rounsaville (Team Leader): "When they sent me up to Roemberpon Island, the one thing we learned real early was that if you're a native and I give you a cigarette you'll tell me all about the Japs, and conversely, the Jap gives him a cigarette also. They'd been around enough, and they had terrible fear of them. They could get enough information if they just knew you were in the area and that would put a kill to our job.

So we go into this Roemberpon Island, a very small island, and we had Rapmund, a Dutch officer with us. And I said, 'We're going to take charge of all the boats immediately.' They brought them all to one place. We were about a mile off the main [route], then I took two of my boys and the natives and went across and looked that place over for a day. There were sixty Javanese, a 'governor' they called him, and his people. We went on in and they were hugged up against this river, and there wasn't any beachhead to ward off any surprise. From the swamp it was just about a mile to the ocean. So, we went in and I gave my report. I recommended that we use two teams, so we'd go back and use two teams."

195

Sgt. Harold N. "Hal" Hard (Rounsaville Team) [Letter - 27 Sep 1944]: "Dearest folks: …We had venison steak for dinner today. Yes sir, real deer. Some of the guys shot it yesterday. I hope there are no game laws around here because it would be illegal in Michigan, I know. Anyway, it was darn good and just like a Sunday dinner. Your loving son, Harold."

U.S. Navy Patrol Report (1944) "PTs 299 and 301 went on a patrol for Wandamen Bay, at 1400 on Sept. 27, 1944, with a special mission to recover Dutch POWs at Point Oransbari, with four Alamo Scouts on board.

The special mission was cancelled but, at 0715 on the 28th, they sank one type 'A' barge, ten miles north of Mios Noem Island. On Sept. 29, 1944 at 1300 PTs 298 and 300 stood out for patrol of Wandamen Bay-Roemberpon. They returned to base at 2015, because both port engine stacks of PT-300 had burned out in rough seas."

Lt. William E. Nellist (Team Leader): "It isn't recorded in the reports but the Oransbari mission was attempted three times. One of the times at night, one of the PT boats struck a log and bent the screws on the propeller, and had to turn back. The next time we went over there we hit a storm and it got really rough. Everybody got sick and we turned back.

The next time everything went smoothly. We got in there, and fortunately, just after dark the full moon came out and helped us a great deal in traveling over to the prison camp… We walked a good part of the night getting in there.

Everybody else turned off and went to the prison, including two of my men, Smith and Asis. They had a special job to do for Rounsaville, and the rest of my team continued with a guide south across this Maori River… and we went a ways and we heard a shot, which was like three o'clock in the morning… out ahead of us which caused me quite a bit of concern. Pretty soon we heard another shot and I had one of my Filipinos with me, Alfonso… and finally I found out the Japs were out hunting pigs."

TM2c Clyde F. Smith, USN (PT-300): "My boat was in there at Oransbari and we didn't go clear into the shore. We went probably within twenty-five yards of the shore because we didn't want to get grounded. We had dinghies [rubber boats] on board, and the other boat with us had a dinghy on it, and that's what we used to row the Scouts in with. A guy named Metcalf and I rowed the Scouts in from the PT boats. Soon as we got into the shore there were two Japanese there asleep with a water-cooled .50 caliber machine gun. Those Scouts immediately cut their throats. The Japs never knew what killed them. Then we went out to sea again. They had a Scout aboard our boat with a radio that kept in touch with them. They went in for about ten miles and released a bunch of prisoners while the Japanese were getting dinner. There were two Japanese parties there several miles apart and they were very quiet not to let the Japanese know they were there."

Pfc. Galen C. "Kit" Kittleson (Nellist Team) [Letter - 1946]: "On the night of October 4, the force left base at 4:30 a.m. and the Scouts joked about the nervousness of the sailors. Sgt. Andy Smith commented, 'Hell, the bastards aren't even going to get off the boat.' The destination was reached at 7:30 pm and the rubber boats were lowered and two teams plus a Dutch officer and two native guides rowed ashore. The boats were taken back and the PTs left.

Native guides found the trails and the party proceeded inland. But we used a different plan than what we started with. Instead of going ashore at the point of the cape, we landed down about two miles and walked eight miles across in the jungle. The trail was difficult to follow, so the natives had to use flashlights to follow it, which of course was very dangerous but necessary. It took us all night up until 4:30 a.m. in the morning to reach the outskirts of camp. Then the party split up.

Lt. Rounsaville's team, plus natives, and the Dutch officer, were going to take on the main force consisting of twenty. Andy Smith and Sabas Asis were to capture a military police officer and one assistant if possible, who were in the building a short distance from main barracks."

Lt. Tom J. "Stud" Rounsaville (Team Leader): "Bill Nellist went up to the mouth of the Maori River with Siason, Wismer, Cox, and Kittleson. We gave them about a fifteen minute head start to cover the mile or so to the beach before we moved out. Andy Smith and Bob Asis from Nellist's team came with my team. We dropped them off at their objective, which was a hut with a couple Kempetai men in it, then we moved on to our objective, which was a larger building where the Jap guards were billeted. We immediately noticed a Jap cook starting a fire. We watched him and four others move in and out of the building."

Sgt. Andy E. Smith (Nellist Team): "It was dark. When you say 'dark' in the jungle you are talking **'dark.'** We used flashlights to come down on the trail to the Maori River. The guides, of course, knew where they were going, but not the Scouts. I was scared. I thought, What in the hell? I've been in the Army before and landed at Finschaven and Lae and already had my Combat Infantry Badge and you dumb clunks around here are carrying a flashlight! But, we'd been briefed on this mission, and we had the plans all drawn up. And actually, it was one mission, but there were three targets. So, we split the teams up.

We started at the landing point with guides and thirteen Scouts, seven in Nellist team, and six in Rounsaville team, and a couple of guys up front had flashlights. The rest were straggling behind with phosphorous or tent rope tied to our belts. We all came down to this river together. It took us from maybe 7:00 p.m. in the night until 3:00 a.m. in the morning. It was muddy all the way, dark jungle, wading around all the way. When we got to a point, the Nellist Team, except Bob Asis and I, split off. Nellist went down to the beach to take care of the two machine guns and the guards. Asis and I stayed with Rounsaville and went up the Maori River to the west a couple miles from the prison camp.

We waded in the river most of the way down with one guide with us. The prisoners were kept back in the compound, and there were about twenty Japs in this one building. And they had no security out anyplace except the beach. So Asis and I split off and Rounsaville team took position around this building. It was a large hut, about thirty feet by twenty feet with a grass roof and bamboo slat beds with a dirt floor runway through the middle. It was open on both ends and the grass curtains were up.

The plan was that Rounsaville open fire, and on that "bang," Nellist opens fire down at the beach. Meanwhile, Asis and I had waded the river and went up right in front of the hut. The door was on one of the ends, and Rapmund had told us that on the left as we go in there were going to be two Japs sleeping, and on the right there was going to be another two Japs sleeping lengthwise. In the back of the hut, there was going to be a Jap intel officer sleeping.

Our plan was that as soon as Rounsaville opened up just across the river and down a few hundred yards, Asis and I would go in. Asis would go to his right and I to my left and I would fire a clip into the first two beds down one end and back the other, then I would drop a clip and put in another. Asis would come up from the other end with his M-1 rifle and do the same thing. We had practiced this for two nights back at rest camp and had actually taped flashlights to our rifle barrels. We turned these on and wherever that spot was, we fired.

We knew that we'd be in there close with the Japs, and that we wouldn't have time to aim. In front of the door was a big tree and Asis and I were standing behind it. When we heard the signal shot we, just walked in, but there was a desk or something stacked high with books right in front of the door that wasn't supposed to be there, and we had to go to the left to get in. Asis then had to go back to the right, so, I was shooting before he was.

The Papuan guide was waiting outside for me to come

out with the prisoner. We were going to tie the Jap up, and this other guy was going to sit on him while we went and helped Rounsaville. We were just going to lay him out on the trail until we got ready to leave.

So, we fired on the men on the sides. To look back, it was a little bit hairy. Total damned darkness; we couldn't see nothing. Scared, *so damn scared* that I don't know how I pulled the trigger on my gun. Habit, I guess. You know, it's different

• *Nellist Team. Awards ceremony at Leyte, New Years Day 1945*
Standing L-R Andy E. Smith, Galen C. Kittleson, William E. Nellist
Kneeling L-R Wilbert C. Wismer, Sabas A. Asis, Thomas A. Siason

the first time you hit something like that—you walk into a building and turn your flashlight on and start shooting. Anyway, Asis said, 'Are you ready, Easy?' I said, 'Yep.' Then I went back and pulled the mosquito net off this next guy and he was sitting there in bed looking at me with a bayonet in his hand. But this guy resisted arrest, and I had my rifle slung and a .45 pistol on me. But he went for me with the bayonet and missed. I didn't have to use my knife, but I did. I don't know why. In fact, I could have shot him just as easily. I had a .45 in my holster. It's funny, but they had taught me enough Japanese to say, 'I am an American soldier. Come with me and you won't be harmed.' Hell, when the time came, I couldn't have told him my name! My God, in a place like that you know, I had just killed my first Jap. Whew! Hell no, no way could I tell him that!

Asis then checked these four to make damn sure they weren't going to wake up and start hurting us, then he pulled the pin on a thermite grenade and threw it against the side of the grass hut. Meanwhile, we began picking out any books, magazines, shoulder patches, maps, insignia, and whatever else that might be of value to headquarters."

Lt. Tom J. "Stud" Rounsaville (Team Leader): "I started the attack. Whenever we emptied one round of gunfire from whatever type of weapons we were carrying, and some carried different types of weapons, we'd throw in grenades. Some carried phosphorous grenades, and usually everyone carried at least one anti-personnel grenade, a fragmentation grenade.

Then we threw in a phosphorous grenade, then I took LaQuier and Vaquilar, the Indian, and Filipino I had, and we went in and checked for dead. Four people got out out of twenty, but some of them jumped into a foxhole at the back of the house, which we knew was there, but it looked like a swamp. It didn't look like a foxhole. We worked them over pretty good in there and one guy ran out the side. It was pretty lively right then and everything was burning. That Jap ran in

201

a circle like a rabbit runs from a dog, and he ran back in. Hard killed him on the way back in.

We weren't supposed to take any prisoners. We didn't have any mission to take Jap prisoners. Then I sent Rapmund into the compound to tell them that they had twenty minutes to get their material, and hadn't heard Nellist shoot yet, so I said, 'Well, maybe during all that shooting, he didn't hear it.' He didn't hear it, as it turned out later, but we were going on up that thing and we heard them open up. 'Goddamn! They must have attacked them!' But he had it well in hand when we got there.

The guard was up there at the head of that river. That's the only way they considered that we could come in, but around the *governor* (Theodoor Beynon) and his people was a bamboo stockade, and they had their little gardens in there. We came in around that and alongside it. The Japs were just living here and they'd get the natives to construct a shack made out of bamboo. They had this opening, and old Smith came back over after popping the *Kempetai*, and he was looking around and found a gramophone, and the record that had been playing was a Bing Crosby record.

They also had a brand new M-1 rifle and one of those cloth bandoliers, which has six clips of eight, and a rifle, brand new. We took that with us. Then we took those people out of there. I told Rapmund, 'Tell them we're leaving in twenty minutes and to take whatever they want to carry. If they can carry it, I don't care how big it is. Carry it out of here.' They had these big bundles on their heads and they were taking out all they owned in this world. We took them up there and put them on the PT boats, and Nellist already had his people set up the security on the way to be reinforced, and they had to be reinforced on the coastal track. They had two tracks, the coastal track and the one next to the mountains. Then we went home."

Sgt. Andy E. Smith (Nellist Team): "After we finished our job in the *Kempetai* shack, we went over to where Rounsaville was just finishing up his crossfire. Some of our stray shots were going through their building, but they were a little bit high. The prisoners had no idea they were going to get released, so the guides and some of Rounsaville's team got them out. Rounsaville and Vaquilar and one other guy went inside the big hut to make sure everybody was dead, and Asis and I went in with them. The rest of Rounsaville Team met on the south side and helped form up the prisoners for the trip out.

In the middle of this building was a runway about ten feet wide with ten-foot doorways on both ends and a dirt floor. A little table sat in there and had an old phonograph and records piled up. In the Pacific, our Red Cross had dropped American records to *Tokyo Rose*, and she played them. She talked about the Alamo Scouts all the time. We were supposed to be a secret organization, but *Tokyo Rose* knew more about us than I did. Now, there was a record by Bing Crosby, *My Melancholy Baby*, so I played it. Boy, I kicked my feet up. I was sitting there leaning back on the corner of the table with my ankles crossed acting like I was playing the fiddle.

All of a sudden, Vaquilar walked out of a room and cut loose with his Tommy gun. Man, I thought he had gone crazy. He didn't miss me by a foot-and-a-half or two feet. I said, 'What the hell you shooting at Vaq? The war's over!' He just nodded. Vaquilar was a great Scout, but he'd say about twenty words a month. He just nodded and turned around and walked away. I looked back behind me and there was this Jap standing up on a bed. He had just come out from behind a curtain holding a rifle and a bayonet and he was just sinking lower. He fell over right at my feet. That ended my record-playing and cut my fiddling off right now. To me that rifle looked like it was four or five foot long with a six-foot bayonet. And you talk about somebody trembling. I almost got the shakes, but I stood there and watched him fall right down where I had been sitting. And I thought, Rufo, thank you very, very kindly. I would have had that bayonet between my shoulder blades.

203

Just about that time, Rounsaville came out from another room and asked, 'What are you doing, Easy?' And I said, 'Trying to get well to get my composure back.' And he asked, 'You got time to come in here a minute?' And I said, 'Yeah, of course.' The building was burning by this time. That was part of the itinerary; shoot through it, get in there, and kill what you see, and the minute it gets too hot, get outside. And if there's anybody alive, get him when he comes out. But we went in and found this Jap lying right in the middle of the floor, and there wasn't as much light as a lamp would make, but you could see him. He was on his knees with his elbows and his wrists and forearms on the floor, and he had his head down on the floor, face down between his hands. Rounsaville says, 'Easy, take a look at this joker.'

Rounsaville put his foot on his hip and pushed him over. He rolled over on his side and popped back up. Now, that was not quite normal. So Rounsaville pushed him over again and he popped back again. Rounsaville said, 'Easy, does this joker look like he's dead?' And I said, 'I don't think he's done for, do you?' And Rounsaville said, 'Easy, I've used every weapon the Army's got except this .45 caliber pistol. If you'll lift that joker's head up and hold it off to the side where I'm not going to hit you, I'll use my .45.' So, I got down there and grabbed this dude under the chin and held his head up. He had crew cut hair but I finally got enough grip on it to hold him up. So Rounsaville took his old .45 out and splattered him. Man, knocked him right out of my hands. I was still kind of unnerved enough that it didn't bother me, but man I'd have a helluva time walking into a situation like that now holding somebody up and letting somebody shoot him.

The village was burning by this time and a few miles through the jungle nobody knew if Nellist fired at the same time, but we found out later that he had fired at daybreak. Alfonso and Rounsaville's team with Rapmund and one of the Papuan guides, took the lead. But Opu [Alfonso] saw some guy coming out of the brush and stuck his shotgun in his face.

The guy said, 'Don't shoot! I'm a Frenchman. I speak English. I want to go with you.' And Opu said, 'Why the hell didn't you say you spoke English!' He said, 'I just did. I got my wife and ten kids here.' He was a prisoner, but when the shooting started, he didn't know what was coming off, so he took his wife and ten kids and got out into the brush. Then he saw us and heard that we were taking the other prisoners to be evacuated.

It was about two miles to the beach down this well-worn trail. Asis and I were in the rear, and Rounsaville's team was walking sides, and Opu was in front. We then made contact with Nellist, and he had waved the PT boats in, so we waded out a ways and crawled on. There was one young lady, fair-skinned and slick as a button; she began breast feeding her baby about the time we got on the boat. It was written that all the Scouts blushed and turned away. I doubt that statement. We might have blushed, but I don't think any of us turned away!

The prisoners were all seemingly in good shape. When we got them on the boats, the Dutch started singing. Rapmund told us it was their national anthem, so we respected it like we wanted them to respect our national anthem. It was good. They sang it out loud and clear. Boy, that made us all feel a lot better because we knew then that we were among friends, and because they were friends, they appreciated it. They appreciated our efforts in doing this."

Lt. Tom J. "Stud" Rounsaville (Team Leader - 1947): "I took half the Scouts and proceeded in advance of the Dutch and Javanese and left half of the Scouts as rear guard. Our Dutch interpreter (Louis) was jabbering like an idiot with the rescuees. We went down the trail toward Nellist, and I dispatched a runner to him with a note for the OK to call the boats, as he had the 300 Radio with him. When we arrived at the beach, the PTs (four of them as two more had rendezvoused with our two boats according to previous plans) were coming in. Dove and four sailors and four Scouts manned four, seven-man rubber boats getting the Dutch and Javanese on board while the remainder of us set up a small protective perimeter 150 yard radius around the mouth of the river. We then went to the beach and left under the protection of PT gun cover, although we had not received any fire or aggressive action. Total time twelve hours."

TM2c Everett V. Nussman, USN (PT-300): "As for the pickup of the prisoners, we went in very close and some of the guys took little dinghies ashore and picked them up. The Alamos sneaked in there and put their shotguns in the windows and shot the Japs. Then they loaded up all the boats with everything they could get hold of, and life being good, the Alamo Scouts and the other group put as much stuff in those boats as they could. I think one of them had to take some stuff out because they about sank bringing what they called souvenirs out of there. Then they put those people on our boat, but they didn't speak much English, and they were looking for stuff too. They could have set our torpedoes off. Those people had our torpedoes armed and we didn't even know it. I think they fed them a little bit.

We didn't have that much food on the boat, but I remember a Dutch woman breast-feeding her child. We all watched that. The baby had to have some food - what the heck! As I recall the people were in good shape, but some of the guys gave them some of their clothes because they weren't very well-dressed. During the trip back I was manning the twin .50s."

MoMM1c M.L. Smith, USN (PT-300): "We were sent out to pick up sixteen refugees (Ex POWs of the Japs). Someone got the wrong signal. There were more than sixty. Those people had all kinds of personal gear. They had everything from pots and pans to one who had a sewing machine. The only thing we had on board for the kids was bread and jam. How clean they were. They were careful not to get their hands on their clothes."

Lt. Tom J. "Stud" Rounsaville (Team Leader): "Sixty-six people on four PT boats. Hell, you could put sixty-six on two eighty-feet long, three Packard engines. Some of them were seventy-eight some eighty [footers]. All of them had three Packard engines before they'd load them down with two torpedoes on each side, and some of them had a 37mm on the nose and a 40mm pom pom on the back.

It was the fastest boat afloat in the Pacific. From the cabin, and that's kind of built over the crew's quarters downstairs, clear on out to the bow of the boat, it's open. They were sitting up against the cockpit, women and children. One young Dutch girl had a young baby and the woman was nursing the baby, and it embarrassed Vaquilar and he turned his head. That's the only thing that happened out of the ordinary all the way back to where we turned those people in. Then we went back to our mission.

One thing to me that was important on this mission, as it was on every other one we pulled, once we made contact on a job we tried to stay that way. So any move you made you wouldn't be caught unaware, so you could plan for any moves they made. So you could change a position here or change a machine gun or whatever...we didn't go in on many of these raids. It really wasn't what we had trained to do. But we worked it just like we did a reconnaissance mission where you could land right in the midst of a Japanese concentration. They even had to sound beaches in Europe. They didn't have any maps or charts on the oceans that would tell the kind of sand, so they had a lot of knowledge we fell in on—on some missions. The thing that I think is important is that we went in on Roemberpon Island, and to the best of our ability stopped any possible contact with the natives, and the Japs would have scared the information out of them if no other way. By rounding up all the boats, they couldn't get across. They weren't going to swim. Going in and looking at it and taking it in, we went out in that swamp knowing we could do it. Went out to see the ocean then came back—went on back in on a PT boat and came out on patrol the next night or late the next day.

We went in - I don't know if we had any clearance from higher headquarters or not, but we consolidated both teams and made up our own little plan and went in. And I want you to know, that is surprise. That is cold surprise, because they don't expect anything from the ocean coming in from the back of them, and those people don't even expect what's coming from the ocean."

TM2c Clyde F. Smith, USN (PT-300): "The Scouts I talked to were very, very nice, but they were very thorough and they knew what they were doing when they went in there. They didn't play around with anybody and they used their knives and killed the cook there and released the prisoners.

One of the prisoners I remember very well was an Australian, and he had been trying to escape from the Japanese. They had burned his feet with a blowtorch, and he walked out of there on those feet that way. They were just kind of round knobs on the bottom of his legs. That's how tough he was. An awful lot of prisoners they brought back were natives, but there were white female nurses, too, and they were thin and in real bad shape. We would load four or five of those in those dinghies and haul them into the boat.

We could only haul two of the Scouts, that was the difference in their height and weight. I don't remember how many or anything because they were only on our boat for a short time before we had them released to authorities to take better care of them. I helped load the prisoners.

They were terrible. They were starved and thin and just worn clear out. Impossible. They were tickled to death, but they were sick. Our cook's name was Raymond Charles Hill, a wonderful guy, and he made hot split pea soup for everybody that was on our boat.

They just ate every bit of it they could get. Our boat was crowded with them, but you know, I just remember two boats because we operated in pairs. But I didn't have any fear of

208

the Alamo Scouts because they were fighting on the same side of the war I was!

When they got back on the boat they had these smaller knives, but they were very, very sharp, and they had blood on them. And I asked this one Scout if I could see this knife which still had blood on it, and he said, 'Yeah, you can have it.' So, I had it for years and years and my wife finally found it and got rid of it."

Sgt. Andy E. Smith (Nellist Team): "A Navy man wanted my knife for a souvenir when they dropped me back off, a knife with blood on it, so I gave it to him."

Lt. William E. Nellist (Team Leader): "There's a lot said about hearing Rounsaville shoot or them hearing us shoot because that's what was supposed to be. We assumed we would hear them but we didn't. In my mind it might have been too far for us to hear them. But what I really think happened is that we shot at the same time because it was at just that stage of light when you could barely see a guy. So, it was up to me to call the PT boat if I heard Rounsaville shoot, but I didn't hear him shoot.

Jack Dove was the contact officer on the PT boat and the code that we used was - I'd say, 'Jack, this is Bill.' He came right in and I told him that we got this place here, but I didn't hear Tom shoot. But I would advise to come on in. So we burned these shacks where the Japs were…The weapons captured at the machine gun nest included an M-1 rifle and a one British machine gun."

Pfc. Galen C. "Kit" Kittleson (Nellist Team) [1946]: "Lt. Nellist, Wismer, Siason, Cox and I were to take the beach guards. The attack was to start at daylight or 5:00 a.m.. At 5:10 the attack was over, all the Japs were killed and no prisoners or men were wounded or lost. I was in the party which took care of the beach guards. We crawled about fifty yards up to a range shack approximately twenty yards away.

The Japs got up a few minutes before daylight to cook breakfast and a guard came in from the beach to awaken other three. When two of them appeared in the doorway Nellist and Cox fired immediately killing the two. The other two escaped out the other side of the building into foxholes, which were dug for protection against bombings. Siason and I located and killed them. We hurriedly searched for souvenirs and proceeded to a pickup point where the other group was already loading prisoners and personnel on the PTs to go back to base. All totaled, sixty-six Dutch and Javanese were rescued by these two teams. It was a great mission."

RM1c William C. Tatroe, USN (PT-300) [War Diary - 5 Oct 1944]: "Well, our boys did all right last night. The Alamo Scouts landed, cleaned up twenty-five Japs (no prisoners) and the boats evacuated the sixty some odd Dutch men, women, and children, all in a pretty bad state, they had been held prisoner for over three years. I guess they were glad to see our gang."

Sgt. Andy E. Smith (Nellist Team): "We got back to Woendi Island and they fed us and the prisoners when we got in. They took us in the mess hall, and these Javanese people had never used silverware, and they looked at that silverware and their eyes got big. 'What do we do with this stuff?' They watched everybody eat with silverware, and finally Rounsaville said, 'Damnit, you don't have to use that silverware, dig in!' So, they dug in. It was kind of funny watching them eat potatoes and gravy with their fingers.

I'm not certain if the Army MPs took the prisoners someplace. They weren't prisoners of ours; they were liberated, and I don't know if they resettled them or if Rapmund took them and sent them home or what, but my Scout team went back to Hollandia for a short time, and then we went back to Woendi Island to wait for another mission."

Lt. Col. Gibson Niles (3rd Director of Training): "The success of the mission depended not only upon accurate and reliable information of the enemy, but also upon detailed planning, flawless execution so as to achieve surprise, and careful coordination between all elements of the team.

As an example of a night attack, although on a small scale, the execution of the mission followed the basic principles of surprise, detailed planning, close coordination, and attack against limited, well-defined objectives. The initial plan was followed to the letter and success depended on each element carrying out its particular task.

It was the opinion of many experienced personnel that it would have been preferable for the team to have landed in the area a day earlier so that a daylight reconnaissance of the area could have been made. In such an event, planning might have been more accurate and many uncertainties would have been eliminated. The use of native guides and an interpreter greatly facilitated the accomplishment of the mission and lessened the time element required for execution considerably."

Lt. John M. "Jack" Dove (Contact Officer): "At the time, I was the Alamo Scouts operations officer at the PT base on Woendi Island. I didn't have much to do with the Oransbari mission other than to act as the contact officer aboard the PT boat and to give advice. Rounsaville and Nellist Teams, and Rapmund and his boys, did all the dirty work. But it was heartwarming to get those people out of there and to safety. Charley Hill and I and some Navy guys were the contact team. We had four PT boats loaded with people on the return trip to Biak.

We rescued sixty-six Dutch and Javanese, which included four young Dutch women and eighteen children ranging from infancy to fourteen years of age. On the way out, we also picked up one Frenchman, his wife, and their ten children. It was one for the books!"

Seventh Fleet MTB Squadrons (Radio Message - 5 Oct 1944): "Special Alamo Scout mission to Oransbari successful. Sixty-six Dutch citizens. Majority Eurasians evacuated and delivered to NICA representative Biak. Scouts killed eighteen Nips during raid."

Sgt. Harold N. "Hal" Hard (Rounsaville Team) [Letter - 7 Oct 1944]: "Dearest folks: Well, after a brief spell, I am back to letter writing. I have been out the last couple of days and yesterday I was too tired and preoccupied to do any letter writing…I'm going to enclose a few pieces of Jap money. The one bill is fifty yen note - what its peace time value is I don't know, but it will never be worth anything again, so I won't worry…Your ever loving son, Harold."

Sgt. Andy E. Smith (Nellist Team): "In less than thirty minutes, thirteen men killed eighteen Japs in three locations, and released sixty-six prisoners who couldn't speak English in less than three minutes. A West Point officer told me that it was the 'most nearly perfectly planned, perfectly executed military mission of all time.' It was our best mission."

• Another team of the Alamo Scouts liberators ready for another rescue mission in the Pacific

Who Were the NEFIS and NICA?

23

• *Conrad Helfrich*

NEFIS - Netherlands East Indies Forces Intelligence Service was a Dutch World War Two-era intelligence and special operations unit operating mainly in the Japanese-occupied Netherlands East Indies. Soon after the evacuation from the Dutch East Indies, a Dutch intelligence service was set up in Australia on the instructions of the Dutch Commander of the forces in the East, Conrad Helfrich.

NEFIS 1 gathered reports, maps, publications, and photos on the Dutch East Indies. On the basis of this information, monthly summaries were issued on the situation in the archipelago.

NEFIS 2 was responsible for censoring the mail of Royal Netherlands Navy and Royal Netherlands East Indies Army (KNIL) personnel. It also checked whether the spouses of Dutch troops in Australia presented a security risk. It was not involved in carrying out secret intelligence operations. That was the task of the Inter-Allied Services Department (ISD), which was set up in April 1942 on the instructions of U.S., General Douglas MacArthur, and was responsible for sending out agents to commit sabotage and gather intelligence in occupied areas.

Two Dutch officers were assigned to the Dutch East Indies section, which, like NEFIS, was based in Melbourne. A few months later, on 6 July 1942, the Inter-Allied Services Department was merged with other intelligence services operating from Australia.

The new service was called the Allied Intelligence Bureau (AIB). It included a division responsible for gathering information on the enemy and carrying out sabotage operations. The Dutch section of the former ISD was incorporated into this division. The Dutch section carried out various operations in enemy territory. NEFIS was not given the task of sending agents on assignments until after the AIB had been reorganized in April 1943.

A new division, NEFIS 3, was created for this purpose in May 1943. It sent secret agents into occupied territory by submarine or plane to gather intelligence on the local political and military situation. If possible, these agents had to make contact with the local population to gather information and set up undercover organizations.

NEFIS 3 had little success with the deployment of secret agents. Despite the training course, the agents lacked experience and expertise. It was also difficult to win support from the local population in the Dutch East Indies, as they feared Japanese reprisals. NEFIS 3, and its predecessor, the Dutch section of the ISD, sent thirty-six teams into enemy territory. Over two hundred and fifty agents were involved in these operations, and thirty-nine lost their lives.

• *HRH Prince Bernhard*

His Royal Highness Prince Bernhard once wrote: *"For example, nothing has been published in relation to the former Dutch East Indies about the contribution of agents in occupied territory with the aim of gathering intelligence to benefit the Allied forces. The Dutch and Indonesians were involved in their lives to contribute to the liberation of the enemy-occupied territory. They often did so*

214

under very difficult circumstances, without preparation in peacetime and without the support of a resistance movement. They deserve our interest and gratitude."

Sergeant Major P.P. de Kock, *Carrier of the Bronze Cross*, also wrote a piece, about his time and experience with the NEFIS. He, from the day the Governorate of the Dutch East Indies declared war on Japan, except for a five-month break in Australia, carried out tasks assigned to him and passed on critical information to the Allied high command in the Pacific War.

Sergeant Major P.P. de Kock had always been at the front with minor interruptions: first as a guerrilla fighter; then as a member of the NEFIS (Netherlands Forces Intelligence Service); and finally as commander of a 150-strong unit somewhere in New Guinea until the capitulation of Japan. In the fight against Japanese supremacy, the Governorate of the Dutch Indie had to surrender within three months. Small units of the army, navy, and air force were able to swerve to Ceylon and Australia. From these remnants, a special unit was formed and bore the name NEFIS.

In early 1943, the NEFIS received the approval of the American commander to operate more independently. It is important that at such a combined forces party there is at least one person who comes from the region or knows the population and speaks their language. Such a NEFIS party was brought to its destination by submarine or by a torpedo boat, or dropped a few times by plane somewhere on the spot. From this summary description the NEFIS is not exclusively a KNIL affair. Navy and air force played an important role in this. But not only the military. The civilians were militarized before the deployment.

Until mid-1943, about twenty-six parties were dropped into occupied territory, among others on the Moluccas, Celebes, Java, and Sumatra. Afterwards, small dozens of parties were broadcast to Sumatra and Borneo. Not all broadcast parties were successful. A large part was betrayed by the population and executed by the *Kempetai* (the Japanese secret service).

A group was commanded by Naval Lieutenant H.P. Nijgh in December 1942 in Ceram. A Moluccas group *Mackerel* was under Naval Lieutenant G. of Arcken in April to south Java and in November 1942 under the command of Naval Luitenant B. Brocks in the Seag Bay. Both groups were betrayed and probably executed in 1943. The group *Goldfish II* was under Sergeant Tahapary in November 1944 to south Celebes. The group *Apricot* under Sergeant Manopo in November 1944 went to Minahasa North Celebes. Also known are the groups of Lieutenant De Haas and of Soeprapto. They were set ashore in Panaroekan but betrayed by the people and then shot by the *Kempetai*.

Before leaving the Philippines, General MacArthur declared that he would come back to defeat the enemy. The first successful counter-offensives of the U.S. forces in the Pacific were the naval battles in the Coral Sea, Midway, and Quadalcanal (the Solomon Islands). Plans were then made to advance from island to island, the so-called *Island hopping or some kind of hare over along the coast of New Guinea, the so-called Leap Frogging* to the west to drive the enemy away. Both plans were maintained.

The independent operation of the NEFIS proved to be a good thing for the Allies. After the occupation of the Solomon Islands, General MacArthur embarked on his bold plan, *the leap frogging*, to advance west.

Madang was occupied in the Australian part of New Guinea in December of 1943. The area further east was left to the Australian Armed Forces. General MacArthur chose Hollandia, on Dutch territory, as the starting point. Months before, a NEFIS party was dropped behind Hollandia. They had to collect data on troop concentrations, positions, and any airfields of the enemy. At this party was also a young man from Hollandia.

The data provided by the party to the U.S. Army leadership proved reliable and on 22 April 1944, the Allies landed at Hollandia. A NICA detachment also participated in this landing. Compared to the earlier battles on the islands, the Allied losses were minor. It was a success. Willem Indey, the Papuan young man from Hollandia, was promoted to sergeant and later assigned to the first established Papuan battalion.

The Americans advanced farther west and in May 1944, they occupied the island of Wake and part of the mainland. Thanks to the NEFIS, American losses were also limited.

Further west, in the Sarmi area, there was a large enemy concentration. This area, like Wewak in the east, was skipped by the NEFIS. The choice fell on the island of Biak and Noemfoor. An advance NEFIS party came ashore. They were ordered to determine the enemy positions and troop concentrations on the island of Biak. One of the members of the party was the Ambonese writer at the district office Wandamen.

He had gone inland in 1942 and had joined Mr. Vic. de Bruin, later known as the *Jungle Pimpernel*. Vic de Bruin and his men were transferred to Australia by plane. The writer, Janes Latumalita, returned after some brief training as the NEFIS man in his field of work. He spoke the indigenous language quite well and looked like a *Wallman.*

When the group sent forces to Biak, he took the place of one of them and went to the heavily-occupied island. He was lucky. The enemy was only interested in the number of forces recruited. In addition to the airport, they were also employed elsewhere. He was able to leave the island just in time and was picked up by a submarine at the agreed place and time. The Japanese positions were bombed from the sea and from the air. After fierce fighting, the airport was taken.

The enemy retreated to the many caves on the island. They were bombarded with flamethrowers and grenades. Janes Latumakulita was promoted to sergeant and received military honours. He remained with the NEFIS until Japan's capitulation. After that, no one looked back at him.

At the end of June 1944, the jump was made to Sansapor, a small town on the north coast of the Vogelkop. The airport on the island off the coast was taken after heavy bombardment. Here, too, the Allies' side suffered few losses. From here, several airfields on the Moluccan islands and the city of Amboina were bombed a number of times.

Prior to, a few NEFIS parties, including those of Lieutenant Tahia and Sergeant D. Watimury, had been dropped off there to gather intelligence on Japanese activities and their positions on the islands.

From Biak, a NEFIS party, commanded by Lieutenant at Sea A. Rasak, was dropped somewhere in the interior of the Bird's Head. The presence of the guerrillas in the interior had been passed on to the authorities by the people in Noemfoor.

Lieutenant Rasak was tasked with tracking down the guerrillas. His mission was successful thanks to the help of the local population, and so the guerrilla fighters were liberated in September 1944. For the people of these coastal regions, the arrival of the Allies with a NICA detachment was a special event. The people wanted to cooperate in driving out the Japanese. The position of the Japanese patrols were passed on to the Americans in good time and destroyed.

Thanks to the NEFIS, the Americans learned there were many large Japanese units on the tip of the Bird's Head at Sorong. Their positions and troop concentrations were mapped and bombed. The airport on the island of Jefman was deactivated. The Americans left this area.

From Sansapor in September 1944, the jump was made to Morotai, an island north of the large island of Halmahera. Everything was then built and prepared for the great leap to the Philipines. General MacArthur has fulfilled his promise to come back to defeat the enemy!

Before the NEFIS handed over their duties to the Philippine scouts, another successful action was carried out on Temate. The Sultan of Temate no longer felt safe between the two fighting parties: the Japanese and the Americans. He and his entire family were liberated by the NEFIS party and transferred by submarine and later by plane via Morotai to Australia. In his book, *De ongelijke strijd in de Vogelkop* (The Unequal Struggle in the Bird's Head), Pieter de Kock described, in a chapter entitled *The New Adventure*, the task of carrying out the NEFIS mission.

NICA: The Netherlands Indies Civil Administration *(Nederlandsch-Indische Civiele Administratie)* was a semimilitary organization established April 1944 for the purpose of restorating of civil administration and the law of Dutch colonial rule after the capitulation of the Japanese occupational forces in the Netherlands East Indies.

In January 1946, the name was changed to Allied Military Administration-Civil Affairs Branch (AMACAB). After the British departure from the Indonesian arena and the disbandment of the SEAC in June 1946, the name was changed into Temporary Administrative Service (*Tijdelijke Bestuursdienst*).

The NICA was established on April 3, 1944 in Australia and operated as a link between the Netherlands East Indies Government in exile and the Allied high command responsible for the area of the Southwest Pacific Area (SWPA). Based in Camp Colombia Brisbane, it originally reported into the Allied command structure.

Early 1944, Dutch Lieutenant-Governor-General H.J. Van Mook and U.S. General Douglas MacArthur, supreme commander SWPA, agreed that areas of the Dutch East Indies recaptured by Allied (U.S.) troops would be put under the civil administration of the NICA. Due to procrastination by the U.S. State Department, it was not until December 10, 1944 that the Van Mook-MacArthur Civil Affairs Agreement was officially signed.

The first NICA detachments went ashore at Hollandia (New Guinea). NICA staff consisted of Dutch, Indo (Eurasian), and indigenous Indonesian military or militarized personnel wearing uniforms. The general management was in the hands of Colonel C. Giebel who had the rank of Staff Officer NICA (SONICA). Each detachment was headed by a Commanding Officer NICA (CONICA) responsible for local government. Before the capitulation of Japan NICA units had established civil administration in New Guinea (i.e. Hollandia, Biak, and Manokwari, Numfur), the Moluccas (Morotai) and Borneo (Tarakan and Balikpapan).

U.S. support and supplies to the NICA virtually ended when it became clear that after August 15, 1945, military command was transferred from the American SWPA to the British SEAC. The two hundred and fifty NICA detachments planned for Java were halted. The reoccupation of Sumatra, Java, Bali, and Lombok became a British responsibility. The rest of the islands became an Australian responsibility.

On 24 August, the Dutch signed the new British Civil Affairs Investment Agreement with Lord Mountbatten's South East Asia Command (SEAC).

In September 1945, the first NICA representatives arrived in Batavia. Because the Republic of Indonesia strongly reacted to the arrival of the NICA staff and its name (Netherlands Indies) in January 1946, the name was changed to AMACAB (Allied Military Administration-Civil Affairs Branch).

NICA's highest commander was the Dutch acting Lieutenant Governor-General Hubertus Johannes van Mook. His most senior adviser (1944) and second in command (1947) was the Javanese nobleman, Raden Abdul Kadir Widjojoatmodjo, a graduate of Leiden University and a prodigy of Professor Christiaan Snouck Hurgronje. Before the war, he was a senior diplomat in both Jeddah and Mecca. In his roles for NICA, he was appointed colonel in the KNIL and the Resident of the Moluccas.

JOHANNES BERNARDUS HERMAN WILLEMSZ.-GEEROMS
(Kediri, 1 October 1902 -
Manokwari, May 1944)
*Dutch infantry captain of the KNIL
was awarded the Bronze Lion*

Willemsz.-Geeroms attended the Royal Military Academy and in July 1924 was appointed second lieutenant of the infantry for the KNIL. On November 15, 1924, he set off on the steamship *Slama* with a detachment of the Colonial Reserve under his command to Batavia. Upon arrival, he was placed at Bandoeng and promoted to first lieutenant.

In November 1931, he returned from a leave of absence and was then placed at Poerworedjo as adjutant battalion commander of the third battalion. On June 30, 1937, he was promoted to captain and in December 1937 he travelled to the Netherlands on the steamship *Sibajak* of the Rotterdam Lloyd. On July 13, 1938, he returned from his leave to the Dutch East Indies on the *Ms Johan van Olderbarneveld*.

When the Japanese landed on the coast of New Guinea, Willemsz.-Geeroms was commander of a KNIL-detachment in Manokwari; he retreated to the jungle with his group of sixty-two men on the day that the Japanese landing took place. Four men on patrol later joined him, including reserve Sergeant-Major P. P. de Kock.

In the first bivouac about sixty kilometers southwest of Manokwari, Willemsz.-Geeroms was able to have food and ammunition collected from three depots that he had formed deeper in the mountains. Sometimes trips were made to agitate against the Japanese on the coast. The group captured three U.S. servicemen from the Philippines (one of whom was wounded and soon died) and a Filipino soldier in their bivouac. In mid-November, the bivouac was raided by the Japanese and four men were killed.

221

Willemsz.-Geeroms decided to leave the bivouac and go through the mountains of the *Bird's Head* to a region closer to the coast, west of Manokwari. The arduous one-hundred kilometer journey to the new location took a month. Sergeant M. C. Kokkelink later wrote about this tour: through uninhabited areas, over heights of 2,800 meters, often without food, dressed in sheets of whipped tree bark. They crossed mountain passes and trekked over wide rivers, stiffened from the cold, and often too weak to walk. Seven men died of exhaustion. That trip lasted a month. In the end, they had to deal with a depleation of salt, so much so that they licked off the crusts of dirt, which had formed out of sweat on their bodies.

Willemsz.-Geeroms was leading forty-two people when he arrived in the region near the coast in January 1943, where he moved into a bivouac. The Papuans in this area were unreliable and received a guilder from the Japanese for every Dutchman they turned over to them, dead or alive. In the meantime, the group continued to fight against the enemy; sometimes Japanese posts on the coast were raided and clothing, ammunition, and medicine stolen.

In the last months of 1943 and the first of 1944, the Japanese took a more active stand against the group. On April 18, 1944, while Sergeant Kokkelink was on patrol with a number of others, the bivouac on the river was raided. Four members of the group managed to escape but all the others were captured or killed. After being tortured by the Japanese, Willemsz.-Geeroms was forced to write a letter in which he urged Kokkelink and his men to surrender. He was then beheaded.

Willemsz.-Geeroms was posthumously endowed with the *Bronze Lion* by Royal Decree of 12 April 1945. He was reburied in 1955 in the *Pasir Poetih* cemetery in Manokwari and later transferred to the Dutch Field of Honour *Kalibanteng* in Semarang.

*Lt. Razak Picks Up Sergeant Kokkelink
and His Guerrilla Fighters*

24

We were finally liberated. I knew we did not look very heroic to our rescuers. Dark skin burned by sun and wind, hollow cheeks, unshaven, wearing rags, and our bodies covered with sores. We carried rifles and *klewangs* (machetes) just like other guerrilla fighters looked after years in the jungle.

We were given cigarettes, bread and corned beef, dried fruit, chocolate, milk, coffee, and more. Our transition was too sudden and too big. Filling our stomachs, we talked about the adventures but also wanted to know what happened elsewhere in New Guinea!

Abdul Razak was a naval lieutenant and was from Sumatra. His group consisted of eight men: Langeveld (Indo), two Menadonese, two Sundanese, one Ambonese, and one from Kei-islands. The rescuers were dropped off by an American plane, and they had tried to find us for over a month.

We listened to their stories of travelling to reach us. I laughed and recalled the hours of wrestling that we had to do to advance just one hundred meters in this impenetrable jungle with meter-high growths of lianas, bamboo, rattan, and weeds. The jungle was filled with poisonous snakes, leeches, and all kinds of vermin.

We were eager to know how they were able to find us. Abdul Razak said: "By accident. We heard that the Japanese motorship *Daito Maru* was found by the Americans in Hollandia. When they inspected the ship, they discovered bullet holes in the bridge and the crew told them they had been shot at from the beach near Wekari."

After we shot at the ship, the Dutch authorities decided to parachute in a military group to find us on the Kebar mountain. That is how the liberators had come to "fall from the sky."

Our liberators told us that Germany and Italy had capitulated, and the Japs would be next. That evening, we slept calmly. A big difference from being on watch in the jungle. The men offered their hammocks, but we declined. We urged Coosje Ayal to take them up on the offer.

I was surprised that the team did not post any watches. Razak said: "We have airplanes flying over the Vogelkop daily and no Japs have been spotted. As soon as we hear of any, another team of parachutists will be dropped to help us."

We woke up to the smell of coffee and fried bacon. Shortly after we were visited by planes that dropped metal containers of clothing, food, medicine, toiletries, and weapons. We finally had our new khaki-uniforms; we shaved and had haircuts. We received new jungle boots, but I felt we could move better in bare feet. There was also a new outfit for Coosje.

The radio operator went on air and passed on greetings to us from Dutch, American, Australian, and English authorities. A couple of days later, we loaded up our Papuans and went to Andjai.

Here we found a truly fancy bivouac where we each had our own hammock and *klamboe* (mosquito net). We got a couple of extra days of resting our bodies.

Lieutenant Razak, with the help of Papuans, built an airstrip. A small Pipercub landed with an American pilot to inspect the strip making sure it was ready for landing a larger plane. Some adjustments were made, and a two-engine airplane landed with a Dutch pilot and an American crew.

They were ordered to fly me and my group to Sansapor

on the northwest coast of the Vogelkop. It was my first time in an airplane.

At Sansapor, an impressive crowd of American officers met us and overwhelmed us with questions. To save myself from embarrassment, I said, "Me no speak English," which was not far from the truth.

An officer stepped forward and introduced himself as KNIL Captain Horsting: "Come with me, and we can have a quiet conversation in my office." It was crowded in that area. "There are about twenty thousand Americans here," he said. "I would like you to see some familiar faces." Quartermaster de Beaufort and soldier Mellenberg entered. I could not believe my eyes. It had been a year since I had seen them last. I thought they were dead. But here they were laughing and shaking my hand. "Yes," the captain said, "They too crawled through the eye of the needle."

Rasak had sent out troops of Papuans and one of them stumbled upon the Quartermaster and Mellenberg on the Wepia River. "We were ready to knock ourselves off when the Papuans arrived," the quartermaster said. "We got into a fishing *prauw* (canoe) and they rowed us to Sansapor."

In the hospital we got a thorough medical examination. The hospital food was excellent and the care by the American nurses brilliant. The girls called me "Dutchy." They were good-looking girls. They asked, "Well Dutchy, how many Japs did you kill?" to which I replied, "Plenty!"

After a week, we got discharged. I was given a medical certificate that stated I was fit for service. The following day, we were flown to Hollandia.

In Hollandia, we were housed in a Dutch camp where a few hundred Hollanders were being trained to operate alongside the Americans. A Papuan battalion was also being trained. I was asked to talk to the troops about my jungle experiences and that captured a lot of attention from my listeners.

The NEFIS questioned me for a period. They were interested and worried about the internment camps and asked me what I could tell them. Commissioner of Police van Eechoud, as liaison officer to the Americans, suggested I return to the Vogelkop to find more internment camps there.

Van Eechoud: "You know the area and with your experience, it occurs to me that you are the only one who can carry out this plan successfully." I discussed this with my fellow comrades in the camp and only Piet de Kock declared himself ready to return to this area.

That is what happened next.

• This picture was taken in Camp Wacol, Australia.
The group of Sgt. Kokkelink. L-R Nuhuway, Sagrang, Soehe, De Mey,
Kokkelink, De Kock, Coosje Ayal, Beaufort, Jaquard, Attinger, and Sandiman

Coosje Ayal:
Liberated. Arrival in Hollandia. Move to the Netherlands

25

On October 4, 1944, we were rescued by Abdul Rasak. He ensured our survival and arranged with three loyal Papuan tribes to prepare a landing place close to the coastline. When the landing strip was ready, a plane landed to pick us up.

In Rasak's army camp, we were welcomed as kings. We ate the rice that was supplied to us like pigs.

After we were ready, they took us to Hollandia, the capital city of New Guinea.

I stayed behind in the hospital in Kota Nica to receive treatment for malaria and malnutrition. Two months later, I was released from hospital and transported to Camp Columbia in Brisbane, Australia.

Here was the Netherlands East Indie Government in exile established. Upon my arrival, I was received by General Spoor of the KNIL and members of the Female Auxiliary Corps of the KNIL. I followed a training for the Women's Corps and then a training for the care of the sick.

After an eight-month stay in Australia, I was transferred to Kota Nica, New Guinea. I first worked in the military hospital and later as assistant to the director of the Orphanage of War, Mrs. Tuhumena.

During a visit to the outpatient clinic in Kota Nica, where I came for a consultation with a few orphans, I met the outpatient clinic administrator, Sergeant E. He had just returned from Balikpapan where he had participated in the landing. It was love at first sight. It turned out that he came all the way from Curaçao.

After a three-month courtship, we got engaged in Kota Nica. Since I am from Ambon, the Ambonese soldiers stationed there had organized a party.

My fiancé was then instructed to set up an outpatient clinic for the Public Health Service in Kampong Ameth on the island of Nusalant. Since I myself was from Titawaay, also a village on Nusalant, I was appointed his assistant, so my fiancé and I left together for the island, which I had not seen for almost five years.

The joy of seeing them again was great. But there was work to be done. The set-up of the outpatient clinic in the village of Ameth went smoothly. The island is not big; there were seven *kampongs* (villages) that we visited regularly. After that, my fiancé and I were transferred to the town of Namlea on the island of Buru. We went there by boat.

Namlea already had a large outpatient clinic under the direction of Dr. Bin Heyder. The staff also consisted of a *mantri* (qualified nurse) and two student nurses. My fiancé was appointed assistant to the doctor and was in charge in his absence. I myself helped my fiancé in the pharmacy.

During our stay there, my fiancé and I were officially married. There was a big party on the tennis court. The soldiers present on the island had donated their drink ration to us to make the party more enjoyable, while the dance music was also provided by the military.

We did really work in Namlea, not only at the outpatient clinic, but also on the tours around the island, where all places were visited as part of the *framboesia* (an infectious tropical disease resembling syphilis) control. Our first child was born here, unfortunately lifeless. My husband and I have had a lot of grief about this.

After almost one and a half years my husband and I were transferred to Tangerang in West Java. My husband was appointed as an outpatient clinic administrator at Tanah Tinggi Youth Prison in Tangerang, as well as at the National Education Institute. I was appointed again as his assistant.

Our eldest son was born in Djakarta during that period and our eldest daughter in Tangerang. After about two years, we left with the "Asturias" to the Netherlands and from there with the KLM to Willemstad, Curaçao, in the Netherlands Antilles.

My husband went to work here at the Shell, and I became a housewife. Seven children were born in Curaçao. I began to feel homesick for my family who I had not seen for so long. I was regularly ill. In the meantime, many family members had come to the Netherlands from Indonesia.

Finally, at my request, my husband wrote a letter to Prince Bernhard with the request to mediate in our repatriation to the Netherlands. The cabinet of the Governor of the Netherlands Antilles was brought in via Minister Korthals.

We were picked up by a social worker with three large taxis and transported to the Maashotel in Rotterdam. This hotel was rented by the Dutch government for returnees from Indonesia. A fully-restored wing was reserved for us.

My husband had a job after three months, and we moved to Ridderkerk. We got offered a new house which was fully furnished. I felt very much at home in Ridderkerk, especially because of the large number of Ambonese who lived there.

I am extremely grateful to the Dutch government for everything they have done for me and my family .... Despite everything, I am a satisfied and happy person. But there are also many things that I will never forget.

I still wake up at night, screaming. In my nightmares, I run away from the Japanese who are shooting at us. I never talked about this with the guys. These fights you must fight for yourself.

Coosje Ayal passed away on March 28, 2015.

• *Coosje Ayal and Beaufort shortly after their arrival*
in Camp Wacol in Australia

• *The flag that was carried by the guerrilla fighters in New Guinea is*
on display in the military museum in Bronbeek, the Netherlands.

Pieter Petrus de Kock:
Hero's Welcome in Australia. Back to New Guinea

26

We looked back at the unfair fight in the jungle that lasted thirty months. Of the seventy-six man who took on the fight on April 12, 1942 in the jungle, only a few survived. That group consisted of ten troops and four troops of the group Beaufort. Of the non-military people who joined the guerrilla fighters, only district employee Seth Nuhawae, his cousin Coosje Ayal, and radio telegraphist Ruhulessin survived.

It was amazing to hear how Beaufort was able to put his story of survival together. Although his body was in bad shape, his mind was in perfect order. He told us that they travelled from Wekari to Sanfarmoen to help the troops there. Because they did not trust the coastline, they travelled through the jungle.

When we arrived in Australia, we were heralded as heroes, and we were told by the commanding officer that he was very proud to have us under his command, and he hoped that after a period of rest, we would be ready again to defend our country.

We had been liberated for a week when Major Spoor, executive commander of the NEFIS, asked for volunteers who were willing to return to the occupied area.

According to the intelligence received, behind Manokwari was an internment camp where someone died of hunger and thirst almost every day. If he, Major Spoor, did not take any action in the short-term, then in the foreseeable future, no one would be left.

He added, "I won't blame you if no one feels like going back now. Remember, your refusal will cost many lives." After that last statement, Kokkelink and de Kock caved. Both agreed and were immediately transferred to the Allied Intelligence Service in Biak.

The entire service unit started running at full speed. For the time being, they had nothing to do but wait and see. Then suddenly, they were picked up and taken to a meeting room. An hour later, the time of departure had arrived. We were handed a closed envelope on board an *MTB* (motor torpedo boat). The instructions on the tasks to be performed and further operations were neatly outlined on a sheet of paper. They were given two weeks to complete the mission. On the evening of the fifteenth day they would be picked up.

They told us about the content of the letter because we were not allowed to keep the letter itself.

All necessary information, from the location of the camp as well as the number of guards and their position relative to those of the prisoners, were recorded. Also, the distance from the camp to the coast suggested that we had to take a route through the jungle. We were able to complete the needed information with the help of the loyal Papuan population.

The end result was that within a month, an action for the liberation of the internees took place. The Japanese were eliminated by our surprise attack. We were fortunate that with our efforts about one hundred people or more were freed (Read the continuation of Sergeant Kokkelink in the next Chapter for more details on this mission.)

Mauritz Christiaan Kokkelink:
Back in the Jungle of New Guinea

27

The next day, Piet de Kock and I were flown to Mios Woendi (nicknamed *Windy*) a small island south of the Schoutens. The American navy had a PT base there. There were two Dutch naval officers with us, de Boer and Berends. They put a map in front of us and asked where we should be landing with the PT boats. I said, "the coast between Sidai and Masno." The next day, we embarked in a PT boat, with an abundance of food, an Owen-gun, a jungle rifle, and a model 45 Colt revolver.

We reached our destination. I thought the two Dutch officers were coming with us, but they told us, "We are at the spot where you wanted to land. Take the rubber boat and destroy it after you have reached the shore. We will pick you up in fourteen days." De Kock and I stepped into the rubber boat and with a pair of oars, we began rowing towards land. On shore, we took off our wet clothing and made a small fire to protect us from a cold night. We wondered if what we planned was going to work. It was too late to turn back and we gathered positive energy to move forward.

The next morning, we found a suitable place to hide most of our baggage as we could not take everything with us. On our way we went. The progress was slow as we carried additional food with us for a second cache further inland. On the third day, we were within a few kilometers of an internment camp. It was raining hard and our shoes felt uncomfortable. I thought we should have gone barefoot. The next morning the weather was better, and we snuck slowly up to the camp armed with our revolvers.

We observed the camp through binoculars and saw women and children, poorly dressed, walking around aimlessly. There were no men with exception of a few Japanese sitting in one of their tents. I made a sketch and said to De Kock: "I believe we have seen enough." De Kock suggested looking for a *kampong* (village). We decided that the local Papuans could tell us a lot more.

We went back to pick up our weapons and looked for footprints or a track to a *kampong*. We found one and by evening, we approached with words and gestures that we came in peace. First the Papuans thought we were Japanese, but soon they found out that we were *belanda* (Dutchmen). We spoke with them and distributed cigarettes. One Papuan was called Peter, and he was from Manokwari. He told us that the *kampong* occasionally exchanged vegetables and bananas with the internment camp for salt. He told us that the camp was only for women and children, about one hundred with thirty guards. "There are more internment camps here, but do not know exactly where," he said. "I can take you to a place where many of them are buried." We trusted Peter and stayed the night in the kampong.

Our plan was to give the Papuans a letter for the internees and tell them we are here. But I changed my mind because I was afraid that the Japanese would get a hold of it. We told Peter to make sure that the Japanese would not be told we were here. We promised him a reward when we returned to attack the camp.

On the agreed day and time, we were in the spot where we had landed fourteen days before. No PT boat came. We stayed on the beach for a couple of days, but there was no boat to be seen. "Well", de Kock said, "Let's prepare to play Robinson Crusoe for a few years." We decided to go to Merenveds. Driven by hunger, we reached the location and were welcomed as we had been before.

A few days later, a Papuan arrived with the news that Japanese were near Sidai. We thought it would be a good idea to have a look. We left in the light of a full moon with a team of twelve Papuans armed with spears, bows, and arrows. With my binoculars I discovered about forty Japanese on the beach talking. No tents and no weapons, we were surprised, but Japs are Japs, with or without weapons.

I had twelve full cartridges for my Owen gun and de Kock had plenty of ammunition for our jungle rifle and 45 Colts. We found a spot within firing range and smiled. "This is going to be something else." We had told the Papuans to stay behind, and at a given moment, we got up from our kneeling position and opened fire. It was all over in a few minutes. Some managed to reach the sea. We counted thirty-four dead. Some we had to give a mercy shot. We examined the bodies but did not find anything useful. The Papuans thought differently, and after there were only a few naked bodies left on the beach.

The next day we finally saw a boat coming towards the beach. "It is our PT boat," I said "I can see the American flag." We were just ready to return to the *kampong* when the boat showed up. We did see a man on the bow of the ship shouting through a horn. He was shouting in Japanese. A vessel was lowered, and six men rowed to shore while the boat aimed a machine gun at the beach.

We ran towards them convinced they were here to collect us. An officer who looked more Japanese than American jumped from the sloop, followed by several sailors who encircled us. But admittedly, we also looked more Japanese than Hollander with our dark hair and skin. "Who are you?" The officer said, "Kokkelink, Holland, Dutch."

One of the men came forward and addressed me in Dutch. He was a corporal drafted by the Americans, and he soon cleared up the situation. They had not come to collect us and had never heard of us. They were instructed to transport a troop of Formosans who wanted to surrender.

"Did you see them?" "I believe so," I said pointing to the corpses a few hundred meters further up the beach. The corporal was shocked. "God almighty, who did that?" "We did." I spoke. "Are they dead?" "Yes." "Damn, how am I going to explain this to the Americans?" "Well, just tell them the truth. How could we know they were not the Japanese, and that they wanted to surrender? Anyway, experience has taught us, it is best to shoot these fellows first and ask questions later."

When the officer saw our grim faces, he tapped me on the shoulder and said, "It's all right old boy, I think you did very well." He asked me what we were planning to do next and we told him we wanted to get out as soon as possible. We asked where they were going. "Sansapor," he replied. "Can we come?" "Yes, of course." "Great."

The officer walked to the place where the Formosans lay. He looked at them thoughtfully, one by one, and then said, "There are two Japanese among them. How disappointing that I did not bring my camera. You do not often see Japanese troops who want to surrender." We boarded the sloop and were soon on our way at full speed. Another rich adventure!

Back in Sansapor, we found Captain Horsting. He was stunned. "How did you get here?" he asked. We told him and he shook his head. "Working with the Americans sometimes leaves a bit to be desired. Come with me to Major Spoor. He will be interested in this case," he said.

Major Spoor listened to our story and asked us "Would you like to go to Australia?" De Kock said, "yes," right away. I answered that I would stay here for a while, at least if there was a plan for liberating the internees. The major asked me to show on the map where the camp was. He said: "Go and do what you need to do, and you will hear from me soon."

The next day, I was called to see Captain Horsting for a meeting with Major Spoor, KNIL Captain of the Artillery de Winter and Lieutenant ter Zee Abdul Razak. Major Spoor told us that the Americans were not prepared for an expedition but did not mind if we took the lead. They promised all the material we needed. Major Spoor said that he had decided to get our own Dutch forces to do this mission. "Captain de Winter will use your advice about a landing spot, which route to follow, how many weapons and so on," he told me.

I then had a lengthy discussion with Captain de Winter and Lieutenant Abdul Razak. At my suggestion, Sidai was chosen as the landing place and from there we would go to the internment camp. The terrain was not too difficult, and I knew the way. Captain de Winter wanted to make sure we had a small but well-selected group with light automatic weapons and be as mobile as possible. Captain de Winter was an amateur guerilla fighter, but his dealings with the troops were always very supportive and encouraging. Like our former Captain Geeroms, he was an able, energetic, tough fighter who inspired his people to sacrifice everything.

A few day later, the Dutch fighters arrived from Australia, including Adjutant Petty Officer Blokland, Corporal Bodegraven, two Indonesian guys, Javanese Sergeant Oeroep, and eight Menadonese, Sundanese, and Ambonese soldiers. Captain de Winter asked the Americans for two mechanized landing boats (LCM) to set us ashore with our equipment. My friend, Barend Mandatjan, was part of the team.

After a couple of mishaps with the landing, we came ashore at Sidai. Among the things, we had was a radio transmitter which we would use to report twice a day to the American commander in Sansapor. He would have a group of paratroopers to help us if needed. We understood that it would be impossible for the internees to walk through difficult terrain. They were all women and children who were very weak or sick and some might need to be carried out. I prepared a path with six men and all the Papuans. It took a considerable amount of time to complete.

We reached the Mangopi River and crossed it easily, following our path to the Warjori River. I knew that crossing a fast flowing river would be difficult. Our Papuan team found a good spot and during the night built a double cable from liana and rattan that enabled us to cross. We arrived at the Woseggi River two days later. In the morning, I went to pick up my friend, Papuan Pieter, who would serve us as guide. The internment camp was at a fork at the confluence of the Prafi and Woseggi Rivers, and the internees were in the narrowest part of the fork. The Japanese tents, within the fork as it widened across the terrain, were about one hundred meters from the prisoner camp.

Pieter brought us to a spot where we could see the whole camp with our binoculars. We made sketches and notes and when we returned to our camp, we had a long discussion. Our best chance was to approach the side where the Japanese were positioned and enact a surprise attack. We were worried about a shoot-out with the internees in the firing line. We judged the Japanese, once cornered, might avenge themselves on the internees and murder them. We decided to cross the Woseggi River and advance as quickly as possible past the internees to the Japanese camp. A group with Barend had to position themselves and the Papuans at the back of the Japanese and capture and kill all those who escaped. "This operation has to succeed," our captain said, "There is too much at stake, not only for our own lives, but also for those of the women and the children."

We were ready at 4:00 a.m. After a solid breakfast, we moved forward with Pieter and me in the lead. Slowly and silently, we snuck forward through the dark, and about an hour later, we reached the outer bank of the Woseggi River. Opposite, not even a hundred meters away, were the internees' barracks, lit by a single storm lamp. We sat in the pitch dark waiting for daybreak.

At sunrise, we moved forward. Suddenly, Pieter stopped and pointed in front of him, I looked straight into the eyes of a Japanese. He was twenty meters away, unarmed, and dressed in khaki shorts.

My God, Japanese here also, I thought. Did Pieter not know? No time to ask. The operation would fail of this man sent an alarm. The commanding officer dove next to me. "Bloody hell, Kokkelink. Why are you stalling; We have to cross that river, fast!" Silently, I pointed at the Japanese. He said: "Grab that guy, but don't shoot."

The Japanese froze. I yelled, "doedoek!" (Sit down!), which to my surprise he did, and we silenced him immediately. But now we saw two rows of three homes fifty meters ahead of us, half hidden in the jungle. There was no one in sight, but there were Japanese living there based on the articles of clothing hanging out to dry. There was also a small shed that was used as a kitchen. I wondered how many Japanese were there? They all must be sleeping, and this guy had gone out to do his business. There was no time to think. We had to act quickly, and everyone understood that.

The captain shouted: "Follow me!" Close to the homes, he roared, "Encircle. Hand grenades in!" a maneuver we had practiced many times. We surrounded the houses, threw our hand grenades and began firing with our automatic weapons. A few Japanese came and were promptly mowed down. A big Japanese who was screaming at the top of his voice came straight for me. I gave him a broadside with my Owen-gun, and he fell in front of me like a tree. It was later learned that he was the commanding officer of the camp, and he was hated and feared by the internees. We entered the houses and eliminated everyone.

We counted thirty-two dead, and no one had escaped. Our internees, alarmed by the shooting and explosions, sat together anxiously in one barrack and the children were crying. We told them, "Don't be afraid. We are your countrymen and are here to free you. Stay together. We will be back."

We heard rifle shots in the distance and suspected our Papuans were engaged in a fight. It was only 10:00 am in the morning. We were satisfied with the outcome.

The commanding officer assembled the internees and said, "I have come to liberate you and now we have to take you to the coast where American ships are waiting to take you to safety." I had never seen such a pitiful spectacle in my life with this collection of wretched creatures with rags around their sick and emaciated bodies. They did not realize their suffering had ended. Dull eyes, apathetic, heavy-hearted, no smiles. Even the children were afraid of us and clung to their mothers.

The commanding officer asked Pieter and his *kampong* friends to recruit as many carriers as possible. There were a hundred and seventy women and children and a few old men. It was obvious that most were in such a bad state that they had to be carried.

We collected food from the Japanese and cooked and distributed it. There was an abundance of rice, tinned fish, and all sorts of food items that had never been given to our people. We left the dead Japanese where they were and set fire to their camps. Our Papuans turned up dancing and singing with the heads of seven Japanese on the points of their spears. They had fled the scene but were cut off by the Papuans and killed. Only a few managed to escape.

Pieter returned later with six kampong friends and made carrying chairs. They were primitive but light and useful. The commanding officer brought all the internees together and radioed Sansapor to get a few LCM's to pick us up at the beach in Sidai. The next morning, we were on our way. We needed to stay together as a group for safety. Some women were not willing to listen, so the captain had to raise his voice to make sure everyone understood. He had also heard from the Papuans that there were plenty of Japanese spotted in the area where we were travelling. He wanted to keep the group together.

After five days, we stood on the banks of the Warjori River. Unfortunately, five women were missing, and nobody knew where they were. We suspected that at some point they had given up and stayed in the jungle to die, unable to cope with freedom and the idea of a new future.

It took a day to cross the river. Each woman and child had to be carried. We did not make it without incident. One woman drowned when a carrier tripped and turned the chair over. Before we could help, the current had dragged her out of sight.

We took a day to rest after the crossing. Barend and I went back to Merenveds to pick up more carriers. We got an additional twelve young strong Papuans who immediately constructed more carrying chairs. Reluctantly, the commander sent groups of people to the next resting place at the Mangopi River. That took four days. The carriers went back and forth to bring all the internees. Finally, we were all together again, and we rested and recovered.

With better food and great improvement in the physical and mental condition of the women, it was still difficult to motivate some of them to carry on. They regularly sat on the side of the path and cried, "Leave us behind." I must have heard it about a thousand times. We did not cover more than five kilometers a day. Three days later, we were within a few kilometers of Sidai.

We could see the sea and hear the surf. Our commander sent a radio message to Sansapor to pick us up immediately. A small patrol was sent forward to wait for the boats while we remained hidden in the jungle. Finally, the boat arrived in Sidai, ready to pick us up. The next day, we were at the beach, and we carried the internees on board in small groups.

In the end, another roll call showed that we missed an additional twelve women. They remained in the jungle.

On board the ship, a group of American doctors and nurses took care of the people, and later that day, we anchored in Sansapor. A group of dignitaries came onboard to congratulate us. The women and children were accommodated in special barracks because they had been diagnosed with infectious diseases. After a medical inspection, we were free to move about. I drank a couple of whiskies before I went to bed, feeling satisfied. I thought, "I hope I wake up in a week."But that was not going to happen.

At midnight, I awakened believing we had a big thunderstorm but realized quickly it was canon fire. "Can't those damn Japanese leave me alone?" It was all over in a short time, and I fell back asleep. One of the troops told me later that three Japanese planes bombed our position but did not inflict much damage and managed to escape.

In the morning, Captain Horsting repeated Major Spoor's suggestion that I go to Australia. I was more interested now especially since Christmas and New Year were approaching. The next day, I flew to Brisbane. Before departure, I visited the women and was relieved to see they were doing well.

A couple of weeks later, they were all transported to Hollandia. My Papuan friend, Barend, wanted to return to the Merenveds district with his people. He asked for weapons to continue fighting against the Japanese. The American Commanding Officer gave him one hundred Springfield rifles. I promised Barend that, if I were allowed, I would join him later.

In Brisbane, I was housed in the Dutch camp 'Columbia' under the command of Lieutenant Colonel de Stoppelaar. Most of my team was there, and we talked late into the night. In the morning I checked in with the camp commander, and he told me that Army Commander Lieutenant-General van Oyen wanted to see me. "It would be a good idea if you presented with the whole team, which would make an even bigger impression." The meeting was arranged the next morning.

At the appointed time, I marched with the group, Coosje Ayal included, to the headquarters of the army commander. I lined up the group and took a few steps forward and said, "Marched out with sixty-two men, two-and-a-half years ago from Manokwari. Of these only fourteen remain, General." I had practiced these words fifty times and delivered them well.

General van Oyen put on his cap and with a short bow gave the military salute. He was impressed. It gave me a great satisfaction to see this happening. The general shook everyone's hand and said to me, "Dismiss your troops Kokkelink, but I still want to talk to you." I gave him a full report of our guerilla war, then he said, "Take a month's leave and then we shall see how we can make further use of you."

Governor-General van Mook and Chief Executive Officer van der Plas received me as well. All friendly and polite, but I did not feel at ease. I went to see every movie that was playing in camp. Drank more alcohol than I had ever consumed and woke up several times in a park or under a bridge. For a while this was appealing, but I had enough and wanted to return to New Guinea. That is where I belonged. Then they asked me ,"We would like to know more about the other internment camps. Do you think you could do something useful there?"

"Of course!" I answered and within days, armed with a letter for the commander in Noemfoer, I was flown to the small island in the Geelvink Bay.

Lieutenant Kouwenhoven, the commander of the Netherlands detachment in Noemfoer, and a few Dutch Airforce officers stationed there, told me that somewhere close to Manokwari the Japanese had a radar installation which they used to shoot down American airplanes. My two missions would be to track down the position of the radar and to find out about the male internment camp by the Prafi River. They suggested a small Dutch fighting force, but I knew that the Papuans would be much better. We decided I would land again in Sidai. Every week an airplane would fly over with provisions, and if I wanted it to land, I should wave a Dutch flag.

I was put ashore and soon I teamed up again with Barend in the Merenveds area. I used the first days to instruct the Papuans on how to handle their rifles better and took twelve men to explore the camp at the mouth of the Prafi River.

On the second day of our mission, we did see twenty Japanese troops coming towards us. We took a position on the ridge and when they passed us in the valley below, we opened fire. The Papuans used hundreds of cartridges, and they would have done much better with bow and arrow I believe. The Japanese returned fire but did not attack us.

We pulled back into the jungle. We bivouacked at the Prafi River a few kilometers from the internment camp. During the night, I had a serious malaria attack and was weak, so I sent a few Papuans to explore the camp. They reported that the majority had died and only a few men were left. But there were a few hundred Japanese troops.

I had seen before how bad the Papuans were in hitting their targets, and I decided to do nothing this time. I rested a few more days to recover from my malaria and returned to Sidai. On the next appointed day, a seaplane flew over. I signaled it to land, which it did close to shore, and I waded towards it. I fastened myself to one of the wings. Told the pilot what I had discovered about the camp and that I wanted to be dropped off in Manokwari to investigate the radar situation. "Just pick me up in two weeks," I said. "Okay," he said and took off again. I heard later that it had been a great gamble for him to land on such rough sea.

We followed the coast to Manokwari where the local indigenous people told me there were at least ten thousand

Japanese. I asked if they knew the location of a radar instal-lation. I did not get a satisfactory answer and decided to search for it myself. I went undercover, dressed like Papuan, naked except for a *tjawat* (loin cloth), a rope net commonly used by the Papuans hanging from my shoulders filled with roots and bananas. The Papuans laughed and said, "We know you are not a Papuan, but you can surely fool the Japanese." With two of the men, I entered the town. We encountered many Japanese on the way, but they did not take notice of us.

I thought the observation post on top of the hill where I was prior to the invasion would be a good spot for a radar system. We decided to move in that direction and when we were close, we got chased away by the Japanese. That was a good sign. I knew it had to be there. I sent one of the Papuans to go and investigate closer as they know how to move silently through the jungle. In the evening, he returned, telling us that he did see a strange large thing. I believed he saw that radar system. The place was cordoned off with barbed wire and guarded by Japanese.

I decided not to stay any longer and went back to Sidai. Hours before the appointed time, an airplane flew over. I was ready with the flag. The plane dropped a parcel that included a flashlight, cigarettes, tinned food, and a letter: "Be prepared. A ship will collect you at 10:00 p.m. tonight. The ship will flash a green light. Answer this in morse with "KOK."

That evening, I saw the outline of a ship under the clear sky and not long thereafter heard the engine of a motorboat. The ship gave the green signal, and I answered by morse code. After saying goodbye to my Papuan friends, I got into the boat. Everything went smoothly, and I was again aboard the ship that brought me here a couple of months ago.

We went back to Noemfoer again. After my meeting with Lieutenant Kouwenhoven and some of the flying officers, I showed on a map where I suspected the radar was positioned. One of the fliers suggested that I should come along for this mission. I was not crazy about flying but agreed to be part of this. A few days later, three bombers took off with jets as cover. I was seated beside one of the pilots and in no time we were above Manokwari. "Is that the place you meant?" he asked. From the sky, the terrain looked so different, and I told him I was not sure. The Japanese activated their artillery and some of the small cloud plumes got really close to the airplane. Suddenly, the pilot took a sharp turn, dove, dropped his bombs, then returned to the sky. He looked at me and said, "There was a radar installation, but not anymore!"

Back in Noemfoer, Lieutenant Kouwenhoven told me I was instructed to go back to Australia. Arriving in Brisbane I was taken to the office of the army commander who told me: "Take a seat Adjutant". "Sorry General, I am only …" He laughed and said, "Yes, you were but no longer. Besides that promotion I want to inform you that Her Majesty the Queen has honoured you with the *Military Willems Orde*. The official presentation with take place soon." He shook my hand. I was overwhelmed by this unexpected good news but did not feel that I deserved it. I thought anyone could have done what I did.

Overwhelmed by congratulations, I enjoyed being recognized now as *stipple* (nickname for adjutant-non-commissioned-officer). It drew a sharp line between superiors and subordinates. I did not find this easy to adjust to. A month later, the official presentation took place with a parade and music. I felt like someone being readied for an execution.

Shortly after, I was transferred to Noemfoer. There were still small groups of Japanese hiding, and they had to be cleaned out. We conducted an intensive drive through the island. In one place, we found a cooking pot with pieces of human flesh and a scattering of chopsticks. The Japanese we encountered did not signal any desire to surrender, so we put them down. It appeared they were relieved to be put out of their misery.

246

When I returned to Brisbane, I heard about the end of the war. It was a madhouse in Australia. Americans were fighting with Australians about who had really won the war. After some beatings back and forth, they celebrated again with whisky and beer.

I had been transferred to the military police, and we had our hands full transporting drunk and disorderly soldiers. Fortunately, in this unpleasant work, I had assistance from a few fine fellows, including Bep van Klaveren, the Dutch boxing champion. Some of the worst offenders got a punch on the jaw from Bep, and when they fell he put them on their back and dragged them to the military police wagon.

The war was over, but there was a more vicious struggle brewing in our colonies. At the end of August 1945, I embarked on the *KPM van Heutz* for Batavia. I participated in the struggle in Java, but my heart was not in it. Why risk my life for a lost cause? I was sent to England to take part in the Victory Parade and had the great honor of an audience with Her Majesty the Queen.

I went back to Manokwari in April 1948. I went to the same place I had been six years before. Only a few poles of my house were still standing. "This land must be built back up" became the catch phrase, and I did that with all my strength.

I often relive the memories of love and sorrow of the war years, and inevitably my thoughts turn to my fallen comrades. What I would not give to be reunited with them. I feel, as it were, as if I have grown roots in New Guinea, notwithstanding its changing climate, its malaria, and stalking sicknesses, and I am happy with my family. What more can one expect from this life?

Sergeant Kokkelink passed away in 1994.

April 12, 1945
No. 7

In the name of WILHELMINA, with the grace
of God, Queen of the Netherlands,
Princes of Oranje Nassau etc.

To award the Military Willems Orde (MWO 4)* to:

Mauretz Christiaan Kokkelink

Militie Sergeant of the KNIL (1913-1994)

 For having displayed, at first as subcommander, later as commander of a detachment initially 58 strong, after the occupation of Manokwari on the island of New Guinea by the Japanese in March 1942, great courage, tactful actions, perseverance, and capabilities. Following the Japanese occupation, having moved into the interior and having inflicted on the enemy, despite difficulties and privations beyond description, great damage over a period of thirty months, causing Japanese authorities to put a price of 10,000 Dutch guilders and a reward of a large amount of rice and salt on his head and dispatching a force of 1,100 men to destroy his band of guerillas. After having reported back to the Dutch authorities, still weak and ill, to volunteer for highly hazardous missions.

The medal was presented to him in Camp Columbia, Brisbane, Australia on August 8, 1945.

London, April 12, 1945

*Military Willems Orde was instituted by King William 1 in 1815 and is the highest military order in the Netherlands. It is awarded to military personnel of all ranks and services as well as to civilians for "most conspicuous acts of bravery, leadership and extreme devotion to duty in the presence of the enemy."

Meity Kneefel:
Liberation of My Parents' Internment Camp

28

One morning, something suddenly happened causing a total turnaround in our everyday routine. A group of women doing laundry at a *kali* (small river) did see a group of soldiers nearby. They had an Asian appearance but could not be Japanese. These men did not shout orders. On the contrary, they sat silently and watched the women from that distance.

Terrified and confused, the women wanted to flee back to the camp. But one of the soldiers gestured with his finger in front of his mouth to keep quiet. Then he snuck closer and whispered that they had to go back to the barracks to prepare the others for a speedy attack on the Japanese.

He pressed upon the women that they had to pretend that nothing was wrong and in no way cause panic. It was striking that the man spoke Dutch (More than likely, the group Kokkelink and De Kock were part of this liberation force.)

The liberators all turned out to come from a certain Indonesian island but were part of a Dutch command. As such, they were mixed into a group of the Resistance.

In Australia, they had received thorough training focused on operations which they would have to demonstrate within moments: short, fierce, and above all, deadly attacks on the enemy.

Plagued by the infected wounds on her legs, Mama sat on her wooden bed. She was not able to get up. The V sign that one of the women made on her return with index and middle finger, meant nothing to her. She was not the only one who did not understand.

Many of the prisoners, predominantly women, were so dulled that they were barely aware of what was happening around them. But just as the unknown soldiers, actually existed, so too did the V sign. It stood for 'victory' and, in their case, also for 'freedom.'

The Japanese were totally overwhelmed by the superior well-trained attackers, assisted by a large group of Papuans. A fierce battle ensued because the Japanese did not want to surrender without a fight. In all the tumult and in between the flying bullets, the women had to be removed from their barracks as quickly as possible.

In the end, the Japanese had to give themselves up. They would later return with reinforcements. But for now, that marked the end of the widespread chaos. One could begin the retreat from the camp. That was not supposed to take too long.

The battle in the jungle could be heard far in the surrounding area. It was almost certain that other Japanese army elements had heard the racket.

The women who could still walk were instructed to join the liberators as quickly as possible, while the sick were taken on the backs of carriers.

When the women told their fellow internees the news of the impending battle which would free them from the camp, my mother struggled. She did not want to leave her husband, who was, without a doubt, still in the woods. That is why she thought it would be good to stay behind while waiting for his return. That was unacceptable to both prisoners and liberators.

Everyone knew Mama was related to a guerilla fighter. If she stayed in the camp, she had no chance of survival. In whatever order it would happen, she would succumb to her injuries, starve to death, or fall prey to the Japanese, who would surely come back.

Even if she were fortunate, there was still a chance that the Japanese would find out that her brother was a guerrilla fighter. That would still mean death for her.

Moreover, there was another reason for the liberators to take Mama with them. The reason was a code of honor which required them to bring every family member of one of their comrades to safety. They remained adamant over Mama's objections.

There was no time available to reach the men in the woods, especially her husband.

Finally, Mama went on the back of a carrier in the hope that Papa would somehow be informed of her departure. She did not have it easy on that strange back because the carriers could not handle the sick very carefully in their hurry.

It was a walk along a narrow path, through thickets of sharp leaves and arid branches to safety. My mother's wounds worsened.

The prospect of salvation and liberation, which was being pursued at full speed, could give her little relief at that time. "Furthermore, the journey was very chaotic," my mother told us later. Imagine a group of excited women who were aware that they were now free to talk out loud again, with no chance of a beating.

Along the way some tried to light a fire to cook rice, which the soldiers were carrying with them. Tormented by hunger, they were willing to take a lot of risks for a little food.

Of course, cooking during the trip was impossible. The fire and the smoke could give up their position (not only for the Japanese, but also to the Allies, who could not distinguish between those for and against).

The women were not happy about that. They made it clear and even strongly resisted. The soldiers certainly would not have had it easy.

Some of the carriers later told us more anecdotes about the trip. All funny. One was about a hammock he was carrying. It was more like a 'hang' sleeping bag which could be pulled shut with a zipper. However, the zipper was applied to the bottom of the bag, which made sense, because then you could easily step out of the bag.

So, our guy wrapped himself in the bag at night and pulled the zipper shut. What he did not know was that a group of women had laid themselves to rest under his hammock. Apparently, they felt safer there.

When he opened the zipper the next morning, it naturally caused a stir and hilarity. The women, who were already tense, must have had a stroke when his body suddenly fell out of nowhere. At the same time, the face of a dumbfounded, sleepy man, floundering between a screaming tangle of women's arms and legs waving must surely have worked on their laughing muscles.

Papa was in the forest together with his mate and a third person who had joined to relieve some of the exhausting sago knocking. There was no mention of the attack on the camp. The trio reached an area where they needed to pass an Indonesian police officer employed by the Japanese army. He was ordered to find and arrest my father. This arrest would undoubtedly be the end for my father.

As a person who never stopped expressing his opinions, my father often told everyone, including the enemy, what bothered him and how he felt about people or things. In his sincerity, he embarrassed many of the Japanese. He would pay a big price for that right now. He was the ideal scapegoat for the Japanese defeat in the camp. This time he would be silenced for good.

But again, he was lucky, because the police officer confessed to him that he did not feel right about the arrest and suggested Papa run away with him. The two others agreed, and they decided to come along.

"All the internees, with the other and the seriously ill, had been taken out of the camp," the officer told them. Their group was left behind, probably because the attackers, whose identities were not known, could no longer wait for them.

What they found on the hill was sad. Those who had been left alive were waiting for death, too sick to react to anything. The dead were unburied. But as horrible as it was to see the soulless bodies lying there like that, my father was forced to turn some of them around and see who they were.

This was the only way to be sure Mama was not one of the deceased. He could breathe a sigh of relief; she was not among them.

His difficult search showed that his wife had been taken by the unknown liberators. It somewhat softened the intense grief about the dying campmates.

It was hard for the men to be unable to help the stragglers and bury the dead. However, they could not dwell on this; the Japanese would arrive soon. The men, therefore, rushed away from the place of doom.

Once out of danger, they decided to follow the path of the internees who had left the camp. Their clearly visible tracks made a chase very easy. Nevertheless, it had to be carried out with the utmost caution. It was still not clear who was behind the operation.

Because Papa was on a wanted list, the policeman had squandered his chances with the Japanese, and the two others were also unsure of what would await them, it became a difficult journey with constant tension, vigilance, and extreme caution.

They walked in the evening through the jungle and slept during the day to avoid a confrontation with any possible opponent.

One day, shortly before nightfall, the foursome had just started their journey, they heard voices from the other side of a bend. It was the swelling voices of a large group of people.

Too surprised to get away in time, the men stood petrified and feared the worst.

Suddenly they came face to face with several Papuans who pointed their rifles at them. There was a deathly silence. Feverishly, the four men figured out how to get out of this predicament. They wondered, anxiously what the Papuans knew about the use of weapons. Only one had to pull the trigger by accident!

Then a miracle happened. Papa slowly pulled away a handkerchief, which he had tied around his head during the trip to protect against sweating, the sun, and the bright light. As he did, a frenzied jeer rose. Several Papuans recognized him from the land of Grandpa where they had worked before the war. A firm embraces ensued and the army took them to a camp that the Allies had left behind. There, the four were lavishly treated with food, drinks, and cigarettes.

The food came from tins, but it was delicious. They could not get enough of it at first. My father later told us that he had gained so much weight in a short time that when lying down, not only his head, but also his cheeks touched the pillow.

The fact that 'Nonnie,' as the rescuers called my mother, had indeed been evacuated by resistance fighters and was already in liberated territory, made him forget all the tensions of the travel.

After a few days, the escaped women and their liberators were taken in by a new group of resistance fighters. They were guided during a short march to a large campement with tents.

An army of soldiers and nursing and other support personnel walked off and on. It was an impressive collection of Americans, Australians, English, and Dutch. The number of Asians was lower. Much to their shock, the women discovered that there were Japanese, among them.

However, they soon noticed that they had nothing to do with the Japanese soldiers from which they had been freed.

Gone was the terror. They were safe here. There was also more than enough to eat here. Nutritious and tasty food.

For them, a life began as in a lazy country. Everyone was physically helped as much as possible. They were treated kindly, put at ease, and could recover peacefully from the atrocities in the jungle.

Awakened from the anesthetic of the abysses in the green hell, sobered by the intoxication of freedom, anger, often anger over the grief suffered, also had to be processed.

Of course, these feelings were directed at those responsible. Such a fit of rage overtook my mother once. A Japanese prisoner of war was the unfortunate one who had to suffer when he happened to be carrying out work on a stretch of road in front of the house where my parents were living.

Mama saw him standing there and suddenly thought of the public beatings of people who had not bowed to the Japanese guard of honor. Now that the roles had been reversed, she thought it was the prisoner's turn in front of her house to make him bow.

It was not difficult for her to order a passing group of Allied guards to give the man a rough beating. It was a powerful rage that hit her. After all, she knew all too well that tackling the Japanese did nothing.

Still turmoil, pain, and despair dominated her life. Her family did not suddenly emerge from the forest and the chaos of her thoughts could not be ordered as if by magic. Curiously, the scene gave her a certain satisfaction and there was no regret whatsoever. Sad how war can embitter a human being. How it can harden the feelings of the gentlest people.

I have heard and read several stories about the Second World War over the years, a chapter in history that must have caused massive nervous breakdowns worldwide (PTSD). The consequences are still evident to many. Great sacrifices have been made with the loss of loved ones and often even of one's own life. This period will not soon be forgotten.

Survivors are still haunted by memories and those events that are etched on their retinas. People want to forget. I notice it with my parents, who no doubt have not told us everything and may not be able to.

• *This map shows the position of three internment camps along the Prafi River. Following along the coastline south from Manokwari, you find Oransbari where the internment camp was of the families of the guerrilla fighters under the command of Captain Willemsz.-Geeroms.*

Pieter Petrus de Kock:
Letter from Queen Wilhelmina. Receiving the Bronze Lion

29

"The existence of these NEFIS (Netherlands East Indies Forces Intelligence Service) units and their activities during the Second World War in South-East Asia were never mentioned in the Netherlands. They remain undiscussed and unknown history to the public," Piet de Kock says.

After our safe return to Australia, Sergeant Kokkelink asked me to come forward to help him give our flag to the Governor General. When we gave him the flag, Kokkelink said: "Your excellence, The KNIL detachment in Manokwari never surrendered. That was the same for the two non-military people who were part of our group. This flag, which we carried with us during our guerilla struggle, we would like to present to our Royal Majesty the Queen."

A couple of months later, we received a letter in person:
"Your thoughts to send me your flag, which you carried
with you during the years of fighting in the jungle has
deeply touched me. I thank you for this gesture with
the utmost respect. You can be assured that your gift
will spur my memory many times to think of you and the
people that were not able to put their name on this flag."
Respectfully, Queen Wilhelmina.

Our guerrilla war finally came to an end in New Guinea, but the fight everywhere else in the Pacific was still going on. The job of a soldier is never ending. It was Mr. F. Coenraad and I. Koch of our group who went to the front lines. They were part of the NICA detachment that together with the Allies were preparing a landing by Tarakan on the island of *Celebes* (Borneo).

Sergeant M. Ch. Kokkelink was appointed as an MP and departed for New Guinea. L. Attinger and G. de Mey were sent to Melbourne and were a part of the motor pool. The rest of the team went to Camp Casino to await further instructions about which troops they would be assigned to. Coos Ayal was assigned to a military hospital to work as a nurse.

I was by myself in Camp Wacol, studying to become an officer. It felt like I had lost my appetite for learning. It seemed to have been lost in the practical form of fighting, working with intuition which kept us alive in our guerrilla war in the jungle of New Guinea.

I was worried, since in my earlier years, I had been a good student. Although it was not easy for me, I always succeeded in the end. But now I seem to have lost that ability. Early in 1945, we were given an exam. I was one of the few that did not make it. All the others who took the course became NICA officers.

I was disappointed that I did not make it, but I never regretted learning and studying.

Mr. S. H. Spoor heard about my failing to pass the course to become an NICA major. He ordered me to see him immediately and asked me to become part of a battalion of Papuan soldiers in Hollandia because there was a shortage of leadership.

The duties of this battalion were to keep peace and control of liberated pieces of land. Their commander was Major Mr. J.P.K. van Eechoud, and I assumed that Mr. Spoor asked the major to have me be part of the troops.

Van Eechoud conducted many expeditions in the Wissel Lakes. He organized patrols from Uta on the south coast to Paniai, and from there northwards to the Nabire coast via the

Siriwo Valley. This continued until the Pacific War started. He was a jungle specialist and managed to escape the Japanese troops. He was the police superintendent in Manokwari and had shown knowledge of combined surveying patrols in the northern mountains with ethnographic studies.

Another young controller at the Wissel Lakes was Mr. J.V. de Bruyn, who during the war earned himself the name of the *Jungle Pimpernel*. They both sent reports on their patrols in the jungle and combined with the aerial survey photographs and military maps during General MacArthur's campaign against the Japanese, contributed substantially to an overall increased knowledge of the geography of Dutch New Guinea.

The post-war restoration of the colonial administration in New Guinea is contained in the written information from Van Eechoud. He had been in the military and later Resident of New Guinea since the landing of the Allied forces near Hollandia in April 1944. He held that position until New Guinea became a Separate Administrative District.

Van Eechoud's appointment as Resident in 1947 did not involve the restoration of Tidorese power over the greater part of New Guinea. The formal separation was not legalized until July 1949.

On December 29, 1949, New Guinea became a separate colony, coming directly under the Dutch Crown (when it was called Netherlands New Guinea) and with a Governor as its representative. This period continued until the territory passed to Indonesia through the involvement of the United Nations in 1962.

I was familiar with the area and knew the local population. I knew the character of the Papuans and always had a good rapport with them. I was proud to see that these local people after the liberation were included in this work, and I was completely in agreement with that. I did not take too long to answer. I assumed they could read it on my face even before the colonel finished asking me. It was exactly what I wanted to do, and I took on the opportunity wholeheartedly. In May 1945, I left as sergeant-major.

Although the war had ended in New Guinea and had moved to Japan, the enemy was still present and continued to be difficult to deal with, to put it mildly. Military patrols were a must.

One day there was a military order telling me that a high-level military recognition would be awarded to me. I had to report the next morning on the center of the base to receive this recognition.

I was called to the office of the commanding officer. It was a pleasure, he told me, to announce that I would be receiving the *Bronze Cross*.

Sergeant Major Kokkelink who was our commanding officer after Captain Geeroms was captured, received a cross of a higher honor, and I was very happy for him.

The next morning at 9:00 a.m. the complete battalion was present to hear of the *Royal Decree* which was read in Dutch as also in *Bahasa* (local Indonesian language). Major Van Eechoud pinned the awards on our military uniforms.

Afterwards, the full battalion marched passed us in honor. I became very emotional and had a hard time keeping back my tears. This simple celebration touched my heart deeply, more than all the other events where we were honored with before. Here our troops fought until the end. I remembered all the people we had lost during the war.

Although it was very emotional for me, I kept myself under control, which might have looked to those around me that I was not moved by this honor. Yes, I kept myself under control, but inside I was fully emotional, and on top of that, there was the emotional roller coaster which we had to endure during our fights.

The commanding officer must have noticed something as he asked me to see him after the event. He told me that the command posts of Biak, Noemfoer, and Takar were ready to be relieved of their duty, and I had to prepare myself for the journey.

The next day I was told I had to go to Takar *(Sarmi)*. The commanding officer, Lieutenant Meyer Ranneft, was close to a nervous breakdown, and I was to replace him immediately. I flew with a *Dakota* (type of airplane) to the island of Wagde where a detachment of American troops was stationed to guard the airfield. From there, I went on to my post.

The detachment of Takar included five platoons. Each one was recruited from the local community, so I had to deal with five different cultures from Sorong, Noemfoer, Biak, Hollandia and Sarmi (totaling 150 troops).

My orders were not to engage in fights, but if the Japanese were showing an attempt to move to Hollandia, we had to stop them. We also had two reconnaissance posts where we sent daily patrols to go to the borders of the liberated territory.

If the enemy tried to move on us, we would be warned immediately. Our officers were part of these patrols and with that created a lot of respect with the different detachments.

On August 15, 1945, we finally got the message that Japan had surrendered. We assumed the fighting would come to an end, but it surely did not feel that way. The news we received told us a different story.

We were forced to bring in more troops. Between Hollandia and Takar, five new platoons were positioned. I was ordered to draw back to these positions if the Japanese attacked.

It would take another two months before the white flags were shown on the other side of the Tor River. The period of nervous days finally came to an end. The strength of the Japanese invaders appeared to be about 12,000 troops. They had twelve light army vehicles and a supply of ammunition to last for another half year.

Within the officers of the Japanese, there were some who understood *Bahasa* and were able to make conversation. They were appointed to be translators to give commands to their superiors. The commanding officer of this large number of troops was a sixty-year-old man.

When the Japanese officers started to follow the commands we sent them, I returned to Hollandia.

There I met with Mr. M.H. van Capelle who before the war was a local officer in Sarmi.

To prepare the population and reduce the risks, we decided to evacuate the whole population for safety. A detachment of troops from Takar needed to be ready to take over Sarmi.

Mr. Van Capelle was to accompany me on this trip. The next day, we left for Takar, and a week later, we arrived with our detachment in the area where the Japanese controlled the area for more than four years.

After the evacuation, done swiftly and without any incident, we started the reorganization of the government posts in Sarmi. Having done that, Mr. Van Capelle returned to Hollandia. While I was waiting for my relief person, I oversaw the military and the local government. This was a big responsibility that sometimes created a situation which was more than I could handle. One day, a Japanese officer spoke to me in *Bahasa* that he needed to tell me about a request from his general. He wanted to have a ceremony take place where the Japanese flag would be lowered with respect and honor.

With honor? Did they treat us with honor? Did they treat the prisoners of war with honor while they decapitated them in front of the people?

I had a dilemma. I assumed that the general was counting on my young age and inexperience. Besides that, they had 12,000 troops, and I had only 150. One Japanese action and we would be killed.

With honor? Of course, that meant that our own flag which was now the symbol of victory would be raised in top. One would respect the other.

I was struggling with this decision. But in the end, I believed that in the light of the troops and the more than three hundred evacuated people for whom I was also responsible, it had to be done correctly.

We decided that the Japanese flag would be raised at 6:00 a.m. and at noon the flag would be taken down. At the same time, the Dutch flags would be raised. The general was very happy with this arrangement.

We placed two flag posts at the old soccer field. The Japanese soldiers made their last military parade, and their flag was raised. There was a complete company with full gear and arms. At twelve noon everyone was returned along with the Japanese general. I had called on two platoons for the ceremony. To be honest, I was a bit scared. What would happen if this was a trick? I kept an eye on everything, but luckily nothing happened.

I instructed the sergeant who oversaw the troops that morning to make sure our troops presented their arms when the Japanese flag was taken down and when our red, white, and blue was raised. It was more than just a symbolic event; I considered it to be a victory.

Here was the advantage of our troops in full view: 12,000 against 150 troops and our flag was in top!

What a disappointment that my friends who died for this war were not present here! After this ceremony, I did not really know what to do next. Did I have to wait for the general to come to me or did I have to go over to shake his hand? The loser of the war or the winner of the war. I decided to walk over to the general.

In March 1946, I was sent to Sorong. We travelled aboard a Japanese ship. I received a lot of respect on board. Not only was the captain's hut given to me, but I was treated like royalty. Underway, we stopped in Manokwari. The city we left more than three years ago was in ruins.

The commander of the detachment of Papuans was Adjutant Officer Piet Bessem, a good friend of mine. Piet

263

Bessem was also a very close friend of Theodoor Beynon. He told me the strength of the Japanese troops was about 10,000! I heard some sad stories. Of the approximately two hundred European colonists and government workers only twenty survived. Of the family members of the guerrilla fighters, there was nobody around to wait for the return of the troops: no wife, no father, no brother, no son, no daughter.

Also, my fiance, who I left behind on April 12, 1942 did not survive the war. She is buried somewhere in the jungle of New Guinea. In the end, after our fight with the enemy, our guerrilla group paid a deep price for our victory.

Here is a list of our guerrilla fighters:

KNIL Infantry Captain J.B.H. Willemsz.-Geeroms, Commanding Officer of the Military Garrison Post in Manokwari: Captured by the Japanese in April 1944 in Wekari and executed in Manokwari.

H. Roborg, Reserve Lieutenant:
taken prisoner April 1944 in Wekari.

Maas, Sergeant-Major of the Infantry:
died 1942 in Meorani of illness.

Kapteyn, Sergeant of the militia: died early 1943 in the jungle.

Van der Muur, Sergeant of the militia: captured in Sorong
and executed in Manokwari.

Mandala, corporal from Timor: surrendered in 1944
to the Japanese soldiers.

E. Griet, soldier: died in November 1942 during attack on Wasirawi.

F. Koch, soldier: died in April 1944 in Wekari.

D. Hamar de la Bretonnier, soldier: died in April 1944 in Wekari.

O. Gijbels, soldier: died in April 1944 in Wekari.

Ch. Ross, soldier: died November 1942 in Tjosi.

Hordijk, soldier: died during a march in the jungle.

Lowisse, soldier: captured by Papuans, killed, and eaten.

J. Hofman, soldier: died in November 1942
during attack on Wasirawi.

E. van Kraaienoord, soldier: died in April 1944 in Wekari.

H. van Genderen, soldier: died in November 1942,
during the attack in Wasirawi.

P. van den Broer, soldier: died in April 1944 in Wekari.

G. Waagenberg, soldier: died in April 1944 in Wekari.

P. van der Star, soldier: died in November 1942
during attack in Wasirawi.
Arends, soldier: died November 1942 in Tjosi.
J. Werdmuller von Elgg, soldier: died April 1944 in Wekari.
Von Biela, soldier: died in 1942 in Wasirawi, Blackwater fever.
E. de Vrede, soldier: died in April 1944 in Wekari.
I. Tuinenburg Sr., soldier: deserted the group.
B. Tuinenburg Jr., soldier: died in 1942 at the Anggi River,
killed by Papuans.
Kalempo, soldier, Menadonese:
died in 1943 in Wekari, reason unknown.
Manenkey, soldier, Menadonese: taken prisoner
in April 1944 in Wekari.
Saep, soldier, Soendanese: died in 1942 at the Anggi River.
Hoessein, soldier, Soendanese: died in 1942 at the Anggi River.
Wardi, soldier, Soendanese: died November 1942 in Tjosi.
Sabin, soldier, Javanese: died November 1942 in Tjosi.
Doellah, soldier, Javanese: died April 1944 in Wekari.
Sahin, soldier, Javanese:
died November 1942 by attack in Wasirawi.
Paiman, soldier, Javanese: lost his mind, drowned in the ocean.
Saddat, soldier, Javanese: executed in April 1943 for sabotage.
Martinus, soldier, Papuan: fought till the end with the guerilla.
Jaki, soldier, Papuan: deserted.
Jaksa, soldier, Papuan: deserted.
Jordaan, soldier, Papuan: died in 1943 by Masni.
Rumsajor, soldier, Papuan: deserted.
Mika, soldier, Papuan: died 1944 by Aroepi.
Mrs. Nahuay: taken prisoner in April 1944 in Wekari
executed in Manokwari.
Matsuro, American Captain of Infantry: died in 1943
in Wesoei of unknown disease.
McFadden, American Lieutenant of the Artillery:
died in April 1944 in Wekari.
Sheahan, American radio telegraphist: died in April 1944 in Wekari.
Augustinus, Philippino: died from ingesting poisonous vegetables.
Unknown, Philippino: died in April 1944 in Wekari.
M. Ch. Kokkelink: Sergeant took over command from
Captain Geeroms and fought until the end with the guerrillas.
De Beaufort, fourier: liberated by the Americans
in September 1944 in Wekari.

Soentpiet, soldier: fought until the end with the guerrilla.
De Kock, soldier: fought until the end with the guerilla.
I. Koch, soldier: fought until the end with the guerrilla.
G. de Mey, soldier: fought until the end with the guerilla.
R. Mellenberg, soldier: liberated in September 1944
by the Americans in Wekari.
T. van Genderen, soldier: fought until the end with the guerrilla.
L. Attinger, soldier: fought until the end with the guerrrilla.
F. Coenraad, soldier: fought until the end with the guerrilla.
R. Jacquard, soldier: fought until the end with the guerrilla.
Sagran, soldier, Menadonese: fought until the end with the guerrilla.
Soeha, soldier, Soendanese: fought until the end with the guerrilla.
Sandiman, soldier, Javanese: fought until the end with the guerrilla.
Frederik Rumberbiar, soldier, Papua:
fought till the end with the guerrilla.
Kasim, Cerammer, forced laborer:
fought until the end with the guerrilla.
Mr. Nahuay, Ambon, government employee:
fought until the end with the guerrilla.
Roehoelessen, Ambon: fought until the end with the guerrilla.
Coos Ajal, cousin of Nahuay: fought until the end with the guerrilla.

• Sergeant Kokkelink back in Manokwari after the war

Original Settlers Want to Return to Manokwari

30

When the original settlers from the early 1930s wanted to return to their homes after the war, they found them either destroyed by the Japanese or taken over by the local population. With exception of two homes, all others were gone.

All food trees were destroyed (picking fruit was done by chopping off branches to make it easier) as well as other parcels, such as coconuts and other essential vegetable crops. All the farm animals had been stolen as well.

On June 16, 1947, the settlers sent a letter to the *Sociale Zaken of Immigration and Transmigration* in Batavia and after communication back and forth, the original settlers who had survived the war were given a parcel of land to build a new farm for their families.

On July 8, 1947 there were only thirteen men, ten women and twenty-seven children who had survived the war.

164 of the original 214 SIKNG immigrants were either killed, died in captivity or suffered terrible starvation.
The following members survived:
Theodoor Beynon and his wife and eight children;
Mrs. C. Herklots-Jacquard and two children
(husband died during the war);
Mrs. Maas with one child (husband killed by the Japanese);
Mrs. De Vreede and five children
(husband killed by the Japanese);
Mrs. De Groot and four children
(husband killed by the Japanese);
Mrs. Ang (no children);
Miss Werdmuller v. Ellg (her father and brother died);
N. Japers and his wife;

Mrs. L de Groeve; Mr. N. Kokkelink; Mr. R. Jacquard;
Mr. F. Coenraad; Mr. L. Attinger; Mr. R. Mellenberg;
Mr. D. Kock; Mr. T. van Genderen; Mr. G. de Mey;
Mr. J. Zeelt; Mr. R. Soumokil; Mevr. Gijbels;
Mr. A.A.J. Hessing and his wife and five children.

The following members of the SIKNG died during the war:
Mr. J. Kapteyn and wife and five children;
Mr. P. Maas; Mr. Peerelaar and wife and child;
Mr. von Ende; Mr. G. Waajenberg and wife;
Mr. B. Gijbels; Mr. N. Gijbels; Mr. E. Soumokil;
Mr. de Mey Sr. and wife and two children; Mr. A de Mey;
Mr. R. de Mey; Mr. Steiginga; Mrs. Bekker;
Mrs. Schuylenburgh and three children;
Mr. Hagenbeek; Mr. F. Koch and wife and child;
Mr. R. Koch; Mr. D. Hamar de la Bretoniere; Mr. O. Duren;
Mr. Telehals and wife and two children;
Mr. Goldbach and wife and three children;
Mr. Bouman and wife and two children;
Four children Engelman; Mr. Johny Werdmuller v. Ellg;
Mr. R. Herklots; Mr Krasjenoord Sr. and wife;
Mr. Krasjenoord Jr. and wife and two children;
Mr. P van den Broek and wife and two children;
Mr. and Mrs. Filet; Mr. H. Lapre;
Mr. Crawford and wife and four children; Mr. de Groeve Jr.;
Mrs. R. Mellenberg and six children;
Mr. de Groeve Sr. and wife and four children;
Mr. Ch. Lapre and wife; Mr. E. de Vreede;
Mrs. Tschirpke and three children;
Mr. E. van Genderen; Mrs. Van Genederen;
Mr. Hordijk; Mr. Lowissen;
Mr. Later and wife and three children;
Mr. Tuinenburg Sr. with wife and child;
Mr. B. Tuinenburg; Mr. E. Tuinenburg; Mr. R. Attinger;
Mr. P. Melenberg; Mr. Jaspers Sr, and wife and child;
Mr. J. Jaspers; Mr. Th. Werdmuller v. Ellg and wife;
Mr. C. Werdmuller v. Ellg; Mr. Groeneveld.

31

In the period from 1945-1968, a large-scale repatriation of Dutch Indonesian people took place. More than 300,000 came to the Netherlands from the former Dutch East Indies. This migration is known as *repatriation*, which amounts to returning to the homeland and must be understood symbolically as a large part of the returnees themselves had never been to the Netherlands before.

On 17 August 1945, Sukarno proclaimed the independence of Indonesia which led to a revolutionary and chaotic situation. Japan had capitulated, but because there was no Allied force in sight, there was a power vacuum.

This resulted in an explosive situation; an indigenous attempt at reckoning with all foreign influence followed, be it British, Chinese, Japanese or Dutch Indonesian.

This period is known as the *Bersiap* (*Bersiap* is the name given by the Dutch to a violent and chaotic phase of the Indonesian National Revolution following the end of World War Two. The *Bersiap* period lasted from August 1945 to December 1946.)

Because the situation for Dutch Indonesian people in the Dutch East Indies shortly after the Japanese capitulation and in Indonesia in the 1950s, after the war of independence, remained hostile and dangerous; they were stripped of their official functions and their possessions were confiscated.

Most Dutch Indonesian people were forced to return to their homeland: The Netherlands. They refused to opt for *warga negara Indonesia* (Indonesian citizenship).

The repatriation had five different waves. The first wave of returnees came to the Netherlands almost immediately after the *Bersiap*.

1945-1950: After the capitulation of Japan and the subsequent *Bersiap*, approximately 100,000 Dutch Indonesian people left for the Netherlands immediately or within a few years. They were mainly survivors of the Japanese occupation (inside and outside the internment camps) and the *Bersiap*. The scheme was initially temporary residence in the Netherlands to recover from the Japanese occupation (1942-1945); 30,000 of them went back to Indonesia.

1950-1957: In connection with the transfer of sovereignty to Indonesia, officials from the administration, the police, the judiciary and the army repatriated to the Netherlands. After the dissolution of the KNIL in July 1950, many KNIL soldiers repatriated.

1957-1958: About 50,000 people left following the New Guinea issue and *Zwarte Sinterklaas* (Dutch name for a diplomatic incident) which resulted in Dutch Indonesian people being declared a state-threatening situation in Indonesia.

1962: In connection with the transfer of Dutch New Guinea to Indonesia, all Dutch nationals residing in New Guinea (approximately 14,000 persons) were evacuated.

During the period, the *UNTEA* (The United Nations Temporary Executive Authority) was established during October 1962 in accord with General Assembly resolution 1752 as requested in Article two of the New York Agreement to administer the former Netherlands New Guinea.

The UNTEA administration ended on 1 May 1963, and a group of about five hundred Papuans, who had been in the Dutch public service, also came to the Netherlands with their families.

1957-1964: *Regrets* were people who had opted for Indonesian citizenship after the transfer of sovereignty, but regretted their choice when the new Indonesian society began to discriminate against them. Until 1958, the Dutch admission's policy was very restrictive for them, but the policy was broadened because of the emergency situation in which the *Regrets* were a result of political circumstances; about 25,000 of them were able to come to the Netherlands and regain their Dutch nationality.

In the early 1950s, the Dutch government encouraged emigration from the Netherlands, due to stagnant economic growth; some 50,000 Dutch Indonesian people emigrated from the Netherlands to other countries.

Repatriation of Dutch Indonesian people to the Netherlands was not encouraged for this reason.

Many Indos found it difficult to settle in the Netherlands. Requests to obtain advances for a boat ticket were often rejected (A single passage fourth class cost around one thousand guilders in 1957.)

In the years 1952-1955, the Dutch government put a brake on the arrival of Dutch Indonesian people, especially Indo-Europeans. According to the government, this group could be poorly assimilated in the Netherlands and had to be protected from itself.

Only in exceptional cases were these families allowed to come to the Netherlands. To do so, they had to submit an application to the high commissioner.

In 1953, the Dutch high commissioner in Indonesia, A. Th. Lamping, returned to his point of view, which he announced in Dutch media two years earlier, saying that the future of Dutch Indonesian people lay in Indonesia. Lamping this time called for the possibilities for arrival to the Netherlands to be relaxed.

The living conditions of Dutch Indonesian people in Indonesia became so problematic that the Dutch government decided in 1955 to adjust the repatriation criteria.

As a result, late returnees and *Regrets* came to the Netherlands from 1955. *Regret opt-outs* had initially opted for Indonesian citizenship, but regretted this and opted for Dutch citizenship upon arrival in the Netherlands.

On 5 December 1957, Sukarno declared the last Dutch (40,000 persons) still present in Indonesia a threat to the state and forced them to leave for good. Dutch companies were also nationalized by Indonesia and *Sinterklaas* (Sinterklaas or Sint-Nicolaas is a legendary figure based on Saint Nicholas, patron saint of children) was no longer welcome. It meant, "Don't unpack, but pack." The anti-Dutch actions are, therefore, also known as *Zwarte Sinterklaas*. It was the climax of years of hate speech by Indonesian fanatics on the formerly Dutch overseas territory.

Almost 40,000 Dutch Indonesian people left in the following months, while economic ties between the two countries were almost entirely severed. In 1958, a group of 10,000 came to the Netherlands.

On 17 August 1960, fifteen years after the declaration of Indonesian independence, diplomatic relations with the Netherlands were severed.

Not all Dutch people came back, especially Dutch Indonesian people who held key positions in business remained in Indonesia. In addition, a group of approximately 5,000 Dutch Indonesian people were left behind, and were not allowed to repatriate to the Netherlands for various reasons. (When Louise and I were in Manokwari, we did meet several of them and they are living in very poor conditions.)

The arrival of the Dutch Indonesian did not end with this. Due to the loss of New Guinea in 1962, approximately 20,000 predominantly Dutch Indonesian people left this last Dutch area in the East Indies. In 1968, the Dutch government permanently discontinued the system for their immigration in the Netherlands.

Although the repatriation of the Dutch Indonesians is known as silent, there were sometimes problems. The vast majority of returnees spoke excellent Dutch, but some of the children who came to the Netherlands in the 1960s had a language deficit. In some Dutch cities, that was almost half the children. The cause was the Indonesian ban on Dutch language education from 1958.

In addition to the group of Dutch Indonesian people, other migrants also came to the Netherlands. A special group during this period formed the *Moluccans*, but also the *Peranakans* and the *Stowaways*.

Moluccans deviated from the large group of returnees because they had not chosen to come to the Netherlands permanently and assumed that they would only be in the Netherlands temporarily. They were KNIL soldiers who did not want to be demobilized on Republican territory. The Republican government objected to this happening to the Moluccas because of the proclamation of the Moluccan republic of RMS in April 1950.

Accordingly, the Dutch government decided in 1951 to transfer approximately 12,500 Moluccans to the Netherlands. Once there, they were told that they were no longer in the service of the army. They were taken care of in former concentration camps, such as Vught and Westerbork (then called Camp Schattenberg).

Peranakans (child of the country) were Chinese who were born and raised in Indonesia or the Dutch East Indies. A few of this group also came to the Netherlands, but had European roots, less often. This group feared for their lives, especially in the time after Suharto's coup; they were accused of communism and persecuted by the Suharto government.

Stowaways arrived throughout the repatriation period. For a variety of reasons, they chose to board the repatriation vessels undocumented. For example, a number of stowaways had Indonesian nationality because of their parents' choices, and could not qualify as 'Dutch.' They feared for their lives.

Others made this choice out of adventurer's urge. In addition, the coup d'état of Suharto on 1 October 1965 brought

Indonesians to the Netherlands who, once they arrived here, were naturalized.

The most famous group of stowaways are *Mr. Samkalden's 70*. In May 1958, after *Zwarte Sinterklaas*, a record number of stowaways were on board the Johan van Oldenbarnevelt. Upon arrival in the Netherlands, they were arrested and housed in Camp Schattenberg.

Most were eligible for naturalization, but in October 1958 the then Minister of Justice decided that about thirty to thirty-seven of them had to go back to Indonesia. They were put on board the *Johan van Oldenbarnevelt*.

Under great international pressure, the Dutch government decided that the group should not disembark in Indonesia, but in New Guinea. They were at risk of persecution in Indonesia. Most of the group came to the Netherlands after the loss of New Guinea (other name used was: *Indo Belanda* or *Peranakan Indonesia Belanda)*.

• *May 2, 1958: Arrival of the MS Castel Felice at the Lloydkade in Rotterdam, the Netherlands, with Indos from Indonesia (from Wikimedia)*

Reburial of Hans Fuhri

32

During the reburial in Ambon in 1949, both of Fuhri's brothers, local authorities, over 1,000 students at the local naval school of the Moluccas, and personnel of the harbor and pilot services were present. The Dutch flag was at half-mast and on a podium, barrels of incense burned, guarded by military personnel. The military band played funeral music.

When the casket, covered with the Red-White-Blue, was carried between a line-up of the honor guard, salvos were shot into the air. The preacher honored the fallen officer of the marines and finished with a prayer that was said by all. With more salute shots, drums, and music, the casket was lowered in the final resting place.

Wreaths and flowers were laid by dignitaries and military officers. Both of Fuhri's brothers laid wreaths; then the commander of the marines, harbor master of Ambon, the commander of the navy in the East and the department of the navy placed some more. The regular public brought many bouquets of flowers to create a large bed to honor this hero.

Hans Fuhri was a *Commander First Class*. Fuhri behaved as we expect from our Dutch navy people. He was a great example of the marine corps and navy code from the Netherlands.

The author of a news article published in the *Soerabaiasch Handelsblad en Drukkerijen* in January 1949 wrote:

"He was more than that; he died as the tradition of the Fuhri's dictated with an overpowering mental capacity especially when it is about honor.

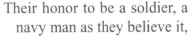

Their honor to be a soldier, a navy man as they believe it, is worth taking on the beating and torture with a steadfast mentality and not to give in.

This event goes deeper if one knows the family history of the Fuhri forefathers. They never learned to bow down to the oppressor out of principle.

Hans Fuhri was well known in Soerabaja, in Modderlust, and the Simpang Club where he was a regular. He was the son of well-known Johan Fuhri, head engineer with a large irrigation company and his mother was the sister of the governor of Soerabaja that time, Mister Halkema. One generation skipped the tradition and did not become officers of the navy, but the sons of that generation entered the service like their forefathers.

Hans Fuhri paid with his life but kept the tradition alive. His brothers served in the navy since 1860 when the first Fuhri settled in Soerabaja as a frigate lieutenant. Little Hans Fuhri grew up in Batavia and as a part of the seal they honor, *the Royal Dutch Marine Corps!"*

West Irian Dispute
Concerning Netherlands New Guinea

33

The West New Guinea dispute (1950–1962), also known as the *West Irian dispute*, was a diplomatic and political conflict between the Netherlands and Indonesia over the territory of Netherlands New Guinea.

While the Netherlands had ceded sovereignty to Indonesia on 27 December 1949 following a struggle for independence, the Indonesian government had always claimed the Dutch-controlled half of New Guinea on the basis that it had belonged to the Dutch East Indies and that the new Republic of Indonesia was the legitimate successor to the former Dutch colony.

In 1950, the Indonesian President Sukarno accused the Dutch of reneging on their promises to negotiate the handover of the territory. On 17 August 1950, Sukarno dissolved the United States of Indonesia (RIS) and proclaimed the United Republic of Indonesia. The Indonesian Republic saw itself as the successor to the Netherlands East Indies

The Dutch argued that the territory did not belong to Indonesia because the Melanesian Papuans were ethnically and geographically different from Indonesians, had always been administrated separately, did not participate in the Indonesian Revolution, and did not want to be under Indonesian control.

According to the political scientist Arend Lijphart, other underlying Dutch motives included West New Guinea's lucrative economic resources, its strategic importance as a Dutch naval base, and its potential role for housing the Netherlands' surplus population (including Eurasians who had become displaced by the Indonesian Revolution). The Dutch also wanted to maintain a regional presence and to secure their economic interests in Indonesia.

Meanwhile, the Indonesians regarded *West New Guinea* as an intrinsic part of Indonesia on the basis that Indonesia was the successor to the Netherland's East Indies government. These sentiments were reflected in the popular Indonesian revolutionary slogan: *Indonesia Free from Sabang to Merauke.*

Indonesian sentiments were also inflamed by the fact that several Indonesian political prisoners had been interned at a remote prison camp north of Merauke (called Boven-Digoel) prior to World War Two. Sukarno also contended that the continuing Dutch presence in West New Guinea was an obstacle to the process of nation-building in Indonesia, and that it would encourage secessionist movements.

During the first phase of the dispute (1950–1954), Indonesia pursued bilateral negotiations with the Netherlands. During the second phase (1954–1958), Indonesia attempted to raise support for its territorial claims in the United Nations General Assembly. During the third phase (1960–1962), Indonesia pursued a policy of confrontation against the Netherlands which combined diplomatic, political, and economic pressure with limited military force. The final stage of the confrontation with Indonesia involved a planned military invasion of the territory.

The Indonesians secured military weapons and political and military support from the Soviet Union which induced the United States to intervene in the conflict as a third-party mediator between Indonesia and the Netherlands.

Following the New York Agreement on 15 August 1962, the Netherlands, under U.S. pressure, handed West New Guinea over to a United Nations Temporary Executive Authority, which subsequently handed the territory over to Indonesia on 1 May 1963. Following a controversial plebiscite in 1969 where West New Guinea was formally integrated into Indonesia.

Between 1950 and 1953, the Netherlands and Indonesia tried to resolve the dispute through bilateral negotiations. These negotiations were unsuccessful and led the two governments to harden their positions.

On 15 February 1952, the Dutch Parliament voted to incorporate New Guinea into the realm of the Netherlands. After that, the Netherlands refused further discussion on the question of sovereignty and considered the issue to be closed. In response, President Sukarno adopted a more forceful stance towards the Dutch. Initially, he unsuccessfully tried to force the Indonesian government to abrogate the *Round Table agreements* and to adopt economic sanctions but was rebuffed by the Indonesian Natsir Cabinet.

Undeterred by this setback, Sukarno made recovering West Irian an important priority of his presidency and sought to harness popular support from the Indonesian public for this goal through many of his speeches between 1951 and 1952.

By 1953, the dispute had become the central issue in Indonesian domestic politics. All political parties across the Indonesian political spectrum, particularly the Indonesian Communist Party (PKI), supported Sukarno's efforts to integrate West Irian into the Indonesian Republic.

According to historians, Audrey and George McTurnan Kahin, the PK's pro-integration stance helped the party rebuild its political base and further its credentials as a nationalist Communist Party that supported Sukarno.

At the urging of President Sukarno, Prime Minister Ali Sastroamidjojo began authorizing limited incursions into West New Guinea in 1952. These early incursions were militarily unsuccessful, and Indonesia did not launch further military operations until 1960.

The first incursions were amateurish. The first infiltration of Gag Island in 1952 led to the arrest of the infiltrators within days. A second infiltration attempt one year later in 1953, this time directed at Kaimana, was promptly contained and the infiltrators arrested.

A third infiltration attempt in 1954 was a more serious affair. A well-armed party of forty-two infiltrators were able to abduct the Dutch police officer, Sergeant van Krieken, and brought him to Indonesian territory. The infiltration force was engaged by Dutch marines, resulting in eleven Indonesian casualties and the capture of the remaining Indonesian forces.

Due to the failure of these armed incursions, the Indonesian government reluctantly accepted that it could not mount a credible military challenge against the Dutch in West New Guinea. It was not until 1960 that Indonesia would again test the Dutch military position in West New Guinea.

Following the defeat of the third Afro-Asian resolution in November 1957, the Indonesian government embarked on a national campaign targeting Dutch interests in Indonesia. This led to the withdrawal of the Dutch flag carrier KLM's landing rights, mass demonstrations, and the seizure of the Dutch shipping line Koninklijke Paketvaart-Maatschappij (KPM), Dutch-owned banks, and estates.

By January 1958, ten thousand Dutch nationals had left Indonesia, many returning to the Netherlands. This spontaneous emmigration had adverse repercussions on the Indonesian economy, disrupting communications and affecting the production of exports.

President Sukarno also abandoned efforts to raise the dispute at the 1958 United Nations General Assembly, claiming that reason and persuasion had failed. Following a sustained period of harassment against Dutch diplomatic representatives in Jakarta, the Indonesian government formally severed relations with the Netherlands in August 1960.

In response to Indonesian aggression, the Netherlands government stepped up its efforts to prepare the Papuan people for self-determination in 1959. These efforts culminated in the establishment of a hospital in Hollandia (modern–day Jayapura), a shipyard in Manokwari, agricultural research sites, plantations, and a military force known as the Papuan Volunteer Corps.

By 1960, a legislative New Guinea Council had been established with a mixture of legislative, advisory, and policy functions. Half of its members were to be elected, and elections were held the following year.

Most importantly, the Dutch sought to create a sense of West Papuan national identity, and these efforts led to the creation of a national flag (*the Morning Star*), a national anthem, and a coat of arms. The Dutch had planned to transfer independence to West New Guinea in 1970.

By 1960, other countries in the Asia-Pacific region had taken notice of the West Irian dispute and began proposing initiatives to end the dispute. During a visit to the Netherlands, the New Zealand Prime Minister Walter Nash suggested the idea of a united New Guinea state, consisting of both Dutch and Australian territories. This idea received little support from both Indonesia and other Western governments.

Later that year, the Malayan Prime Minister Tunku Abdul Rahman proposed a three-step initiative which involved West New Guinea coming under United Nations trusteeship. The joint administrators would be the three non-aligned nations of Ceylon, India, and Malaya which supported Indonesia's position on West Irian.

This solution involved the two belligerents, Indonesia, and the Netherlands, re-establishing bilateral relations and the return of Dutch assets and investments to their owners. However, this initiative was scuttled in April 1961 due to opposition from the Indonesian Foreign Minister Subandrio who publicly attacked Tunku's proposal.

By 1961, the Netherlands government was struggling to find adequate international support for its policy to prepare West New Guinea for independent status under Dutch guidance. While the Netherlands' traditional Western allies (the United States, Great Britain, Australia, and New Zealand) were sympathetic to Dutch policy, they were unwilling to provide any military support in the event of a conflict with Indonesia.

On 26 September 1961, the Dutch Foreign Minister Joseph Luns offered to hand over West New Guinea to a United Nations trusteeship. This proposal was firmly rejected by his Indonesian counterpart, Subandrio, who likened the West New Guinea dispute to Katanga's attempted secession from the Republic of Congo during the *Congo Crisis*.

By October 1961, Britain was open to transferring West New Guinea to Indonesia while the U.S. floated the idea of a jointly administered trusteeship over the territory.

On 23 November 1961, the Indian delegation at the United Nations presented a draft resolution calling for the resumption of Dutch–Indonesian talks on terms which favored Indonesia.

On 25 November 1961, several Francophone-African countries tabled a rival resolution which favored an independent West New Guinea. Indonesia favored the Indian resolution while the Netherlands, Britain, Australia, and New Zealand supported the Francophone-African resolution.

On 27 November 1961, both the Francophone-African (52-41-9) and Indian (41-40-21) resolutions were put to the vote and failed to gain a two–thirds majority at the United Nations General Assembly. The failure of this final round of diplomacy in the UN convinced Indonesia to prepare for a military invasion of West Irian.

As the dispute began to escalate, Sukarno developed closer relations with the Soviet Union which shared Indonesia's anti-colonial outlook.

In July 1959, the Indonesian government adopted a policy of Confrontation *(Konfrontasi)* against the Dutch. According to the Indonesian political scientist, J. Soedjati Djiwandono,

Indonesia's *Confrontation* policy involved the use of political, economic, and military force to induce an opponent to reach a diplomatic solution on Indonesian terms.

Later that year, the Soviet government decided to supply warships and other military hardware directly to the Indonesians. By 1965, the Indonesian navy had grown to 103 combat vessels and other auxiliaries (including a cruiser, twelve submarines, and sixteen destroyers and frigates). Due to Soviet military aid, the Indonesian navy became the second most potent force in East Asia after China. The Indonesian air force also benefited from an infusion of Soviet military hardware and training, developing long-range capability.

Bolstered by Soviet military weapons and equipment, Indonesia had begun to reconsider the viability of renewing military operations against Dutch forces in West New Guinea.

On 9 November 1960, Indonesia launched a seaborne incursion into the territory, but this operation proved to be a failure. Of the twenty-three infiltrators, seven were killed, and the remaining sixteen were captured within four months.

On 14 September 1961, a new attempt was launched, but once again the infiltration party was promptly intercepted and defeated by Dutch forces.

Following the failure of diplomacy in the United Nations and persistant Dutch efforts to prepare the West Papuans for self-rule, Indonesia's *Confrontation* against the Dutch in West New Guinea reached a new crescendo.

On 19 December 1961, President Sukarno gave orders to the Indonesian military to prepare for a full-scale military invasion of the territory (codenamed *Operation Trikora)*. He also ordered the creation of a special People's Triple Command or Tri Komando Rakyat *(Trikora)* with the objective of 'liberating' West New Guinea by 1 January 1963. Trikora's operational command was to be called the Mandala Command for the Liberation of West Irian *(Komando Mandala Pembebasan Irian Barat)* and was led by Major-General

Suharto, the future President of Indonesia.

In preparation for the planned invasion, the Mandala command began making land, air, and sea incursions into West Irian. General Suharto also planned to launch a full-scale amphibious operation invasion of West Irian known as *Operation Jayawijaya* (Operation Djajawidjaja).

In response to Indonesian aggression, the Netherlands increased its military presence and intelligence-gathering efforts in West New Guinea. Since 15 April 1954, the Royal Netherlands Navy had been responsible for the territorial defense of West New Guinea.

A signals intelligence agency known as *Marid 6 Netherlands New Guinea* (NNG) was established in April 1955 to provide the Netherlands New Guinea authorities with intelligence on Indonesian intentions towards West Irian. One of Marid 6 NNG's successes was providing early warning of Indonesian plans to seize all KPM ships and facilities in December 1957. This enabled the Dutch authorities to evacuate forty-five of these eighty-three ships.

Later, Marid 6 NNG helped Dutch naval units to recapture the KPM ships. In 1962, the Royal Netherlands navy deployed a sizeable naval task group including the aircraft carrier *HNLMS Karel Doorman* to West New Guinea.

On 15 January 1962, the Indonesian navy attempted to land a force of 150 marines near Vlakke Hoek on West Irian's south coast. The Indonesians had intended to raise the Indonesian flag on Dutch territory to weaken the Netherlands' position during the ongoing negotiations in New York. However, Marid 6 NNG managed to intercept Indonesian radio messages and learned about the Indonesian plans.

In response, the Dutch authorities deployed a Lockheed Neptune patrol aircraft and three destroyers to intercept the three Indonesian motor torpedo boats (The fourth boat had experienced engine trouble and did not participate.) During the ensuing *Vlakke Hoek incident*, one of the Indonesian torpedo boats was sunk, while the remaining two boats were forced to retreat.

The operation ended disastrously for Indonesia with many crew members and embarked marines being killed and fifty-five survivors taken prisoner. Among the casualties was Commodore Yos Sudarso, the deputy chief of staff of the Indonesian navy.

On 24 June 1962, four Indonesian Air Force C-130 Hercules jets dropped 213 paratroopers near Merauke. Throughout the year, a total of 1,200 Indonesian paratroopers and 340 naval infiltrators landed in West New Guinea.

By mid-1962, the Indonesian military had begun preparations to launch *Operation Jayawijaya* around August 1962. This operation was to be carried out in four phases and would have involved joint air and naval strikes against Dutch airfields, paratroop, and amphibious landings at Biak and Sentani, and a ground assault on the territory's capital, Hollandia. Unknown to the Indonesians, Marid 6 NNG had intercepted Indonesian transmissions and obtained intelligence on Indonesian battle plans.

However, a ceasefire agreement known as the *New York Agreement*, which facilitated the transfer of West New Guinea to Indonesia control by 1963, was signed by the Dutch and Indonesians on 15 August 1962. As a result, the Trikora Command cancelled *Operation Jayawijaya* on 17 August 1962.

By 1961, the United States government had become concerned about the Indonesian military's purchase of Soviet weapons and equipment for a planned invasion of West New Guinea.

The Kennedy Administration feared an Indonesian drift towards communism and wanted to court Sukarno away from the Soviet Bloc and communist China. The U.S. government also wanted to repair relations with Jakarta which had deteriorated due to the Eisenhower administration's covert support for the Permesta/PRRI regional uprisings in Sumatra and

Sulawesi. These factors convinced the Kennedy administration to intervene diplomatically to bring about a peaceful solution to the dispute which favored Indonesia.

Throughout 1962, the U.S. diplomat Ellsworth Bunker facilitated top-secret high-level negotiations between the Dutch and Indonesian governments on August 15, 1962. These protracted talks produced a peace settlement known as the *New York Agreement.*

As a face-saving measure, the Dutch were to hand over West New Guinea to a provisional United Nations Temporary Executive Authority (UNTEA) on 1 October 1962 which then ceded the territory to Indonesia on 1 May 1963. This formally ended the dispute.

As part of the *New York Agreement*, it was stipulated that a plebiscite would be held in 1969 to determine whether the Papuans would choose to remain in Indonesia or seek self-determination.

While U.S. diplomacy averted the escalation of the dispute into a full–blown war between Indonesia and the Netherlands, Washington failed to win over President Sukarno. Buoyed by his success in the West New Guinea campaign, Sukarno turned his attention to the former British colony of Malaysia. This resulted in the *Indonesian-Malaysian Confrontation* which induced deterioration of Indonesia's relations with the West.

Ultimately President Sukarno was overthrown during the Indonesian coup attempt of 1965 and was subsequently replaced by the pro-Western, Suharto. In addition, the U.S. mining company, Freeport-McMoRan, was interested in exploiting Western New Guinea's copper and gold deposits.

Following the *Act of Free Choice plebiscite* in 1969, Western New Guinea was formally integrated into the Republic of Indonesia.

Instead of a referendum of the 816,000 Papuans, only 1,022 Papuan tribal representatives were eligible to vote, and they were coerced into voting in favor of integration.

While several international observers, including journalists and diplomats, criticized the referendum as being 'rigged,' the U.S. and Australia supported Indonesia's efforts to secure acceptance by the United Nations of the pro-integration vote. That same year, eighty-four member states voted in favor of the United Nations to accept the result, with thirty others abstaining.

Due to the Netherlands' efforts to promote a West Papuan national identity, a significant number of Papuans refused to accept the territory's integration into Indonesia. They formed the separatist *Organisasi Papua Merdeka* (Free Papua Movement) and have waged an insurgency against the Indonesian authorities, which continues to this day.

• *The 1st of December marks West Papua's original Independence Day when the Morning Star flag was first raised in 1961. The flag is recognised as the national flag of West Papua and continues to be the defining symbol for a 'Free West Papua.' It is illegal to raise this flag in West Papua. The picture was taken a couple of years ago in Melbourne, Australia.*
(source: Free West Papua Campaign, Australia branch)

• *Picture of family Beynon in 1947: L-R top: Hendrika and her husband Wim, in her arms Sylvie, Margaretha, Suze, Nancy, Jeanne. L-R bottom: Olga, Guustaaf, Mama, Carla, Papa, Eddy. The oldest son Johan is missing.*

Beynon Family Back in Manokwari:
1948 - 1962

34

When the war was finally over and the Beynon family, with the help of the SIKNG, was able to return to their home on the Fanindiweg in Manokwari. Life was getting back to normal. The Beynon sisters, Suze, Nancy, and Olga remember the years leading up to the departure of the family to the Netherlands.

Suze: "Our father worked in Manokwari as an electrician. With *pasar malams* (celebrational markets) and other parties where my mother was always asked to prepare food. After the 1950s, more Indos came to New Guinea. The Papuan women who were all bare-chested carried their pigs in front and babies on their backs. Some came down from the mountain to sell fruit or traded for tobacco or sarongs.

Our father had a large mustache, and all the Papuan people knew him very well. They always said, *Itu papa Beynon sama kumis besar* ('There goes Papa Beynon with his large mustache').

The Beynon girls were well-respected by the Papuans and many times they were called to the front at celebrations, and the leader of the Papuans said, 'These are the Beynon girls, and they are always to be respected.'

Together with our older brother, Eddy, my father build his house. We had a *goedang* (storage room), bathroom, toilet, kitchen, and bedrooms. In the beginning, all the girls' beds were side-by-side. Only my father and mother had a separate bedroom. We built a guesthouse behind our home. We had to bring fresh water down from the mountain.

The girls had to do all the heavy jobs in the household. The boys were working regular jobs and one was with the Dutch marines.

We designed a water pipe with pieces of bamboo whereby the water would be transported from the mountains to our home. In the bathroom, we had a big water barrel that we used to wash ourselves.

We had a big garden including a soursop tree and a large lemon tree. We used the lemons for cooking. Mother loved flowers, and we had many pots with a variety of flowers and plants. We also had a *djati* tree (ironwood). We used the young branches to color our lips and colored our nails red. My father did not like that, but we were never allowed to go out without an escort from one of our brothers.

We had to use a *patjol* (cultivator) to plant vegetables and take care of the fruit trees. We also had a banana tree. We had goats, ducks, and chickens.

My brother would bring the goats to the forest so they could eat there. Sometimes he asked us, 'Shall we ride on top of them?' We did, but he fell off and bounced on his head. We also had a lot of snakes in the garden, and I must have killed many of them. We had to make mountains of dirt to plant the peanuts.

One day mother was bitten by a scorpion. I ran over to my father as he always had 'stones' (powerful stones which had healing powers) that would take care of snake or scorpion bites. 'Dad,' I said, 'I need your stone.' He gave it to me and I ran home again.

In the back of the house right by the end of our property was a small *kali* (river). We always went there to wash clothes or get water for the garden. Father put a small dam in the *kali* so the water would stay in there for the clothes to clean. We always wore sarongs. And sometimes after the wash was done, we took baths in the *kali*. Some boys knew that and tried to have a peek. But there was nothing to see…

From my sixteenth year on, I had to help with the cooking. Right after the war I had to cook for sixteen people. My mother was pregnant with our last sister *Loes* (Louise). Together with another sister, I was always helping Mom in the kitchen. We had no servants in the house and knowing my father, he said, 'We have enough girls in the house who can help.' We did have a Papuan boy who helped bring vegetables to sell in the city. As we did not have any bikes, we had to walk to school every day.

We had Dutch teachers, and we always spoke Dutch. We knew everything about Holland and the Royal Family. In our school were people from the Moluccans and Eurasians but no Papuans. There was a separate school where teaching was in *Bahasa* and there was also a school for Papuans. We had a catholic and a protestant church. We always had to be on guard as we lived with many men in our area.

One day a young Papuan boy wanted to attack me. My father, who taught self-defence to many boys and girls in Manokwari always told me: 'Look them straight in the eyes, it will make them nervous and they won't know what to do.' That is what I did and when he was not ready, I kicked him right in the groin. When I met my husband, he was prepared for a meeting with my father. 'I will go to him and ask for your hand in marriage.' He said later to me, 'your father just looked at me standing there and it looked like he was ready to punch me.' I had to laugh as I knew how my father was. A short time after we got married."

Bastiaan Opdenkelder recalls his father-in-law: "Paatje Beynon, was a well-known *Pencak Silat* (Chinese Indonesian fighting art) teacher in Manokwari. He built a special training facility beside his home and young students would come weekly to learn more about the martial arts which included techniques for armed and unarmed combat. At the age of seventy-two, with his powerful legs, he demonstrated the kicking techniques to many younger students who were not able to imitate him. The relatively restricted nature of the school has long contributed to the fact that little was known about his

• Guru Paatje Beynon left. Right the teachers of Silat Barongsai in Etten-Leur (2000). We recognize Theo v.d. Hijde, Jeffrey and Leonard van Schukkmann and Bastiaan Opdenkelder (middle)

style. Former pupils who were taught by Paatje Beynon for shorter or longer periods of time were, for example, the founder of *Pukulan Rowo Belong;* also Don Kessing of *P.S. Manyang* had taken lessons from Paatje Beijnon in the past. Paatje Beijnon was a *guru* (teacher) of the old traditions. His motto was *Good wine does not need a wreath.* The current school *Silat Barongsai* was founded in 1970. The two founders, the cousins Leonard van Schukkmann and Roy van der Hijde († August 1995) both of whom first practiced Karate Kyokushinkai, which Leonard taught for several years, started the lessons under the guidance of their grandfather Paatje Beynon. Paatje Beynon emigrated to Canada in the late 1970s and died in 1984."

Paatje Beynon was honored in 1999 with a *Grandmaster Certificate of Pukulan/Silat* with the following text: "Chinese Grandmaster Peh Tangkiam was the source of the Pukulan/Silat *asli* (Kung Fu: The Tong Kune) in Indonesia. Under very strict rules Bapak Djimoen was taught this secret fighting art in the 1900s. Paatje Beynon was his only student. After learning several other fighting styles, he was given this *asli-spel* as he was very committed to learn. Paatje Beynon introduced Pukulan/Silat *asli* in Breda (the Netherlands). He gave his pukulan/asli *spel* in 1969 to his two grandchildren Leo van Schukkmann and Roy v.d. Hijde."

292

35

More than 25,000 Dutch soldiers from the army, navy, and air force served in New Guinea. A book published by the army museum in Delft contains the little-known story of the Papuans who served in the colonial army. They felt cheated by the Dutch Government in the end.

Every time Dutch soldiers arrived in Hollandia, Papuan boys stood along the quayside curiously looking at those pale men. "Baroes; new!" they shouted with a laugh.

Demian Prawar was one of those boys. "I thought at the time, there are enough of us to defend our country, right? With Dutch officers, can't we deliver the troops ourselves, instead of letting them come from the Netherlands?" Demian Prawar joined the Papua Volunteer Korps (PVK) in 1960. The only way to do that was to lie about his age. He was only sixteen years old but successfully posed as a twenty-year-old.

Prawar wanted to join the corps so badly as he considered it the forerunner of our own national army. He believed New Guinea would become independent. "The flag had already been chosen; we already had an anthem, so we would be ready when independence came." The Papua Volunteer Corps served as a reinforcement of the Dutch army and marine corps. The Dutch really needed that help.

In the late 1950s, infiltrators from Indonesia made Dutch

New Guinea unsafe. Indonesia claimed New Guinea, and now the Dutch colony had to become part of the young Republic of Indonesia. The Papuans helped to defend Dutch New Guinea. After all, they knew their *own* country, even if it was a colony, better than the boys from the Netherlands. "They saw a lizard instead of a crocodile," Prawar laughed. The Netherlands had previously deployed Papuan soldiers to secure Dutch New Guinea. The Papuan battalion served between 1945 and 1955. At its peak, the battalion had about one thousand soldiers.

Pieter de Kock, an Ambonese soldier, was a petty officer in that battalion. He explained that he was asked by Colonel Spoor, later the commander of the Dutch army in Indonesia, for the post. "I was immediately promoted to sergeant-major. Spoor liked me because of my guerrilla experience against the Japanese."

De Kock had been part of the KNIL unit that had been waging guerrilla warfare against the Japanese troops in the New Guinea jungle for thirty months during World War Two. "In the Netherlands, the army had capitulated after five days, but we have kept the Dutch flag afloat throughout the war in Southeast Asia." The guerrilla battles were an unimaginably difficult period that left deep memories for De Kock. Of the sixty-six men with whom we had moved into the interior of the Bird's Head, fourteen were left after the war. "Psychologically, you were a wreck." After the war, Pieter de Kock joined the Papuan battalion led by Major J.P.K. van Eechoud.

The Ambonese De Kock got along well with the Papuans. He had worked in the Vogelkop area before the war. "I could understand the Papuans better than other petty officers because I knew their culture and customs. The framework consisted of an Ambonese, a Javanese, and a Sumatran, but that did not cause any problems with the Papuans. We lived in suspense and did not have time to think about things like that."

At the coastal town of Sarmi, De Kock was given command of 150 men after the Japanese capitulation. There were still Japanese soldiers across the Tor River. The U.S. military had moved on. It was a bizarre situation: in front of the 150-strong Papuan unit, there were about ten thousand Japanese soldiers. "There were no confrontations, but if the Japanese had known there were so few of us, it would have ended differently. We were near a nervous breakdown." The Japanese did not surrender until October 1945, two months after the official capitulation.

The Japanese did not want to negotiate with De Kock and his fellow American commander. "We were not in a war with the black people," was the incredulous reaction of the Japanese side when seeing De Kock and his American colleague. The white major, Van Eechoud, had to be called in to complete the surrender. After the war, the Papuan battalion was led by the KNIL. That did not work out as well with the Papuans.

De Kock: "The attitude of these KNILers was too militaristic; they had a different mentality. During the war, many Papuan boys were used to the guerrilla style of warfare: sneaking, waiting, shooting, and then retreating. You should not be exercising with that." De Kock led the reconstruction of Sarmi with the help of Japanese soldiers and equipment.

He joined the interior administration in Sorong in 1946, again at the request of Van Eechoud who had now become a resident of New Guinea. "The management work appealed to me more than the military company." The Papuan battalion remained (at last, no bigger than a company) until 1954.

Demian Prawar knew of the battalion through his Uncle Matthew with whom he once stayed in Biak. "After 1954, Uncle stopped us from getting sweets," Demian recalls.

Uncle Matthew had little respect for the Dutch because they had disbanded the battalion without a proper arrangement for the Papuan military. Uncle said, "You do not have

295

to join the Dutch army. That's where you're going to get screwed." Demian changed his mind in 1960 when he saw recruitment posters all over the colony to "go for your country and people in the army." New Guinea seemed to be heading for a certain autonomy.

Queen Juliana promised the Papuan people self-determination in her speech in 1960. The elected New Guinea Council would make that happen. In this time of euphoria, Prawar enlisted in the Papua Volunteer Korps.

Thousands of men queued at the police station in Hollandia; only one hundred and twenty were hired. "The Old Guard were humiliated: they were simply sent away. In their eyes, we were just children."

It was not until the end of 1960 that Prawar received a call to go to Manokwari where the Papuans of Dutch marines ("Hard, but also sweet and correct") learned to shoot and exercise. The training had little to do with jungle fighting, as did the equipment with a jungle rifle and Uzi pistol machine gun. "In fact, we were just forest runners." But the Papuans knew the area like their back pockets and were therefore called to aid in tracking down Indonesian infiltrators.

A Papuan Volunteer Korps unit was dropped on the island of Gag (disputed by Indonesia). "We saw it as an illegal action by Indonesian President Sukarno. According to Papuan law, that is where the death penalty is implemented. They waited for their supplies to run out, and they showed up."

"We had to officially ask permission to shoot. What kind of army is that? You must be able to decide for yourself. We just shoot. It was him or me. Shoot first, then talk."

Prawar did not regret his performance for a second. "I was happy to defend my country. And the villagers on Gag were also happy. They said: "Finally, here come our boys who speak the language."

Six Papuan soldiers were killed in the fighting and an unknown number were wounded.

The Dutch Government never gave any appreciation for their efforts. "Now I understand clearly that my Uncle Matthew was right. I should never have reported to the Dutch army."

Prawar says, "It's too late for recognition now. I can never accept that." The Papua Volunteer Korps found an inglorious end in 1962.

The Netherlands under great international pressure transferred the governance of New Guinea to Indonesia. The Papuan soldiers were left unemployed. Some may or may not have forcibly transferred to the Indonesian army. Others, such as Demian Prawar, fled to the Netherlands in a struggle to build a life there. The frustration with the fate of their homeland and family members in present-day Papua is undiminished.

Prawar cites Juliana's Throne Speech from 1960: "The Netherlands has not kept its promise of self-determination. The New Guinea Council was kept out of everything. We've been screwed."

Queen Juliana:
September 20, 1960
"In the coming year, the Netherlands New Guinea will enter an important new phase in its development towards self-determination. For as soon as the New Guinea Council, which will consist in the main of representatives of the native population, has been set up, administration and legalization will be possible only with its co-operation."

• *Queen Juliana meeting with a delegation of Papuan leaders*

• *Papua Volunteer Corps*

The Morning Star:
History of the Liberation Flag for the Papuan Population

36

The supplemental *Morning Star* flag of Netherlands New Guinea differed from the flag of the Netherlands.

It was first raised on 1 December 1961 prior to the territory coming under administration of the United Nations Temporary Executive Authority (UNTEA) which started on 1 October 1962.

The flag is used by the Free Papua Organization and other independence supporters. Under Papua's *Special Autonomy Law*, ratified in 2002, the flag may be raised in Western New Guinea (West Papua) region so long as the flag of Indonesia is also raised higher than the *Morning Star* flag. The flag consists of a red vertical band along the hoist side, with a white five-pointed star in the center of the band, and thirteen horizontal stripes, alternating blue and white. The seven blue stripes represent seven customary territories in the region.

After territorial elections in February 1961, the New Guinea Council, a representative body consisting of twenty-eight members, was sworn into office by Governor Dr. P.J. Platteel on 1 April 1961. The Council's inauguration on 5 April 1961 was attended by representatives of Australia, France, the Netherlands, New Zealand, the United Kingdom, and other Pacific Forum nations (with exception of the United States).

The Council appointed a national committee to draft a

manifesto expressing the desire for independence and to design a flag and anthem commensurate with this desire. The design of the flag is credited to Nicolaas Jouwe.

The full New Guinea Council endorsed these actions on 30 October 1961, and the first *Morning Star* flag was presented to Governor Platteel on 31 October 1961. The Dutch authorities recognized it only as a *landsvlag* (territorial flag), not a national one.

An inauguration ceremony was held on 1 December 1961 with the flag officially raised for the first time outside the Council's building in the presence of the Governor together with the Dutch flag.

On 1 July 1971 at *Markas Victoria* (Victoria Headquarters) in West Papua, Brigadier General Seth Jafeth Rumkorem, leader of the militant independence group *Free Papua Movement,* proclaimed unilaterally Papua Barat or West Papua as an independent democratic republic. The *Morning Star* flag was declared as a national flag.

Presently, now the *Morning Star* is flown by Papua independence movements and supporters across the world. Special ceremonies take place on 1 December of each year to commemorate the first flag raising in 1961. The flying of the Morning Star is seen by Indonesian authorities as advocating independence and challenging Indonesian sovereignty.

Two Papuan men, Filep Karma and Yusak Pakage, were sentenced to fifteen and ten years respectively for raising the flag in Jayapura in 2004. Pakage was released in 2010 after serving five years of his term. Karma was released in November 2015 and claims alleged abuse at the hands of prison authorities during his incarceration.

Amnesty International considered both men prisoners of conscience and named Karma a 2011 *priority case*. Thirty-four people were arrested during celebrations of Papuan flag day across Papua and West Papua provinces in 2019. Other sources say more than one hundred.

Introducing: **"The Birds of Paradise"**

37

The birds of paradise are song-birds of the family Paradisaeidae. They live in eastern Indonesia, Maluku, New Guinea, Torres Strait Islands, and eastern Australia.

They live in tropical rainforests, swamps and moss forests. They build their nests (typically placed in tree forks) from soft materials, such as leaves, ferns, and pieces of vine. These birds are best known for their remarkable plumage and the talented behavior of the males. They are an extreme example of how sexual selection works.

Females choose males that they instinctively see are fine specimens of their species. The colors of the plumage, the construction of the nest, the song and the mating dance all play a part.

In some species, the pairing is monogamous, and in others the males are polygamous. If they are monogamous, the males look much like the females. If they are polygamous, the males are very much flashier than the females. In both cases, it is the female who makes the choice of partner.

Hunting for plumes and habitat destruction have reduced some species to endangered status. Habitat destruction due to deforestation is now the main threat. In most species, the diet is mostly fruit, but riflebirds and sicklebills also prefer insects and other arthropods.

Louse and I were in New Guinea in 1999, but we were not able to see these birds of paradise. I did find this wonderful article written by *Een Irawan Putra* and wanted to share it:

ARFAK MOUNTAINS, Indonesia. Seblon Mandacan scampers with ease up the slippery footpath through the forest in the Arfak Mountains. I follow slowly. It is about 4:00 a.m. and the sky's still dark. Wearing headlamps, we cut through the forest mist here at an elevation of about 1,900 meters (6,200 feet) above sea level.

I find it a struggle to get up this early and steel myself for the walk. The wind knifes through the multiple layers of clothing I have put on, and the cold cuts to the bone.

It rained the previous night, making the trek that much more taxing. I must grasp tree trunks and branches to avoid slipping, and step gingerly to make sure the ground is solid. But that is the price I am willing to pay to reach the "playground" of the greater superb bird-of-paradise, known locally as *nyet*, a bird species endemic to the Papua region of Indonesia.

"They start to flock to the playground between 6:00 and 7:00 a.m.," says Seblon, pointing to a moss-covered fallen tree that the birds are said to frequent.

"Let's hide under this blind so the birds won't be able to see us," he says. We wait in silence beneath the tarpaulin for about an hour and a half, not moving even to smack the mosquitoes landing on us, for fear of making noise. I have heard that this bird species is very sensitive to noise and difficult to encounter.

And then, faintly, there is a chirp from afar.

Seblon points to the fallen log again, where a superb male

bird-of-paradise has now perched. It looks around for a bit, appearing to be assessing any threats, before calling out to its female partner.

When the latter arrives, a spectacular show immediately gets underway. The male flares out the patch of shiny blue feathers on its neck, which glow against the legendarily void-like black of the rest of its body, and dances around the female. With every passing minute it puts on a different act, none of which I will ever forget.

When the dance is over and the birds are gone, I cannot stop thanking Seblon profusely for the experience that I have now captured on camera.

Seblon is one of many people in Minggrei village, in the mountainous district of Manokwari, who work as guides on bird-watching tours. The birds-of-paradise are the village's main draw, and tourists keep coming to see these spectacular species.

One of my fellow travelers during my trip is Tim Laman, a world-renowned wildlife photographer. He is here with Ed Scholes, an avian researcher from the Cornell Lab of Ornithology; it is their second visit to Minggrei. They stayed for three weeks last time and are likely to do so again this time.

"I started working as a wildlife photographer more than twenty-five years ago," Laman says. "I came to Papua for the first time in 2004." For him, what makes the birds in the Papuan forests particularly special is that they occur nowhere else on Earth. The birds-of-paradise and the bowerbirds are some of the most well-known of these endemic species.

On this trip, Laman wants to take pictures of the Vogelkop superb bird-of-paradise, a bird once thought to be a subspecies of *L. superba* but described as a distinct species in its own right only last year.

He is also on the lookout for the western *parotia* (Parotia sefilata), the magnificent bird-of-paradise (Diphyllodes magnificus), the *black sicklebill* (Epimachus fastosus), and the *Arfak astrapia* (Astrapia nigra).

"Plenty of species to photograph here," he says.

The remoteness of this region and the lushness of the primeval forest have allowed the birds-of-paradise and other species to thrive here even as wildlife in other parts of Indonesia face the growing threat of extinction from habitat loss.

Keeping the birds' habitat intact is what will keep the tourists coming to Minggrei, a concept that village head Aren Mandacan fully understands. He has ordered the villagers to protect the birds and stop cutting down trees in the forest.

The bird-watching tours have had a massive impact on the village's welfare. "We haven't had to buy any rice in the past three years," Aren says. "We get to eat for free together with the guests. Plus, we get to make some money."

It was Aren who first pitched the village's bird-watching potential to Shita Prativi, the founder of Macnificus Expedition and the *Papua Bird Club*. Shita, in turn, had learned how to guide bird-watching tours from her husband, a tour guide in Papua since 1992.

Birdwatching in Arfak really took off in 2007, Aren says, thanks to positive publicity and travel accounts written by visitors enchanted by the diversity of the local bird life.

"In Minggrei, the [natural] potential is incredible; the range of birds-of-paradise species is quite complete here," Shita says. "There are also many other bird species. A single tour can involve twenty-five locals, so the people really benefit from protecting the birds."

She says a typical five-day trip for eight visitors can generate up to thirty million rupiah ($2,100 US) in revenue for the people of Minggrei village — a small fortune in a region where the minimum wage is only about $200 a month. The cost covers accommodation, meals, guides, porters, transportation, and the use of the bird blind. Shita says tours are

• *Papuans love to use the feathers of the Birds of Paradise.*

fully booked until 2021 (The COVID outbreak must have devastated their income.)

Like Aren, she says that protecting the birds will benefit the people of Minggrei in the long-term in a way that will not require destroying the rich natural resources of the region.

Other regions in Indonesia have adopted ecotourism to boost their economic growth, in most cases, almost as an afterthought. In the Arfak Mountains of West Papua, though, local leaders have mandated that substainability and conservation be prioritized as part of the region's economic development.

In October 2018, the provinces of West Papua and Papua, which together compose Indonesia's half of the island of New Guinea, signed the *Manokwari Declaration*. The agreement changes two regions' development framework from *conservation* to *sustainable development* (a subtle shift that de-emphasizes the central government's control over local land issues). By making this alteration, they hope to place responsibility for substainability more firmly in the hands of local governments, who are more in tune with the rights of their indigenous constituents.

Scholes, the bird expert, says he is impressed with the people of Minggrei village for their hard work in protecting the forests and natural resources.

"You don't have to be a bird expert to come here and watch the birds-of-paradise. Anyone can come and see them," he says, adding that he hopes future generations of visitors will still be able to see the birds and hear their calls ringing out through the forests in Minggrei.

• *Celebrational flag raising in Manokwari, Dutch New Guinea*

38
INDOS IN THE UNITED STATES

Many stories of the Indos who left Indonesia shortly after Independence were lost with the passage of time. Legend has it that they went to Holland, but some found a second home, or perhaps a third, in the United States.

Michael Hillis, a part-time teacher and history buff who resides in Portland, Oregon, estimates there are around 200,000 Dutch-Indonesians, or Indos as they call themselves, living in the United States.

"Not many people in America know about them," Hillis told *The Sunday Post* during a research trip to Indonesia. "They left Indonesia and headed to The Netherlands shortly after Independence. But when they got there, they faced racial issues."

The Dutch-Indonesians repatriated to Holland between 1945 and the 1960s. But it seemed that Dutch society was not ready for an influx of postwar Eurasians hailing from the former Dutch East Indies colony.

Their ability to speak fluent Dutch raised questions from people who were not aware of their origins. Hillis said that the Dutch Indos simply answered that they had learned the language during the journey by ship.

"In my opinion, I think they probably realized that they had gone through terrible things," he said. "They lost their homes and their money in Indonesia. On the other hand, they had to cope with new issues, such as eating potatoes, instead of rice, and racial tension."

He said that after arriving in Holland, most Indos learned

martial arts to defend themselves, such was the extent of the attacks on them. Unable to bear the continuing discrimination, an estimated sixty thousand Indos immigrated to the United States in the 1960s.

"Once they arrived in the United States, they took any kind of job they could get and they worked really hard," Hillis said. "For them, the United States was a place where they could work and live in freedom. They did not have to worry about people trying to discriminate against them."

Nowadays, he said, the Indos in the United States are into their third generation. Los Angeles is home to the largest Indo community, with some 100,000 people. The first generation of Indos still speak Dutch, as it was the language they were born with, Hillis said, adding they also speak Indonesian because they spent a lot of time with their nannies, servants, and helpers.

"Many of the first generation came from wealthy families. They used to have several maids in their houses. When they reached the United States, they decided that they had to make it there, so they learned English," he said.

"These people would have loved to stay in Indonesia but they had no choice, they had to leave. Many of them still live in Holland but I believe there are many who left for the United States, Australia and Canada, or perhaps other countries." Members of the second generation speak English; the third generation don't speak Dutch and are unaware of their Dutch-Indonesian roots. The Indos quickly assimilated into their new country, marrying people outside the community. Most never returned to Indonesia.

Hillis first came across the issue of the Indos when he read Jan A. Krancer's *The Defining Years of the Dutch East Indies 1942-1949*. He contacted the writer, who introduced him to Bianca Dias-Halpert, an Indo residing in Seattle. Dias-Halpert invited Hillis to an Indo community gathering.

The Indo community often holds gatherings where they

cook Indonesian food and do line dancing to Indonesian music played on small guitars, which, Hillis said, sounded to his ears like Hawaiian music. They also publish a bulletin about their community activities, all written in Dutch. "When I first saw them, I was wondering who these people were," Hillis said with a smile. "They look like Hispanic people, speak Dutch, eat Indonesian food, and sing Hawaiian-like songs."

As the younger generation immerse themselves into America's melting pot multicultural society, the older Indos are concerned that the young ones will forget their roots. As Hillis learned more about this concern, he was inspired to make a film about the Indos. "I have a strong relationship with this movie, because I'm married to an Indonesian woman," Hillis said. "I want my daughters to understand the history of Indonesia during hard times."

He said that the movie would take audiences to the World War II base of American general Douglas MacArthur on Morotai Island, as well as to other places of interest. "Most Americans know little about Indonesia. We hope this movie can show them that Indonesia and America have a historical relationship," he said.

.

Ray van Broekhuizen: I hope this film will remind us not to hurt each other. Every time I read or hear about war, wherever and whenever it is, it always brings such a huge sadness in me. When I look back at the past, and when I look at what happens now, it's always the same: Many people are killed. Why can't we live in harmony, without hurting each other? Sometimes I believe nationality and race place us in different boxes. If my nationality is A and yours is B, then I'll do my best to bring all glories to my country, even if it will bring misery and suffering to country B. That still happens today. Let's live in peace!!! May peace be spread all over the world and to all people.

Calvin: I am that second-generation Indo. I will be seventy this year. Lived in Holland for four years. Saw my dad go through many racial situations with the Dutch, since he was pretty dark. We moved to Oregon City, Oregon when I was eleven, and there were a total of three Indo families who lived there at that time. I am still in contact with them today (fifty years later). The three were De Water, Rhemrev, and the other Bouwens. I believe they still live in Oregon, but my family moved to Southern California in 1992 since we love warm weather. My wife is American (Italian-French), and we have four boys. She can cook Indonesian food (thank God) and my kids eat that as well besides all kinds of other foods. They don't speak Dutch, but they know my mom as *Oma* and they do know their roots because I share them with them. I have three brothers and four sisters all over the United States. We recently went to Bali to visit, and it was awesome! Yes, I am all for keeping these Indo roots. My mom shared with me recently that they were the last true Indo generation who moved from Holland to America for a better life and I thank them for it. I love all you Indos out there. Be proud of who you are because we are a special people!

George K: I think it is not only Americans who need to learn about *Indische Nederlanders*, but also Indonesians. The fate related to them is simply unnoticed in the standard Indonesian history line (which is not surprising, regarding their small population which was not more than one percent from all Indonesian population at that time). However, some Indos contributed a lot in national building of Indonesia. They can start from this point.

Ronald van Hek: I agree with Michael Hillis, as to his comments and analysis of the plight of the Indos. In Holland, they could not expect any mercy. They were not welcome there; only their money was most welcome. I am glad that Mr. Hillis is making this movie, and I for sure, am looking forward to watching it. Thank you, Michael, for this great and wonderful initiative and plan. May God bless you always!

Roy van Broekhuizen: I have been interviewed by *Cogis* from the Netherlands and a book was printed, called *Verlaten Verleden* (Left The Past) which was written in Dutch. I came from Holland to America in 1957 and raised a family here.

Paolo Scalpini: I am very intrigued with your movie. I was born in Jakarta in 1948 and went to a private Dutch school. Both my parents were of mixed blood Dutch, Indonesian, Chinese, Okinawan, spoke both Dutch and Indonesian growing up, fled to Holland in 1957 in the middle of winter (November). Because of racial issues and discrimination, my parents opted to immigrate to the United States in 1961. My first time back was in 1976. When the tsunami hit Banda Aceh, Sumatra, Indonesia, I was asked by Saddleback Church (We are active members since 1997) to be a tsunami relief coordinator, bringing volunteer teams and distributing funds we collected on the first weekend of January 2005. My contract ended February 2006. My wife felt that we needed to stay so we started a small handbag factory/training center with twelve women. Today we are able to support more than three hundred tsunami survivors.

Helena van der Winden: I suppose I should call my son an Indo, having an Indonesian mother and a European father. Or does the term Indo as origin stop in 1945? Does it really matter so much? I suppose nationalism, racism, and later religion have led to the situation that people need to associate themselves with a certain ethnic/racial/religious identity. Then, if you fall somewhere in between, it can be hard for some people. I certainly would like to understand better under which conditions the Indos left Indonesia. We only get two patriotic versions of the history (Indonesian/Dutch). It would make the story more colorful to explore the perspectives of other identities. Regardless whether it is the case for the Indos or not, it seems that so many people have lost their original homes and countries. Some of their stories are well-known. Others are less-publicized. Some have started a military struggle against their (in)voluntary displacement (like some groups of Mollucans). Others have fought back in another way, working hard to make a living in their new home to become part of the society. The Indos deserve the credit for their positive struggle and contribution to society in spite of their loss.

Louis Vanderveen: For people who are interested in knowing more about Dutch-Indo heritage/community in Indonesia, I suggest you to visit places like Bandung, Bogor, Malang, and Batu. You'll be amazed that some of the third generation still speak Dutch fluently, while at the same time they are proud of the Indonesian culture.

Jane van Beers - Heim: For many in my first generation of Indos, we have been told the stories both good and bad about our history and the plight of the Indos. My mother lived during the occupation of Indonesia and saw and experienced many great horrors. My father was a guest of the Japaness army along with many other Dutch citizens recruited to fight the invading army. Though my parents came from vastly different sides of society, their paths would intersect during the happy time after the war. Unfortunately they, like thousands of other families, found themselves in the middle of a revolution that would end up putting them in a cold and less then welcoming society. The story of my family is only unique if you are not an Indo. For all of us growing up in America, we became Americans. Many have done well. I for one have never forgotten the stories both good and bad told to me about our journey.

Martin Westerlink: I am second-generation Indo...and am re-searching and writing our family roots and stories for the rest of my siblings, totalling six of us. I was born in 1953 in Surabaja. Three of us were born in Indonesia, two in Holland, and one in the United States. We came to Los Angeles in 1962...I'm proud to be an Indo!

Charles L. Pieters: Being a second-generation Indo and was born in Surabaja, in 1955, when I was still an infant of eight months, my parents also immigrated to Holland. They had two boys then, myself and my older brother. I believe that was in 1956. When we lived in Holland, there were four other siblings born. It was in 1962 that they decided to immigrate to the United States. When they immigrated to Holland, we had family that lived there. It was two Westerlink brothers, with their wives and children, who made that bold move to the United States. All of the children from both of the West-erlink families were fluent with the Dutch language. As a child, I could understand the Indonesian language my parents spoke, but could never really have a conversation with them. However I did know all the cuss words! I can remember the days that family would get together and gather, as this was really the only family we had. As I think about what our par-ents did for us, all I can think is how hard it was. They did not speak English, and they did not have any technical back-ground, but they took on jobs that today we would not even think about doing. But our fathers did that for us, for their children to have that better life. I have also been asked what race I was, and have always proudly said that I am an Indo ninety-nine percent. Even today, I have been assessed of being Mexican, Hawaiian, Native American, and then so-me...But deep down inside, I know where my roots are, and isn't that all that matters? There is so much more to discuss in being an Indo. I could keep typing until my fingers turned blue, and the reality of writing a story could actually happen one day.

Hans Hayer: I am a third-generation Indo. My grandparents came from very wealthy sugar plantation owners and they grew up with servants and maids and gardeners and cooks. The family members who survived the war left Indonesia in 1949. Some went to Papua New Guinea others like my *Oma,* went to the Netherlands. We stayed there until 1960, then moved to the United States where the third generation was born but as first generation Americans. It's nice to put a face on our identity. We now know who we are culturally!!

• New generations of Americans with Indo-European lineage, at some point in their lives, have a desire to rediscover or know more about their origins and (multi-) cultural background.

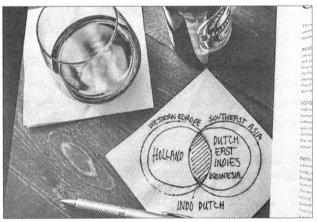

• Explaining Best of Both Worlds - Indo Dutch: Hybrid Culture & Fusion Cuisine (from the cookbook Indo Dutch Kitchen Secrets)

39

WAR STRESS AFFECTS
FUTURE GENERATIONS

Marcel van Doorn is an expert therapist in psychotrauma-tology and specialized in intercultural relationships. As an experiential expert, he knows all about the influence of war on future generations.

Van Doorn says both my Dutch Indonesian mother and my Dutch father experienced the Second World War up close as teenagers. This has had a great deal of influence on them unconsciously and consciously. Later, that also affected our family. So there are traces in me, and in my siblings. The traumas of that war that took place in two different hemispheres of the world. My father with the Germans; my mother with the Japanese and Indonesians. Transgenerational war traumatization is actually a post-traumatic stress disorder, or PTSD.

Personally, I call it a *Post-Traumatic Colonial Disorder*.

For the time being, the Western medical world has been and is mainly addressed by medication and re-traumatisation. Only conversational therapies don't help in the end. As a specialized trauma therapist and experience expert with extensive knowledge of Indonesian history, I struggled with this fact myself years ago. For example, I wore out three psychotherapists, two psychiatrists, and five psychologists, before I met my German trauma therapist. After years of searching and hours of conversations, I ended up with him and within fifteen minutes, I was lying on a bench under a blanket. He finally let me experience peace and quiet in my body.

A number of large studies have now shown that the DNA in our cells ensures the transmission of trauma. Where we always assumed that it would only be a few generations ago, these studies show that the trauma is passed on as long as we do not resolve it. Abuse in the family can still play a role in current behaviour. A repeat of this trauma could easily take place in the history of various families, which come from that family.

Trauma is in your body, in your DNA.

So it is of the utmost importance to subject your family to an accurate examination. Do this without hesitation and do so without being reproached or judged. Do this out of love for the family and for healing the trauma. This is always my first assignment to a new client who comes to me with PTCD complaints.

Create a *genogram* (a family tree that comes alive) and talk to the family members who can still tell you all sorts of things. After a few sessions, I usually suggest doing a family set-up based on the desire of the heart. The heart is the oldest brain organ of the body and therefore possesses the wisdom needed to heal.

Because of PTCD, there is a lot of confusion about taking your own place in the family, the family of origin. And all out of love for that family, even when there are arguments, addictions, incest, mental health problems, and discomfort.

Much has been destroyed by not recognizing children in the past or by sending the mother, the *njai* (women who were kept as housekeepers, companions, and concubines in the Dutch East Indies) away. The *apartheid* introduced by law made for the recognizable trap-thinking as Marion Bloem describes it. And today, that is still current. To get out of there, you do not have to yell at that Jap or agree with him. I am not a victim anymore because I do not want to be. Each of us is presented with the choice to be what you want.

Sometimes you can use some help with that, and you need

316

courage for that. It's very powerful to ask for help. The fact that you always ask at the right time is one of the most beautiful things I've learned over time. You're never too late, no matter what your age. My mother, then eighty-two, wondered why her mother was always so mad at her. When we started researching this with a family set-up, it turned out that my mother went to school and could go to work and dance while my grandmother, her mother, was not allowed to. The belief at the time was that a woman was supposed to do the housework.

Today, they call this a multinational collateral damage. The Indonesian community and I, as an Indo, are a little more than that. I have two worlds in me, and I'm proud of both. It makes me rich in wisdom to unite these worlds in me, without judgment, without reproach. At the same time, I am not going to let myself be put away and demand recognition just because I am.

• *Early 1970 Breda, Holland. Mama Beynon (right) with her daughters Nancy (left) and Louise (middle). Mama Beynon died at the age of 72. I believe the stressful move from New Guinea to the Netherlands had contributed to her early death.*

Badplaats Pasir Poeti Manokwari

40

PASIR PUTIH MANOKWARI

*In this final chapter, I like to include a poem that was
written by one of our dear friends, Alex Bal.
It is fitting that this will be the final chapter as many
Manokwari friends that have lived in that
beautiful paradise will always remember the place
by the ocean called Pasir Putih.
For my English-speaking friends, I have tried to
translate it, but it will never contain the heart
that is full of memory in the Dutch language.*

Manokwari, Pasir Putih

De zon laat het spierwitte strand van Pasir-Putih schit-
teren. Ontelbare lichtpuntjes bespelen vrolijk het wiegende
water. De baai is kobaltblauw getooid. Het wit bruisend
schuim bespeelt het zilverstrand, waar kreeftjes nog even snel
een goed heenkomen zoeken. Lichte golfjes fluisteren de taal

van de zee, strelen het zilver laken en trekken zich dan weer langzaam terug in de schoot van Pasir-Putih.

De temperatuur is tropisch, het water verkoelend. Het mooiste plekje op aarde is nog even vriendelijk als altijd. Ondanks het ontberen van aandacht en liefde, gaat ook zij haar nieuwe toekomst tegemoet. Woelige tijden heeft zij doorstaan, afgewisseld met tijden waarin zij werd aanbeden om haar schoonheid en geborgenheid. Gastvrijheid bood zij overdag, maar ook na zonsondergang. Menig stel waande zich hier onbespied en leerde elkaar beter kennen. Vele geheimen werden haar toevertrouwd en bleven verborgen...

Ik laat me verleiden door de waterlijn, die mijn voeten bij ieder stap beroert, loop langs het licht hellend strand, die in de felle zon vibreert. Niemand in de buurt. Ik ben alleen, maar niet vervuld van eenzaamheid.

Het roestige motorblok al decennialang een spontaan standbeeld als eer aan de slachtoffers van de Japanse invasie in de tweede wereldoorlog, houdt ook nu nog stand. Dit monument, door de natuur gekoesterd en geteisterd, met zoveel karakter en wilskracht, zal nog lang in menig geheugen gegrift blijven. Dit 'standbeeld' is stille getuige van mijn jeugd en die van nog vele anderen.

Ik neem een duik. Het water is helder en heerlijk als altijd. Geelzwarte visjes schieten mij nieuwsgierig tegemoet, een zeepaardje doet moeite om onherkenbaar te blijven, verbergt zich achter een drijvend *ketapangblad*. Vertrouwde beelden voor mij. Dan sta ik oog in oog met een langbaardkwal, zo noemde Nono ze altijd. Die weet ik nog maar net te ontwijken.

Als ik mijn hoofd weer boven water steek, rust een sliert drijvend wier als een krans op mijn schouders.

In de verte springt een school tonijnen speels uit het water, even later zijn zij weer één met het zilte nat. Een visser roeit zijn prauw alsof zijn leven ervan afhangt dwars door het feestelijk gedruis.

Dan is het weer snel rustig en haalt de Papua zijn vislijn binnen. Hij heeft beet, heeft weer te eten of handel om mee langs de huizen te gaan.

Het eiland Mansinam ligt er mooi groen en vredig bij, ontneemt mij het uitzicht op de voet van het Arfak-gebergte, het veilige oord voor stenentijdperk-krijgers.

PASIR PUTIH (English Translation)

The sun makes the muscular white beach of Pasir-Putih shine. Countless bright spots cheerfully play the rocking water. The bay is cobalt blue. The white bubbly foam plays on the silver looking beach. Lobsters are still looking for a quick return. Water ripples whisper the language of the sea, caress the silver sheet, and slowly retreat into the beach of Pasir-Putih. The temperature is tropical, the water cooling. The most beautiful place on earth is still as friendly as ever. Despite lacking attention and love, she too is facing her new future. She endured troubled times, interspersed with times when she was adored for her beauty and security. She offered hospitality during the day, but also after sunset. A lot of people thought they were completely private here and got to know each other better. Many secrets were entrusted to her and remained hidden.

I am tempted by the water line, which strokes my feet at every step, walk along the light slippery beach, vibrating in the bright sun. No one around. I am alone, but not filled with loneliness.

The rusty engine block has become a spontaneous statue for decades to honor the victims of the Japanese invasion in the Second World War. It still holds up. This monument, cherished and ravaged by nature, with so much character and willpower, will remain etched in many memories for a long time.

This 'statue' is a silent witness to my youth and that of many others. I dive. The water is as clear and wonderful as ever. Yellow and black fish shoot by me curiously; a seahorse makes an effort to remain unrecognizable, hiding behind a floating *ketapang* (leaf). Trusted images for me. Then I am face-to-face with a long bearded jellyfish, that is what *Nono* used to call them. I only just managed to avoid this one.
When I put my head above water again, a floating string of seaweed rests like a wreath on my shoulders.

A school of tuna playfully jumps out of the water in the distance, a little later, they are one with the silver wetness of the ocean. A fisherman rows his *prauw* (canoe) as if his life depends on it, right through the festive waves. Then it will quickly calm down, and the Papuan brings in his fishing line. He has caught some fish, food to trade and sell by knocking on doors.

The island of Mansinam is beautifully green and peaceful. It deprives me of the view of the foot of the Arfak mountains, a safe place for stone-era-warriors.

.

"Moment of Solitude"
A small beach between Pasir Putih and Bakaro in Manokwari
Painted by Coen Robert Kokkelink

Coen told me that he often went fishing with his father, decorated
KNIL Sergeant Mauretz Christiaan Kokkelink, who guided guerrilla fighters
through the jungle of New Guinea during the Pacific War

• Out of deep respect for his heroism during the guerrilla warfare in Manokwari (New Guinea) and to recognize his birthday (one hundred and third!!) a picture was taken by Pieter de Kock. (May 2021) This decorated World War Two army veteran is not yet ready to fade away. May God continue to keep him in His grace.

BEYNON FAMILY

Pa Beynon had fourteen children; Ma Beynon thirteen

Theodoor Beynon (1902-1984)
Married Marie Retelaer (1905-1976)
Went to Holland
Theodoor went to Canada

Emmi Beynon (1922-1942) born in Batavia
Father, Theodoor Beynon, mother unknown

Johan (Nono) Beynon (1925-1981) born in Batavia
Married Frouwke Vecht (1929-2013)
Went to Amsterdam
No children

Margaretha (Nini) Beynon (1927-2021) born in Batavia
Married Joop de Rooy
When he passed, she married Rinus Mollinger
Moved to Papua New Guinea (Port Moresby)
Went to Australia
Children: Grace

Hendrika (Ika) Beynon 1928 born in Batavia
Married Wim van Schukkmann in 1946
Wim was a KNIL soldier
Went to Holland
Children: Sylvie, Leo, Eugenie, Jeffrey

Otty Beynon (1929-1929) born in Batavia

Eddy Beynon 1930 born in Batavia
Married Hildegonda Otto (1937) in 1964
Went to Holland and to Australia
Children: Bert, Sandra

Suze Beynon 1932 born in Batavia
Married Cornelis van Geenen (1927) in Manokwari 1953
Cornelis was a KNIL soldier
Went to Holland
Children: Rocky, Maureen, Vicky, Sandra, Patsy, Sheila

Albertine Beynon (1934-1937) born in Manokwari

Jeanne (Sjane) Beynon 1935 born in Manokwari
Married Johnny Vetter in 1954
Went to Holland
Children: Lindie

Nancy Beynon 1936 born in Manokwari
Married Cornelis van der Hijde (1929-2000)
in Manokwari 1955
Went to Holland, then Canada
Children: Roy, Theo, Jim, Gina, Peggy

Olga Beynon 1938 born in Manokwari
Married Jack Visser (1932) in 1958 in Manokwari
Went to Holland, then Canada
Children: Brenda 1960, Robbie 1962

Guustaaf (Ventje) Beynon 1940 born in Manokwari
Married Sonja Kruger (1945) in 1963
Went to Holland
Children: Andy, Glenn

Carla Beynon 1943 born in Oransbari
Married Johan Hesselink (1934-2013) in Manokwari 1960
Went to Holland
Children: Ineke, Rickie, Richard, Francie, Jackie

Louise Beynon 1948 born in Manokwari
Married Bastiaan Opdenkelder (1948) in Breda 1970
Went to Holland, Spain, and then Canada
Children: Claudia 1970, Griselda 1975

The following pages contain some pictures of
the Beynon family in Manokwari after the war.

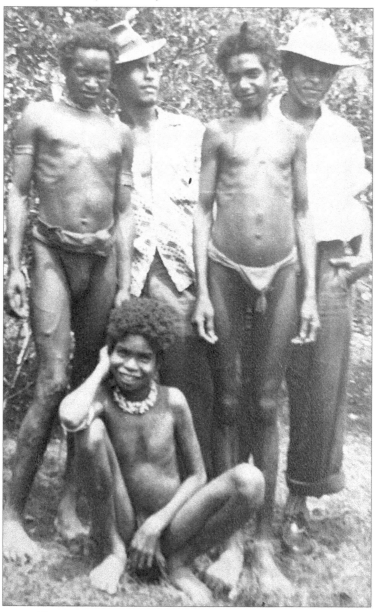

• *Eddy Beynon with Isaac (foster brother) and three local Papuans*
who helped in the gardens

• *Wedding picture of Nancy and Cor Van der Hijde. Top left to right:*
Rien Mollinger, Frauke Vecht, Mama, Cor, Nancy, Papa
Middle left to right: Johan (Nono) and Margaretha (Nini). Bottom left ro
right: Peter Mouthaan, Louise, Grace, Guus (Ventje), Olga and Carla

• *Mama Beynon with Carla, Louise, and Guus*

328

• *Beynon family. Top left to right top: Jack Visser, Olga, Margaretha (Nini),*
Rien Mollinger, and Carla (Meighty)
Bottom left to right: Grace Mollinger, Papa, Mama, and Louise

• *Wedding picture of Carla and Johan Hesselink. Top left to right: Eddy, Olga, Mr. Hesselink, Jack Visser, Mama, Nancy, Johan Hesselink, Margaretha (Nini), Carla (Meighty), Cor van der Hijde, and Papa. Bottom left: Louise and Grace Mollinger*

• The following family members are recognized in this picture: Top row: Family Vetter; Family van Hien; Mevr: Verlinden, Tjalie Verlinden, Mr: Hesselink, Nancy holding baby Jim van der Hijde, Cor van der Hijde. Bottom: Grace, Louise, Theo en Roy van der Hijde, and Wally van Hien

331

• *Louise's birthday party with the following friends: Sonja de Kock, Janie Wagemakers, Mieke Kempees, Trees Baum Bletterman, Uckel Buck, Sanny van Maren, Dinant Kempees, and three children of the Loomans family*

• *Left to right: Olga, Guus, Jack Visser, Mama, Roy, Nancy, Margaretha, and Grace*

• *Guus, Eddy, and Isaac. Louise is hiding behind Eddy*

• *Eddy teaches Roy van der Hijde his first steps in pentjak silat*

Vaarwel Mijn Dromenland
Geschreven door A. Holten

Ik heb zo'n heimwee naar dat verre land
Ik verlang terug naar jou
Met je palmen en jouw witte strand
Ik hou van jou

Waar melati zoete geur verspreidt
In je maanverlichte nacht
Als ik terugdenk aan de mooie tijd
Dan huil ik zacht

Vaarwel mijn dromenland
Jouw oceaan
Vaarwel mijn dromenland
Ver hier vandaan
Vaarwel mijn dromenland
Nee hoor, 't doet zeer
Vaarwel mijn dromenland
Ik zie jou nooit weer

Aan de bloesem hangt het pareldauw
En de wind speelt door het riet
In gedachten ben ik steeds bij jou
En zing dit lied

Vaarwel mijn dromenland
Jouw oceaan
Vaarwel mijn dromenland
Ver hier vandaan
Vaarwel mijn dromenland
Nee hoor, 't doet zeer
Vaarwel mijn dromenland
Ik zie jou nooit weer